CENTURY STORY

By the same author:

Brighter Bondage Chatto & Windus 1935

Vagabondage Chatto & Windus 1941

China Mending & Restoration by C.S.M. Parsons & F.H. Curl, Faber & Faber 1963

CENTURY STORY

Claudia Parsons

Foreword by Sir Anthony Parsons

The Book Guild Ltd
Sussex, England

The Book Guild Ltd.
25 High Street,
Lewes, Sussex

First published 1995
© Claudia Parsons 1995
Set in Baskerville
Typesetting by Acorn Bookwork, Salisbury

Printed in Great Britain by
Bookcraft (Bath) Ltd.

A catalogue record for this book is
available from the British Library

ISBN 1 85776 027 1

CONTENTS

ACKNOWLEDGEMENTS

I would like to thank my friends and family, particularly Emma Parsons and Anthony Parsons, for their invaluable support in this venture. I would also like to thank Jean Mann for her patient typing, retyping and finally computerising so faithfully the whole manuscript.

This is a story of the twentieth century, starting at the beginning, in 1900. Young women had by then begun to emerge from the sheltered life to go to universities or to take any jobs that were allowed to them in a man's world. Further careers, men reserved for themselves. Setting out with little more than the proverbial shoestring, I sought a paid job that would also give me knowledge of the world. This led to my breaking through the man-made constraint but, by good fortune, I won a great part of my ambition over the years. It gained me a reputation as a traveller in distant countries, yet this is no travel book in the normal sense. Starting in India, it is an autobiography of an eventful life.

C.P.

FOREWORD

I am delighted that my cousin Claudia has taken her elder sister Betty's advice and has written her autobiography. When, in her late eighties, Betty had made this suggestion, Claudia was doubtful, regarding herself as 'a clownish character and a charlatan in most of the jobs I took up, but managing to be successful in the end'. It is difficult to reconcile this self-deprecating description with the elegant, literary, world-travelled non-agenarian whom we all know. But who am I to query Claudia's self-characterisation? Betty was right in seeing her sister as 'one who had broken the ice of convention that held women down to certain jobs but denied them others, and at a time when to the majority of people the world was unknown'.

Century Story is the story of Claudia Parsons's life from her birth in 1900 to her last trips – China, the Yemen and the Danube – in her late eighties. It is lucky that she delayed writing the autobiography for so long, otherwise we would not have had the account of her riding pillion on a motor-cycle in the Yemen at the age of eighty-six! Her tour guide, an old friend of mine, told me recently that he was sure that he would have a corpse on his hands. No question of that. Claudia ends her book by saying that she is now happy to sit at home and wait for the undiscovered country 'whenever that may be'. But I would not be surprised to hear of her turning up in Latin America, the only part of the world she has yet to visit.

Mine and Claudia's family are the embodiment of George Orwell's 'imperial middle class', the Anglo-Irish who, generation after generation, served the East India Company, the Indian Raj and the Empire as a whole. I must be one of the last to spend a lifetime in the service of the Crown. Claudia's genetic inheritance took her in a different direction. Obviously a brilliant mechanic and craftswoman from her early teens, she was one of three women amongst 300 men who graduated from Lough-borough as a civil engineer shortly after World War I. She spent the inter-war years – the heart of the book – as a chauffeur-courier and chauffeur-companion. This was very much a man's world when cars, although built to last, were unreliable on long journeys. Punctures, especially on poor or non-existent roads, were frequent as were broken springs and more serious internal injuries whose rectification demanded surgical skills as well as physical strength. Fortunately for her clients Claudia had both, as her journeys took her through Europe, to the Balkans and, in the 1930s, much further afield.

The high point is the circumnavigation of the world in the late 1930s. Claudia begins by driving a customer in a hired car across the United States. She decides to continue westward, arriving in Japan with the war against China raging. After selling most of her clothes and writing for a Japanese newspaper, she forged on to Calcutta, where her younger sister and husband were stationed, via French Indo-China (Cambodia) and Thailand. En route she fell in with a young male American psychoanalyst. After working briefly on a social anthropological project, they reached Calcutta and decided to go back to England together by car. It was 1938. They bought a 1925-model Studebaker for ten pounds, and set off. Hair-raising adventures, breakdowns and crises followed as they ploughed on through India, Afghanistan, Iran, Iraq, Syria, Palestine, Egypt, Libya and Tunisia, crossing to Marseilles and thence across France to her base near Guildford in Surrey. It was a truly epic journey, but their life of carefree adventure was shortly to be curtailed by World War II.

Claudia's talents were rightly engaged in factory work throughout most of the war, after which she briefly resumed her driving career. However, the next ten years were mainly spent in making money as a professional china mender and restorer, ultimately culminating in a book which took its place alongside a successful novel (1925) and travel book (1941). In the 1970s and 1980s she resumed travelling although, with age, she was obliged to abandon the car for the conducted tour.

Century Story is much more than a travel book. It is an exploration of an indomitable character whose resolution and unquenchable optimism carry her safely from adventure to adventure, while she never overlooks the stability and love provided by the family 'back at the ranch'. There is also no lack of what I suppose is called human interest. Claudia accumulated a host of friends, both male and female, and was indifferent to the conventions of her age in regard to travelling only with a male companion. Why did she not marry? She obviously had plenty of opportunities but nothing came of them in the end beyond lasting friendship. Perhaps she valued her independence too highly.

I can recommend *Century Story* without any prejudice due to family loyalty and my affection for my redoubtable cousin. Claudia's prose style is straightforward and unadorned. The story races along and, even on a second reading, I found it difficult to stop turning the pages and take a break. She was unconventional, yes. She was ahead of her time, certainly. But she manifests no trace of irritating militancy and succeeds in bridging the old and new worlds without strain. The wide range of people, in and out of the family, who both respected and loved her, is testimony to her quality. Claudia has had a wonderful life. Long may it last. My only sadness is that virtually all the characters who crowd her pages are now dead. Thank God she has lived long enough to produce this excellent and entertaining book.

Anthony Parsons

Anthony Parsons was the British Ambassador in Iran 1974–1979 and the UK Permanent Representative to the United Nations during the Falklands conflict in 1982. His publications include They Say the Lion *about his time as a diplomat in the Middle East and* From Cold War to Hot Peace *on the role of the United Nations*

America – June 1937

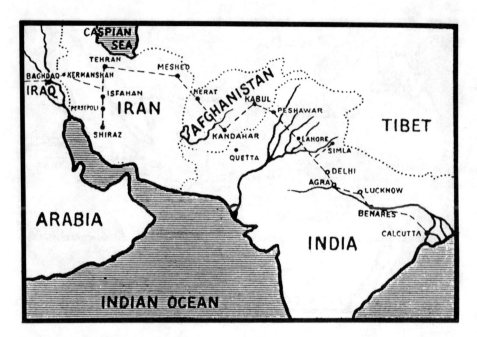

India and Afghanistan – April 1938

Palestine and Egypt – June 1938

1900–1912

CLOWN

It all began on the fifteenth of August 1900, in Simla, in the hills. India was then under the 'wicked British Empire'; an Englishman's word was still credible, and Queen Victoria had yet a few months to reign. On that day not a son but a daughter was born to Clement George and Grace Florence Parsons, fulfilling the prophecy of the local Indians, outraged by the action of Major Parsons in shooting sacred animals.

The annual migration had taken place, the Indian Government moving for the hot weather from Delhi to what was still virtually a modest hill station, with road and rail connections, an English church, a market town and an ever-increasing number of cool bungalows, with thick walls and deep verandahs, reaching out into the wooded hills. Such was Simla, to which a Viceregal lodge had been added and numerous Government offices; but the flavour of the hill station persisted, with jackals howling at night, with netting across windows to keep out the monkeys and, punctually with the arrival of officials and their families, an infestation of diseased and starving cats. In pitiful condition and in search of refuse, the cats were immune from molestation, but the kindest solution for many of them was a painless and instant death. Major Parsons, an accurate shot, took upon himself to deliver a number of them from misery, with the dire consequence foretold.

As there was already a daughter in the family, and certainly Grace had hopes this time for a son, a second daughter seemed to have wrought confusion. On the very day of the christening no name had yet been chosen or, if chosen, at the last minute not thought suitable, and the father of the child addressed himself to a dictionary of names, with only time to reach as far as C before pronouncing Claudia, sister of the Roman emperor to be a satisfactory female. So the name Claudia was chosen, one more Anglo-Indian was established, and I was that child.

At that time the term 'Anglo-Indian' applied to anyone born in India to a British father and mother, but the term loosely embraced anyone British working out there. So the number was legion, for India was then the great source of honours and advancement for the brighter and hardier sons of Britain, also a source of eligible husbands for British daughters. The fruits of

1

service, under the Indian Government, were safe if not spectacular; one had to reach high office before they became at all lavish, and in the meantime husbands had had to pay the sea passages to and from England for wives and children, and many of the husbands died before high office was attained.

My forebears, on both sides of the family, had for generations served in India, suffering in the earliest days excruciating hardship, and always the disintegration of family life for the time that the children, for their survival and education, had to be farmed out at home.

The home of the Parsons family had for generations been Ireland, each generation following on in a similar pattern; a few sons entering the service of the Indian Government, marrying and producing vast families, who were then sent home at intervals in batches to the care of Irish relatives. On reaching maturity, many set out again for India.

Clement George's father, James Edward Parsons – my grandfather – had entered the Punjab Civil Commission from a Bengal regiment and had married the daughter of a fellow officer in the regiment: Miss Tempé Susan Beckett. Married at sixteen, she bore him nine sons and two daughters during their term of service. They broke with tradition only on retirement when, instead of returning to Ireland, they settled at The Gables, a large house then standing alone on the coast at Southbourne, Hampshire, with accommodation for at least some of the displaced grandchildren. But the home base was still Ireland when Clement George, third of the nine brothers, was shipped back as a small boy to Irish relatives, though later, along with other of his brothers, he was educated at Dulwich College.

Like his father before him, my father entered the Indian army and later the Punjab Commission, probably not so much in a spirit of Empire-building as for the adventure of India and the sport that it offered at attainable cost. In fact he was so enthralled by the country that he sacrificed some of his early home leave to explore it on foot and on horseback, encountering at times such formidable terrain that he came to value the local advice always to venture with a companion. Inevitably he wrote letters home describing these expeditions, but they have not survived, yet some of these ventures were later to fire my imagination in the all too brief time that we had together.

Grace Florence, my mother, was also born in India, the daughter of Hungerford Meyer Boddam, and the Boddams were again an Anglo-Indian family whose India-going forebears reached even further back into posterity. Among the most noted was Rawson Hart Boddam, who had entered the service of the East India Company and in 1784 was made the first Governor of Bombay. It was Rawson Hart's ambition while he was Governor to enlarge Bombay's existent harbour, which he saw as a potential and magnificent opening for Indian trade with the West, replacing Calcutta, then the

2

main port but more distant and more difficult of approach. With the concurrence of the East India Company, he drew up plans for this enlargement since Bombay was singular in having a tide-rise of fourteen feet, which permitted docks on the scale envisaged. The British Government, however, remained indifferent and the necessary funds were withheld. When a few years after his retirement his plans were adopted and Rawson was offered a title in recompense, the sop was refused with great bitterness of feeling. In fact it was exactly a century before the first of the big docks was opened.

Rawson Hart Boddam retired to a family seat, Capel House, at Enfield, north of London, where he settled down to cultivate some two hundred acres of surrounding property, and there was a marriage between one of his daughters and a son of the Meyer family of an adjacent estate, Forte Hall. Both estates are still intact; the Capel estate is now a horticultural and environmental centre, and the interior of the house much embellished by later owners.

In 1788 large houses, remote from the main water supply, either continued to rely on earth closets and water carried to the hip-bath and bedroom, or they had hand or steam pumping to get a head of water to an upper floor. Outside the eastern extremity of Capel House a well, surrounded by a pathway, is evidence of a pony or donkey being used to gyrate round the well, raising and pumping water to a header tank supplying closet and marble bath on an adjacent upper floor. More than likely this was introduced by Rawson, to whom gyrating camels or bullocks to draw water in India would have been a familiar sight.

Ill health drove Rawson finally to Bath, where he took a small property shortly before his death in 1812, when the Capel House property was sold. If the mass of glowing tributes to him are correct on a tablet in Bath Abbey, where he is interred, he must have been an exceptional man. 'Rawson Hart Boddams' thus occur plentifully among succeeding generations, many of whom have served in India.

*

General Hungerford Meyer Boddam was issue of the Boddam–Meyer marriage, and was my grandfather. Retired from the Punjab Commission, he had large ideas and a lot of large furniture inherited from Capel House, but a diminished fortune through being twice married and raising two families. Though the first family was off his hands, on his retirement he was still educating three daughters and a younger son of the second family, and therefore rented a house not far from Dulwich College, convenient for his son's education. This house was capable of housing a dining-table eight feet in diameter round which the East India Company had once held meetings, and two flawless mirrors reaching from ceiling to supporting console tables.

3

He had married, as his second wife, Louise Husband – of whom more later – and there were two sons and three daughters in this younger family, most of them born in India, including Grace Florence, the second daughter – my mother.

As seemed customary at the time, girls in their teens, after education with governesses, were sent to school in Germany, where they were wont to suffer merciless discipline and hardship, but those who survived the ordeal seemed to derive great benefit. Tinie, Grace and Muriel Boddam all went to school in Germany, and were survivors; for the rest of their lives they seemed able to withstand any amount of cold, heat and fatigue, the younger two surviving into their nineties. All three of these willowy girls held themselves superbly on return from this schooling, where they were made to march with a pile of books on the head and penalties were levied each time a book fell. They had acquired a complete knowledge of German, besides a good general education, and each came back with an exquisite sampler of all forms of stitchery diligently worked by candlelight. A further attribute that each possessed, but owed to heredity, was an abundant head of hair growing beautifully off the forehead and reaching – in a long plait in school days – to well below the waist. This, combined with Tinie's classical features, made her a considerable beauty.

During the years at Dulwich College, Clement George Parsons and his brothers had met the Boddam family and they were all well known to each other by the time Clement George came home on short leave from India in 1885. He was thirty-four years of age, a Major in the Indian Staff Corps, took his service very seriously, and was fluent in Urdu. Now able to support a wife and family, he proposed to Grace in Dulwich early in that year.

Grace was a diarist; from the previous year till she was well into her eighties she annually filled a diary with short factual extracts each day, meant as a memory aid and not an expression of deeper thought. Feelings nevertheless intrude, and though the proposal occupies no more than a sentence, it is evident it is not unexpected, that affection between these two had been growing over some time. Further entries reveal pleasure on both sides of the family as Grace accompanies 'Clem' to Christchurch, the station for Southbourne and The Gables, where General James and Tempé Parsons are now living in retirement along with visiting or resident members of that numerous family. In a month's time Clem is due to return to India, the hot weather before him, and it is arranged that Grace shall join him in the autumn, marrying him on arrival in Bombay, as many brides did at that time.

Grace, who was twenty-seven when she made this journey, was used to travel but a very bad sailor, and there were then no effective seasickness remedies. Her diary reveals the wrench it was leaving her family, but there appears no apprehension about the journey ahead. She could remember

India, had friends and relatives there, but none travelling with her, yet with fewer feet on the ground and the customer always given first consideration, she probably had an easier time than she would have today. She booked in at an hotel in Marseilles, ordered a *chaise* to go up to see Notre Dame de la Garde, and boarded the P. & O. the next day. There is no indication that the two impeccable ladies whom she found in her cabin – described in her diary as 'very nice', but never mentioned again – had been personally arranged or were in any sense chaperones. The P. & O. cabins were larger than today and solidly comfortable, and Grace suffered only two days of bad weather. The night of a fancy dress ball, for which she made her own dress, is described: 'Lovely dance. Dress much admired. Won first prize.'

On the fifth of December, fifteen days out from London, she arrived at that gateway of India that her great-grandfather had been defrauded of building for her, and Clem met her on board; they were married that afternoon in a chapel of the cathedral, with quite a few friends attending. Two nights later they started their long train journey across India, stopping off in both Agra and Delhi, and it was in the evening of the eleventh of December that they reached Amballa, where Clement was then stationed. The diary records: 'My own home at last. Everything so lovely.'

*

The life which followed, seventeen years of service in India, embraced all the lures of the present-day travel brochure, for Clem and Grace had access to India's greatest treasures and, serving in the Punjab, they were posted to hill stations such as Dharmsala and Dalhousie, close under the backdrop of the Himalayas and enjoyed mostly a temperate climate. But not all the time. They had their share of tropical heat and equally of cold when camping in the hills, where water could be boiling at its base but freezing on its surface. Clem would be sent on fact-finding expeditions to remote areas – some of these are now being made suitable for tourists to visit at a favourable time of year. If not withheld by duty to her children, nothing gave Grace greater pleasure than to accompany him, particularly to Chamba State on the route to Ladakh, the ageing Rajah of Chamba having requested Clem to be ward to his grandson and heir. Without this protection there was little hope of the boy achieving his inheritance, so a state visit to Chamba at intervals had to be made, when Grace rode beside her husband and visited the wives and people of the neighbourhood.

Office life would also be interspersed with camping, in the grand manner: camels bearing tents and equipment from one camp-site to the next, Clem and sometimes Grace riding horses or elephants according to the nature of the land. Thus virtually a magistrate's court reached communities to which there was no road.

5

The first of these camps is described eulogistically in Grace's diary. They were to become a constant source of enjoyment and interest. When her babies were old enough, she had a low-slung pony cart made to transport the children into camp, the ayah and the Indian groom in charge. At leisurely pace the cart followed the camels, but the rough ground was not unknown to overturn it, spilling out nurse and babies. However, as no one seemed the worse for it, Grace decided it was good training for the children.

In contrast to this outdoor life there were, of course, long periods of social duty, which increased with seniority. And in addition to this, India imposed an oriental hospitality towards the passing stranger. Not only did one house the horses and dogs of one's friends when they went on leave, but it was customary, with so little accommodation available, and even after hotels had increased in number and standard, for those who had rooms to spare to be asked temporarily to house visitors, known or unknown, but with some connection with India. To Grace, who had an innate hospitality, this was no hardship. Her kindness was proverbial; also her efforts to bring greater interest and diversity to Indian wives in purdah. By slow degrees she extracted permission for Indian wives of different households to come and meet together in her house with carefully selected English wives. Wearing their finest jewellery and saris, the Indian wives came in closed conveyances, looking forward more and more to these assemblies, occasions remembered long after with touching gratitude.

That was India at the turn of the nineteenth to twentieth century and very different from India today. There was then not only a greater abundance of hostile animals, insects and reptiles, but protection against malaria and sandfly fever depended on quinine, the mosquito net and the joss-stick. There were all the problems of a hot country without electricity and refrigeration, though by 1912 large fans were gyrating slowly in the ceiling of a few public buildings, and other electrical appliances filtered in slowly. Air-conditioning of homes and offices barely preceded the close-down of Empire.

Mainly the Anglo-Indians were protected from the heat by the thick walls and deep verandahs of their bungalows as well as the rhythmic swish of the punkah motivated by hand. For the majority there was migration to the hills, but the junior official remained in office his first years wherever it was. The visitor to India, choosing the most salubrious time of year, would never know that burden of heat like a cloak reaching maximum weight in the long, still time of waiting, all ears cocked for that harbinger of relief – the distant roll of thunder – all life crying for mercy and not a cloud in the sky.

*

6

Perhaps because of their early apprenticeship, as it were, both having been born in India, neither Grace nor Clem suffered the fevers and disorders to which, not unnaturally, Anglo-Indians were prone. They escaped with nothing worse than prickly heat and, for Clem, often headaches at the end of a long working day. Their first daughter, christened Grace after her mother, but for some unexplained reason called 'Betty' for the rest of her life, was a fine, healthy baby with the Boddam abundance of hair and every sign of being intelligent. This was a great joy to Clem, who spent what time he could with her, as she advanced to an age when she could understand what he told her. He was not so happy with his second daughter, much smaller at birth, with a very white skin and hair the colour of a spring onion. This child had her own ideas of entertainment; the bearer's shoes, outside his entrance door on the verandah, were a source of deep fascination and she could barely walk when she first put her diminutive feet into them and shuffled them back and forth along the verandah in deep concentration. 'Grace, d'you think she's quite right in the head?' her anxious father remarked.

He had cause for his apprehensions: she was noticeably left-handed, a condition then looked upon as a deficiency needing swift correction. Time also revealed a strong element of the clown and, not unsuitably, Grace dressed her as a clown for Lady Curzon's fancy dress children's party, Lord Curzon then being Viceroy. Indeed the name Claudia did not seem to fit on these shoulders and she remained 'Baby' or 'Missi-Baba', according to the speaker. The person who seemed to understand her best was her elder sister, who, contrary to the usual pattern of resentment towards a younger member, had from the first enjoyed playing with her and had adopted a protective attitude. Betty at three had taught herself to read and was reading avidly all that came her way, but Claudia's intellectual advancement was to receive a severe shock on being moved suddenly to a totally different environment at two years of age.

In the upper Punjab, schooling, rather than climate, was the prime cause of sending children home, and Betty and Claudia could have remained some years yet with their parents but for a steady deterioration in Betty's health. She was losing weight, was prone to sickness, and the suspicion that the ayah was giving her opium to send her to sleep – hotly denied by the ayah – was in fact true. The ayah was dismissed, an Eurasian nanny supplanted, but Betty failed to regain strength. It was soon evident she must be taken home, but as both parents had recently been home on leave with them, it fell to Grace to take both children, and make the agonizing decision whether to leave Betty only, making both children miserable, or whether to return to India alone. She finally chose the latter.

Anglo-Indians always looked to relatives to care for their young, assuming that blood relationship must be the most protective and best. Grace's parents would have been mortified if she had left them elsewhere and there could be no greater, more warm-hearted affection than Louise, Grace's mother, would bestow. All the same there must have been much pain in Grace's mind as she returned to India alone, leaving a baby of just over two years.

Hungerford Meyer Boddam had moved from Dulwich to a solid red brick house which he rented, built on what had been part of the Onslow estate, the Merrow side of Guildford. The builder had embellished the high ceilings with elaborate plaster work and installed a noble main staircase but, like much architecture of the time, the house ignored the best aspect for sunlight and managed to engender a powerful amount of draughts. The Boddams, who were its first occupants, called it Capel House, after Rawson's estate, and housed the eight-foot round table (with leaves for extension) in the dining-room, and one of the flawless mirrors, but the console table had to be abandoned.

It was here that Grace left her daughters to the care of, so she thought, two grandparents and an aunt, but the grandfather died soon after Grace reached India. Differences of opinion between Muriel and her mother led to Granny gradually withdrawing from the scene. Subject to bouts of giddiness, Granny became an invalid in her bedroom for the next thirteen years.

*

The aunt was Muriel, youngest of the three sisters educated in Germany, who had always had the greatest affection and admiration for Grace, along with a not always concealed contempt for her beautiful eldest sister, Tinie, whose mind was practical rather than scholarly. Muriel herself had a quite exceptional brain; it was like living with a little encyclopaedia, her nieces were later to assert, claiming that it made one lazy, as one had only to turn to the aunt for the source of a quotation, the name of an author, or the location of a country, and it was nearly always supplied without further reference.

Clearly Muriel was designed as a career woman, but the species at that time had scarcely been recognized. She had begged her father to allow her to go to college, and he had refused. One suspects that in him was a strong element of the snob, a yearning for the grandiose, and he considered it unseemly for daughters to earn their livings or even fit themselves for doing so. During his life of service he had paid into an archaic pension scheme for the two families he raised, which helped with their education and finally paid £100 down as each came of age. This was considered sufficient to equip sons for the services and to send daughters to India, where they would get married. Muriel had indeed visited Clem and Grace in India, but she had not got married. She was now dependent on the parental roof, and

8

on a modest allowance paid to her by her father, while not far ahead lay the obligation of the unmarried daughter to look after the parents in old age.

All I can remember of 'Burra Daddy' is a shadowy figure with a red lining to his dressing-gown, but I have tender memories of small, frail Granny, Louise Husband as she had been on marriage, and who, surprisingly, until her husband's retirement had lived all her life in India. This was because her father, George Macdonald Husband, servant of the East India Company and stationed in the North-West Provinces, when his wife died had felt unable to cope with two infant daughters, Louise, barely two, and a slightly older sister. He had other children at home in England and decided to despatch these two to join them, with an ayah and a volunteer escort of other people making the same journey.

In 1840 this was a formidable pilgrimage; no railway system spanned the whole journey and Calcutta yet lacked a regular shipping service. Nor had the telegraph service yet been introduced, so vital to Anglo-Indians for speedy communication. It was therefore a very long time before the father learnt that the cortège, on reaching Calcutta, had found that city in the throes of a virulent cholera epidemic to which the ayah and other members had fallen victim. Neither child had caught it but, in the ensuing chaos, had got separated from their party. Thus their identity was unknown when nuns, rescuing survivors from the heat and the infected area, took them to a mission station in the hills near Darjeeling. This undoubtedly saved Louise's life, but her elder sister died, and she remained for a considerable period an unidentified refugee, while her father was trying to trace his children.

After this, Louise remained in India and an elder sister, Jane, came out from England to look after her father and be both mother and governess to Louise. Inevitably Jane married and the husband, Augustus Fraser Baird, a generous character just twenty-one on marriage, was quite ready to take on a five-year-old as well as a wife. The father died while still in service, and as Jane's marriage was childless and they were billeted up in the hills, they were only too happy to keep Louise with them, and, as she grew up, she was frequently referred to as Miss Baird.

Augustus Baird, who eventually rose to the rank of General, was a ready artist and wit; he illustrated his letters with humorous sketches, he embellished his wife's invitations to croquet, and he has depicted Louise's love of animals in a sketch of her lying in bed with dogs, cat, mongoose and monkey disposed about her room, some even inside the mosquito net. At eighteen Louise married Hungerford Meyer Boddam, who must have been very much older than she was as he had already had three children by a former wife. One imagines thereafter the pets were denied the bedroom.

This small, gentle woman, who could only have been in her middle sixties when we reached Capel House, had in her an immense reserve of

9

courage, which she quietly kept to herself save when, thinking she heard a burglar, she descended to the ground floor, riding crop in hand. At first she was active about the house, but when conflict drove her upstairs she ranged the upper floor only, became a face at a window, or the occupant of a chair in her bedroom, the door of which was always open and the room a sanctuary for children, dogs, cat, kittens.

In that room, on a shelf at floor level under the dressing-table, was a line of neat little shoes which became a happy substitute for the bearer's shoes in India. I played with them ecstatically but presently began asking where were Granny's dresses and coats. It was explained that these had been sent away as they were no longer necessary, leaving me with the idea, which I communicated to any neighbour asking after Mrs Boddam, that my grandmother couldn't go out − she had no clothes to put on.

Granny was wont to refer to me as 'that little scrap'. She often tied up our hair with gay coloured ribbons when we went to parties, which were promptly taken off again by Muriel downstairs. She tried teaching us to sing hymns, but with little success. Interestingly, though her room was a sanctuary it was never a retreat for consolation. No questions were ever asked, no information ever given on what happened downstairs, though some of it must have been clearly audible.

*

It must have been very distressing for our mother, toiling back again from India the following year to see the children she had left behind, to find the baby quite indifferent to her. Left at two years of age, that baby naturally clove to the one person she knew. I had adopted Betty as my mother with a tenacity greater even than the usual veneration of the younger child for the older. Betty could manage her small sister where others failed.

Muriel was in her late twenties when she took charge of both house and nieces. She fully felt the responsibility and, in her way, was fond of us. 'Don't ever take them away from me' is written in one of the copious letters, covering glossy thin paper that caught the weekly mail between Capel House and India. Her aim was to turn us out obedient, tidy, truthful, well-mannered children, but her methods defeated the aim. She herself had been an overindulged youngest child, getting her way, if not with her father, certainly with her mother, shouting and going into sullen moods until she got it, and the German school, probably never shown this side of her character, had done nothing to correct it. It was the shouting that first troubled us, particularly in front of other children or in a public place. We were sensitive types and appalled when she shouted at Granny, after the austere influence of Burra Daddy had been removed.

10

Amongst her contemporaries our aunt was popular, enjoyed their company, went to dances – reputedly she was an excellent dancer – and frequently went to London for the day. An aura of peace then settled on the household, with relaxed supervision from the staff, the schoolroom soon in glorious confusion and muddy footprints across the hall. Maud, who looked after us, would make restoration later but never in time, and the evening, which Muriel probably intended to enjoy with us, ended in a tedious remedial exercise, the brunt of reprimand falling on Betty.

The remarkable thing was our acceptance, our loyalty. The stiff upper lip was the pattern of the day; one covered up injury or hurt; moreover, the child of those days wanted to be liked, which made them more malleable material than a later type to whom this was unimportant. So we continued to believe that everything was our fault; but when she was in a good mood, we did in fact enjoy our aunt's company.

When Muriel had visited India, Betty's early efforts to say 'Auntie' had got no further than 'Unnie', the name by which we continued to call her for some thirty years. At that point a friend of the family started referring to her as 'Auntie Bod', which caught on both inside and outside the family, and by which she is generally remembered, but until that time it is perhaps simpler to continue to call her Muriel.

Like other children born in India, Betty and I were wary of group entertainment. We looked to ourselves for diversions. We had no appetite for parties among a lot of strange faces, when I could be guaranteed to escape, either by bursting into tears or being sick, events with which Betty had learnt to live. She had early taught herself to read, lived in a world of books, of making up stories and inventing wonderful games. When out for walks she liked to walk alone and I, running up to join her, would be told I must walk either in front or behind. 'Front or behind' became the stock phrase in later years for the desire for privacy.

I lived in a dream world of imagination. I had considerable powers of mimicry and an entertainer's sensitivity to an appreciative audience. I had an exceptional memory for Betty's stories, for the amusing incident; could remember a ship with a green sail fetching passengers off the ship for Southampton on returning from India, but I had no powers of concentration for anything being taught or for story-books read to me.

Betty alone managed to instil the alphabet into my brain, and Granny conscientiously plied me with *Reading without Tears* – a heavy tome and the accepted book on teaching the young to read. It conveniently supplied small line-drawings beside the lists of elementary words, and I appeared to be showing promise as we went down the column: MAN, PAN, RAN, but VAN was the give-away. I said CART. This inability to concentrate troubled me all my life, in a more or less degree, but in the early years I made no effort to conquer it and it was readily assumed I was a dunce.

In contrast, Betty had reached a stage needing serious teaching, and a young girl living locally was engaged as governess to come every morning. It is probable that Miss Furlonge was scarcely out of her teens, but she was intelligent, competent, much liked, but not at all strong. Rheumatic fever had left her with a weak heart and within two years she suffered a heart attack and died.

The tragedy was heightened by her dying at a time when we had breached a number of the many laws that beset us, and Muriel used this untimely death as a lesson. She assured Betty that Miss Furlonge's dying words were: 'Oh, Betty, how can you be so naughty!' The implication was that Betty had killed her.

This indeed was cruel. For weeks the kind-hearted Betty could scarcely lift her head for shame, and it was many years before she could bring herself to tell me this, as I seemed not to be implicated in this unwitting homicide, though I would have thought teaching me was far more likely to bring on a heart attack. Thanks to Miss Furlonge, I could now write the name by which I was called, in capital letters, but had not yet been weaned from using my left hand. In the flyleaf of some of my nursery books was written YBAB from right to left, the natural movement of the left hand; however, this was progress.

Miss Culverhouse, the next governess, was older and came from Bath, but Muriel, not wishing for a living-in governess, engaged rooms for her in Guildford, from which she walked a couple of miles daily in all weather, as people then did unquestioningly, and spent the day at Capel House. She was a rather easily offended spinster, but a most conscientious governess, and I was to be all my life grateful for her determination. She would sit in front of me, holding hands, her face so close to mine that my eyes could not wander nor my hands fidget, and recite: 'Twice one are two, twice two are four...' until times tables were indelibly fixed in my memory, and the basis of a career was established.

*

The schoolroom at Capel House opened into the hall close to the main staircase, which we were not allowed to use. We had to go along a passage, through a baize door, up a steep staircase and more passages to reach bedroom, bathroom or lavatory. The downstairs lavatory was forbidden to us.

The house was full of draughts, doors left open soon shut or were slammed by an impetuous niece, thus an exercise book came into being with pages of lines: 'I must not slam the door or I am punished.' The first line, written by Muriel herself, had to be exactly copied and written with the right hand at least twenty times for each offence. They evidence the struggle of the left-handed to become right-handed, but they did teach me to become ambidextrous.

I was still a small underweight object with snow-white skin, even my cheeks rarely tinged with colour, and as yet not a hint of yellow in the hair. I looked like a plant reared in a cupboard and was a cause of constant anxiety to my aunt. Obviously I needed feeding up, but appeared to have no appetite, for it was the pattern of the times to administer to the young what was good for them rather than what they wanted. Those two compulsory pieces of bread and butter, spreading out like the desert of the Sahara before one could attain cake, took me almost half an hour of steady plodding to consume.

There was no lack of appetite, however, when we went to one of Miss Clifton's parties. Rose Clifton and her sister Mrs Wilson lived half a mile distant, and both understood and delighted in children. In the summer they gave haymaking parties in the field adjoining their house, and working parties in the winter, when about a dozen children sat round a table employed in various forms of stitchery; but whatever the occupation there were always the most delectable things to eat for tea, remembered by the guests long after, when they were grown men and women. These parties held no terrors for us as the children were all culled from the neighbourhood and we already knew each other.

Miss Clifton inspired membership of the League of Pity, a charitable confederation which issued a personal card to each member with an apple-tree on it, and each time you subscribed sixpence you marked it on the apple. Membership spread like an epidemic even if the objective was not so much to feed the starving as to be first to fill in all the apples. Unfortunately a pious music mistress had conscripted Betty and me already into a 'Holy Ministering Children's League', which seemed to extort much more and offered no apple-tree. There was thus no evidence of Christian feeling, and it didn't sound convincing to say you were a Holy Ministering Child.

Betty was always a rewarding child to feed. On arrival home from India she had at once regained her health and hearty appetite, and would help me out with the bread and butter if this could be achieved unseen. Muriel believed that if she denied us sugar in our tea we would grow up never to require it, but in the pantry the contents of the sugar-bowls had a habit of disappearing. Here also were dishes containing balls of butter, beautifully patterned, and to put one of these into the mouth was to reach a stage where it was hardly bearable, but once past this stage, it was delicious.

The kitchen staff were all on our side: Maud, who sang 'Becorse I love you' whilst bathing us, Myrtle, who knew which were our favourite puddings and told us when these were due, and a parlour maid, who probably knew about the sugar but said nothing. When promoted to the dining-room, I sat on a high chair at the East India dining-table nearest to the service door, and was inclined to turn towards this door in moments of expectation. That prompted another exercise book full of lines. I have it yet, and there are at least six pages filled: 'I must not watch the puddings coming in.'

I have no quarrel with my aunt in those early days; she had been foisted into a job for which she was unsuited and which carried with it heavy responsibility, bringing her much anxiety, especially when with monotonous regularity we caught the prevailing infectious ailments: mumps, chickenpox, scarlet fever etc. At the outset we had one singular illness to ourselves, when someone gave us a pedigree kitten and no one detected that it had ring-worm. Maud, Betty and I caught it in varying degrees but mine was so bad I had to have all my hair taken off by X-ray, when the infection could be properly treated. I was then rising four.

To me this was an exciting adventure; I travelled to London with Muriel, went in a hansom cab from Waterloo to Harley Street, passing the statue of Boadicea in her chariot – very impressive – to sit under a glass globe with a snout to it that was concentrated on my head. I was warned to sit very still, and a flashing blue light, making a lot of noise, came through the globe. My hair fell off in handfuls, and this was repeated in several visits until my scalp was bald as an egg.

After each visit my aunt would shop at the Army & Navy Stores, then in full flower, supported on Anglo-Indian investment. I was left to have my midday rest in the ladies room, on a horsehair sofa so smooth and round it was difficult to stay on it. There was a large-bosomed attendant, but rarely did more than six people come in.

Betty never had her hair removed, save in the infected patches treated at home, but white close-fitting caps were made for us to appear in in public, when we looked like a couple of small nuns. Soon I had a tremendous crop of thick golden curls, quite out of character and making me look much older than my years, but it all came out again with the next epidemic – scarlet fever – which all but killed me the following year.

On this occasion I alone was the victim and Betty went to stay with friends. A trained nurse was imported, while I had a hard struggle but finally held my own; Muriel meanwhile was distraught.

As ever, when Betty and I re-met after separation, I exerted my consider-able imagination in describing wildly exciting events that, generally for lack of sufficient research, were manifestly untrue. On this occasion I was so rash as to say I had read books. Betty was highly sceptical. What books? That bubble was soon pricked. But our aunt's method for bringing us up – instant punishment for transgression – also encouraged untruthful romance, in fact turned me into an accomplished liar. To avoid the consequences I would skilfully embellish denial, or invent an elaborate excuse if the foot-prints across the flower-beds were of an incriminating size. One might argue that the trouble I took implied a basic regard for the truth, where a slipshod evasion might show indifference. Certainly my industrious pains to cover up felony only endured during my aunt's term of office, but it never shook Betty's basic honesty or moral courage. These she had inherited from her father, but I seemed only to have got a token share.

*

It would seem that the curse laid on my father at the time of my birth still endured. In the autumn before the scarlet fever epidemic, my mother had a third child, also a daughter, but one so beautiful its sex could be forgiven, and the following summer parents and baby came on leave.

As the extent of Clem's leave was limited, Grace came in advance with Nurse Eva and the most contented, blue-eyed, pink-cheeked, rounded baby one could wish to see. When the birds had sung in the garden in India the baby was wont to sing too, and thus had been christened Avis, and at an early age had begun to walk.

Betty and I contrasted poorly in appearance with this new addition, Betty having been clamped into a plate with a gold bar across protruding front teeth, and I had wide gaps in gums awaiting second teeth, and though the crop of abundant hair was still enduring, I remained a thin white specimen whose aunt was wont to describe as a most extraordinary child, sometimes lovely, sometimes downright plain. It was possible the changes were influenced by Muriel's prevailing mood, but also this was consistent with my character.

There was no jealousy of the actual baby, whom the sisters were equally ready to adore; it was the attitude of the grown-ups that left us feeling unimportant and still the butt of Muriel's accusations, so that we who had waited so long for Heaven's gates to open, found Heaven not so glorious after all.

One morning Eva, being busy, had left the baby with us in the schoolroom and we had taken her out on to the verandah to play. This, discovered by Muriel, brought the usual 'How silly you are!' – a refrain that was to echo through a good part of the century. But on this occasion, far worse, the rebuke was quietly endorsed by our mother, for there was an unguarded drop of some feet from verandah to flower-bed below and the baby was at the toddling stage. She was rushed away and Betty and I retired to the schoolroom, where I discovered that Betty was silently weeping; and if Betty's feelings were hurt this was unbearable, and I gave much louder vent to my feelings.

For Grace it must have been a soul-searing situation, this divided command of her children; she was inclined to take the same passive attitude adopted by Granny for, quite apart from undermining Muriel's authority, to

15

criticize Muriel's method would lead to loud argument or long sullen moods. In any case, Muriel was shortly to go for a long-deserved rest to friends in the Isle of Wight and Clem, who always had wonderful ideas for holidays, was soon going to arrive.

He did arrive, and one of his first duties was to visit his mother – Granny at Southbourne, now a widow. To do this he hired a victoria with coachman and pair of horses, and we all proceeded by road. It was a lovely route through the New Forest, then both dignified and lonely; he and Grace sat facing ahead, Betty and I sat on the little seat opposite, and I remember being troubled that there were no doors to keep us in. At intervals we got out and walked, saw new flowers, birds and animals, and spent the night at a hotel in the Forest.

This was indeed heaven; no wonder Jane Austen had so favoured this form of holiday, but in this case it only lasted two days. Nurse, baby and all heavy luggage were despatched by Muriel on the second day by train, and Clem met them at Christchurch station that evening. A carefully planned expedition, such as I was to emulate in later years.

Southbourne provided a sandy beach on which to play, and a host of cousins. Every summer brought some of the nine sons and two daughters born in India back to the family home. They were now nearly all married and with children, and those who could not be housed at The Gables occupied local lodgings. These were plentiful though Southbourne was rapidly expanding into a place of permanent residence.

My golden locks, legacy of the X-ray, had turned into lank straight hair, so spiritless that Grace cut it short like a boy's to give it impetus. This, combined with frilly cotton dresses and brown button boots, resulted in the oddest-looking little creature, but at that time expedience prevailed.

*

The sojourn at Southbourne may not have rivalled the method of getting there, but there was to be a further extension of Heaven when Clem, Grace, children and nurse all arrived at Scole Lodge, up a slight hill from Scole village in Norfolk. This was a comfortable eighteenth-century house separated from the main Ipswich to Norwich road by peaceful parkland, studded with oak-trees, where bullocks occasionally grazed. Tinie, the eldest of the Boddam daughters, had married the owner of this property, one Richard Crawshay, a confirmed country squire who farmed a goodly acreage around Scole Lodge. In Tinie he had the ideal countryman's wife, with her store of practical knowledge and her good will towards neighbours and tenants; her dinner parties were much sought after. They had one adored son, Eric, a few years senior to Betty.

The only flaw in the marriage was that Aunt Tinie and Uncle Dick were first cousins; our Granny in Guildford was a sister of Uncle Dick's mother, but it would be hard to say which was more responsible for Eric's instability, the close relationship or parental devotion, as Eric had early learnt how to dupe his parents. Both grandmothers were now invalids, the one at Scole occupying a large bedroom with an attendant in the adjoining dressing-room, and as there were other guests at the Lodge, we children with nurse Eva were housed at the home farm.

This was Thorpe Parva Hall Farm, once a place of importance, which Dick rented from an owner unwilling to sell, but with its big farmyard behind it and its barns, it made an ideal home farm, housing Debenham, Uncle Dick's foreman, and his family. As the Debenhams only occupied part of the house, we could spread ourselves, and Betty and I had a lovely big bedroom with a sloping floor. Its windows, looking out over a moat and an orchard, had such broad sills on the outside that we climbed on to them, and sat so close to the swathes of swallows and house martins flying past we could almost touch them.

It would be impossible to enumerate all the joys of that summer, with rides in the farm carts, hay in the barns, learning to play conkers and making a raft from an old bit of fencing which sunk under our weight, but there was more mud in the moat than water. It was only hard on Eva getting us to a standard of cleanliness to go and pay visits to the Lodge.

I had my sixth birthday during this time and with four benevolent adults asking me what I wanted, I asked something far beyond the price of the usual birthday present, but everything at this stage seemed possible.

In the Army & Navy Stores list, then the size of a family Bible and covering all conceivable desires, I had seen a picture of a child's tricycle, and it offered – in my eyes – access to the great world; it symbolized an independence I had sought to establish ever since arrival in England when, on a grassy walk, the hub-cap had come off the wheel of my pram and, while nurse and Betty diligently looked for it, I slipped away and, by animal instinct, found my own way home.

I did not receive the tricycle, and indeed had little hope of it, but the time was approaching for parents and Avis to return to India. Clem, now a Colonel, was Deputy Commissioner of Lahore, a title deeply impressive to us though we have no idea of its meaning. Shortly he would be Commissioner, and there was no question of his leaving the upper Punjab, thus no reason for not taking back with them that robust baby daughter. Why, if Avis was being taken, could we not all go back together? The boring matter of education was produced as a deterrent, but picture postcards sent from Marseilles to the deserted daughters are evidence of the agony suffered by Grace and Clem.

That visit to Scole, however, proved a landmark in our lives for it had been agreed that we should now go there every summer for our holidays. And to soften the feeling of being left behind, the green tricycle was delivered to Capel House for Christmas, and promptly on presentation I was skimming round the garden on it. I was then seen heading for the drive, whereon Muriel emerged to say it was on no account to be taken on the road.

This was devastating. I felt utterly defrauded; the tricycle had symbolized independence. Inevitably there were infringements of the regulation in Muriel's absence, until the day when she was thought to be in London but came swinging round the corner at the lower end of the road, to find me careering down the hill on the tricycle. Hoping to save the situation, I came on past the gates of the house towards her, saying with a winning smile, 'I've come to meet you, Unnie!' It did not help. The tricycle was forbidden for several weeks, and Myrtle turned a blind eye to it being ridden round and round the scullery.

*

A small school, mostly for day girls, had been started not far from Capel House, and Betty was sent there, with favourable result. It was attended mostly by our personal friends, Anglo-Indians at that, for a veritable pocket of them lived in this area and, not surprisingly, I believed India was the place where everyone was born. As Betty enjoyed the school, at nine years of age I was also sent, and heartily loathed it.

All my growing years I felt that school stopped you doing anything useful, and certainly anything you wanted to do, and the programme of things I wanted to do, by nine years of age, was prodigious. There were dolls, faithfully got up, dressed, fed and put to bed; there was a magazine, *The Jester*, of which I was sole subscriber, illustrator and reader, though sometimes Betty derived entertainment from it and even subscribed a poem. There was carpentry, the result of watching an old carpenter at Scole, and a firm called Hobbies sold, at modest prices, a few elementary tools, which became my next desire after the tricycle, and were given me by Uncle Dick. This interest flourished mostly at Scole, which offered greater facility, as saw-marks on the side of the schoolroom chair seats led to firm discouragement of the craft at Capel House. Also there was gardening; we had a square patch separated from the kitchen quarters by a small shrubbery. Seeds flourished on Betty's side but not so much on mine as I got side-tracked into making a water garden, using an old pipe I had found lying around to bring the constant drip from the cistern of the servants' lavatory to a trench dug to receive it. That it sometimes worked is amazing, as plasticine was responsible for the connections.

All these occupations school interrupted, but at about this period the family doctor was consulted on my lack of appetite and he suggested giving me to eat what I fancied. No gain in weight resulted, but sausages, scallops, scrambled eggs now disappeared with a rapidity that relieved the tension of getting to school by nine o'clock, which the slow consuming of porridge, bread and marmalade had rendered nigh impossible.

By now I could read and could write flowingly from left to right, even if the spelling was often unorthodox. Because of my inattention I still lacked whole vistas of knowledge I was assumed to have absorbed, and was keenly aware of this. I was, however, determined to live down my backward reputation and succeeded for a time at the school in acquiring the highest marks in class, though at first there was no serious competition. As the class grew in size and others usurped my place, I was content with being third or fourth but was all the time yearning for the weekends on my own, and elated when an epidemic broke out and there was a blissful period of quarantine.

I had no team spirit but wanted to be liked by my friends. I also wanted the approval of the teaching staff, but some of them I found terrifying, particularly a Miss Messervey from the Channel Islands. She had a highly explosive temper and, her hair being prematurely grey, I assumed she had not long to live and prayed nightly for death to be hastened. The wise Lord, however, saw fit to preserve her for heroic defence of her fellow islanders through two world wars, and I soon gave up praying about her as hopeless.

There were school games in the afternoons but neither of us went back for them; I preferred to plough through boring homework and have at least the evenings to myself, while Betty blissfully deferred homework till the last minute, despatching it with enviable ease and efficiency before bed. As Muriel was just as keen that the homework should be completed, there was no hounding off to games, and in any case no fear of our not getting exercise. As the school outgrew its premises it moved to a larger house further away and, unless coming from an impossible distance, all schoolchildren then walked to and from school. Nor was Sunday any exception for Capel House was a good two miles from church and, starting out with Muriel, by the time forgotten gloves, prayer-book, handkerchief, offertory had been retrieved, often requiring successive missions, the walk to church could be increased by another mile. Muriel's hope of teaching by experience seemed unavailing.

*

There were only two school subjects that stirred my interest: Drawing and Composition. I also tolerated Arithmetic, thanks to Miss Culverhouse's patient grounding. Composition, however, was a glorious challenge, for there existed in many members of the Parsons family a compelling urge to write. Clem had it, and handed it on to his daughters, and it was already evident that Betty had considerable talent.

I had copious ideas for stories but no paper to write them on. *The Jester* owed its being to pages torn from exercise books, but Composition supplied books for the purpose and was the only homework I found inspiring.

As I increased in years, but perhaps not in wisdom, my class reached a level where English was taken by the head of the school, a tall, imposing woman of whom pupils were much in awe. Mrs Kitto happened also to be a friend of Muriel's and therefore came at times to Capel House, a displacement that we found rather disconcerting and which led in due course to an unprecedented scene. From time to time compositions were set as homework for the English class, and when Mrs Kitto gave out as the subject for the composition: 'God tempers the wind to the shorn Lamb', I felt duly inspired and covered several pages with what I thought was an exceptional essay. It was.

A breathless moment: Mrs Kitto's entrance with the pile of exercise books, the better essays usually at the top. But mine was not among those given special mention. The subject had been discussed for some time before Mrs Kitto drew an exercise book from the bottom of the pile saying, 'Well, here we have a rather different point of view. Claudia Parsons appears to put her own interpretation on the word "tempers". Her essay seems to imply that no sooner has God descried a young lamb bereft of protection than He sends a furious blast. . . .' No shorn lamb could have felt it more keenly. The general merriment was most mortifying.

Yet worse was to come.

Mrs Kitto had a habit of coming as an onlooker to classes that were not her own, and rumour had it she was coming to one of Miss Ashby's Shakespeare classes, which were in themselves terrifying enough. Miss Ashby was an even greater menace than Miss Messervey, whom, having failed to eliminate, I had now grown used to. But Miss Ashby used a sarcasm that could peel the skin off even the most brilliant Shakespeare pupil, which definitely I was not. Shakespeare belonged to that vortex of ignorance that I was always trying to keep hidden from discovery. I had laboured the whole afternoon with Mark Antony, making notes in my rough book to counter the questions that would be shot around the class; anyone failing to answer was held up to derision. Now the class had settled in place and I found I had not got that mainstay of knowledge; I had left the rough book on the window-sill of the staircase when other books had fallen from under my arm and I had put it there while I picked them up. Without it I was in a panic, my mind a blank, and there was Mrs Kitto already at the door.

Mrs Kitto had dined the previous evening at Capel House, and it was customary for me to come down after my bath to have my hair brushed in Muriel's study. It was at this point that Mrs Kitto had been ushered in, to receive from me no doubt a self-conscious smile, yet sitting in the armchair her manner seemed to soften, and possibly in my nightclothes I looked more angelic than at school. The relationship seemed to ease. Now, here she was at the door of the classroom, but only to tell Miss Ashby not to wait. She had to fetch some things from her office. She would be with us presently.

Does a drowning sailor to whom a rope is thrown stop to consider the type of rope? 'Oh, Mrs Kitto, as you're coming down, would you bring my rough book? It's on the window-sill....'

It was the deadly hush, the frozen silence that gave me the first inkling of the enormity of the indiscretion. Mrs Kitto, always exceptionally tall, looked taller than Nelson's column as she gazed down at me. 'And do you expect *me* to fetch and carry for you....?' What else she said I was in no condition to imbibe. The only relief that could be derived from this frightful gaffe was that it left even Miss Ashby speechless. No following sarcasm; was there in fact the ghost of a smile on her face as she rallied the pupils to get on with the lesson? Clearly, I had yet much to learn besides Shakespeare.

*

Betty and I were now spending our summers at Scole Lodge, summers that were, and continued to be, a wonderful bonus for us, the life of restraint replaced by one of incentive. It opened up fields of knowledge and skill, some of which were to influence my whole life. Scole also grew peaches and grapes for the dining-table.

My first skill came through the discovery in the stables of a small, child's bicycle, long since abandoned by Eric, on which I speedily taught myself to ride and, though the roads were forbidden, in the grounds of Scole Lodge was abundant territory for exciting riding. This kept me happy for a couple of years but I was getting impatient with this low-seated, low-geared machine, and could now reach the adjusted saddle of an adult bicycle. At home, Betty was allowed to use Muriel's bicycle for approved missions, but it was denied to me for fear I would use it in a neighbour's garden for bicycle polo.

I was approaching my tenth birthday and Aunt Tinie wrote to Muriel asking what she thought I ought to be given, and there came an almost unbelievable answer: 'I think Claudia ought to have a bike for her birthday.' The whole of life was altered; I lived in a dream world, holding imaginary handlebars, while we awaited Muriel's decision on whether this should be bought in Norwich or Guildford. The reply came at breakfast and was read out: 'I did not say a "bike". I would never use the abbreviation. I said a "Bible". Claudia is anyhow too young to have a bicycle.'

They gave me a Bible.

But there is a sequel. Shortly after that troubled birthday, Betty and Uncle Dick went to Norwich by pony and trap and returned with a lovely wide string hammock. Betty knew that another of my ambitions was to sleep out under a great beech-tree that stood beside a lawn in Scole garden, though even this ambition had to wait for an evening warm enough for Aunt Tinie to grant permission. After that, one of my most treasured memories is that great tree, stretching above me like fan vaulting, the lawn soaked in moonlight and all the night sound around me; owls hooting, bullocks coughing. However far away these bullocks were across the park, however silently I came out of the house, they knew and crept up stealthily till I could see their eyes glistening on the far side of the railings. Later I would hear a horse trotting homeward along the Norwich road, the sound rising in a small crescendo and then fading in distance. It was all so still, so peaceful, so safe.

We were now approaching 1911, an eventful year, primarily because it was bringing Grace and Clem on leave with Avis and an Eurasian nanny. Excitement was such that the infection had spread to the school and one child asked her parents to go away, it would be so lovely when they came back.

Avis, now six years old, integrated easily with both of us, though very different in character. She was a happy extrovert, naturally demonstrative, whereas we found it difficult to express affection, and she was forthright and outspoken, where we were oblique. It would be hard to say how much this contrast was due to upbringing; certainly she had always had the protection of her mother, but the severity and criticism we had suffered was not always a bad thing, save in destroying self-confidence – a precious asset in a competitive world. Meanwhile Avis showed a satisfactory veneration for her elder sisters and I found it highly agreeable to have someone to whom to tell my stories and to order about.

This was the year of the coronation of King George V and Queen Mary, a day that began with a dawn exit of Clem, Grace, Betty and me in a hired chauffeur-driven car. We two were joining relatives in seats along the processional route, while it was hoped that Clem's invitation to the Abbey, prominent on the windscreen of the car, would secure priority in the London-bound traffic. As every time the police cleared a passage, however, the engine invariably failed and there was an ignominious hold-up, so progress was not so regal after all. Yet all reached their destinations in time.

To me the crowning glories of that day were Hammersmith Bridge, which I had never formerly seen going to London by train, and after that the Royal coaches, particularly the one containing the Royal children, for at the moment of passing, Princess Mary's coronet fell off. It slid from her fair hair which was not yet 'up' and, indeed, with all this gracious bowing, it was a miracle it stayed on at all. It was adroitly fielded and handed back to her by the future Duke of Windsor, sitting opposite. An elderly man seated next to us in our stand told me to tell my grandchildren that I had watched this procession next to a veteran of the Crimean war.

Then came an event of even greater excitement; seeing the naval review from the deck of HMS *Africa*, the flagship under command of the Admiral of the Fleet, Prince Louis of Battenberg. Clem and his family were privileged to be invited on board and the chief memory in the minds of the young was when a squall blew up, just at the hour when the Admirals were calling on the Admiral of the Fleet. Betty and I watched fascinated as pinnace after pinnace, dancing on the choppy waters, arrived at the ship's side and Admirals leapt on to the ship's companion, trying not to fall into the water, to preserve their dignity and protect their masses of gold braid. Luckily, the *Africa* remained firm as a rock, unmoved by the squall.

Glorious as it was to range the deck of a battleship, it was terribly near the naval guns when they fired a salute as the Royal yacht steamed proudly down the line of vessels. No guns in the later air raids ever made such a devastating noise.

*

That summer was spent in Scotland, and the reunion with mountains, even as mild as those in Perthshire, must have stirred my memory. Scotland was not then laced with tourists, and the unfettered loneliness of the country challenged my inclinations to explore on my own. I would go off on the spur of the moment and generally in footwear quite unsuited to the exercise; Grace, anxious but understanding, raised no objection save when I returned from climbing a waterfall with uppers and soles of indoor slippers barely hanging together. What induces her to go off like this, my mother wondered. Betty said it fed my soul. It certainly emphasized the contrasting sides of my character, since for my eleventh birthday I chose to take my dolls to a picnic organized beside Loch Earn. Birthday cake was spread before the dolls, and Clem saw fit to assure the local padre, who happened to alight from a rowing boat at this cove, that we were not practising idol worship.

Clem's soul was also fed that summer since he joined friends for the Glorious Twelfth, and when we all returned to Capel House to release Muriel for a holiday, he took a long solo bicycle ride up to the Lakes, a ride such as he had enjoyed in bachelor days. He was now fifty-one years of age and whilst at home had his health checked with a view to insuring his life. Leave was now rapidly coming to an end and deep responsibilities lay ahead as the Durbar for King George and Queen Mary was due early in 1912.

A highly recommended boarding-school had been chosen, to which Betty was to go the following autumn. Avis was going back with her parents and I again pleaded to be taken, though knowing I hadn't a chance, embroiled in all this schooling. So slowly this precious leave had approached; so quickly ended.

Durbars occurred twice in Clem's career and he was involved in both. In 1902 it had been his duty to find and requisition suitable ground on which to mount marquees, tents, cantonments, stabling and all the paraphernalia for the Durbar of King Edward VII and Queen Alexandra.

This he found could not be accomplished without taking land already under cultivation by the Indians, which entailed compensation and promise of return, to which Clem gave his word. Unfortunately Kitchener, visiting Delhi and seeing this vista of territory laid out for the Durbar, decided it would be ideal acreage for the future placement of his troops, and he applied for it. The application filtered through the usual channels and was finally blocked by Clem, then a mere Major, who would not yield. On reaching Simla that year he was greeted by a fellow officer, 'I say, Parsons! You're for the high jump! Kitchener's seething – his plans held up by a minor official.' This was not comforting news for a married man with two daughters under five. There was a long and harrowing wait while the matter was referred to the India Office in London, which, surprisingly, upheld Clem's commitment.

In 1912 Clem, by now Commissioner of Lahore, had no spadework but far greater involvement besides responsibility for King and Queen. Shiploads came out from England for it, and at the height of the ceremony there was a distant and ill-advised cry of 'Fire!'; at that moment, had the fire been serious, it could have ripped through that canopied area, wiping out Royalty, Viceroy, Rajahs and all other statesmen and leaving few if any officials to receive the blame. A young woman seated near Grace began shaking. Grace muttered, 'Look at the Queen!' Of King George and Queen Mary not a muscle stirred. The fire later proved to have been insignificant.

Nevertheless many sighed with relief when it was all over and the liners were leaving Bombay, packed with returning visitors. It was at this point that Clem suffered a severe heart attack. Whether it was the extra work of the Durbar or the long years of service in the Indian climate, the doctors were adamant that he must be got back to England immediately; but how? Thanks to Grace's fervent prayers, miraculously some reservations were cancelled, and she, Clem and Avis sailed for England.

At the time of going on board neither Clem's speech nor movement were visibly affected, and no doubt Muriel, at home, was being supplied with all news by the marvellous telegraphic communication, which compressed information on every conceivable subject into booklets of short coded words. She told us Clem was not well, but not till their ship was in the Red Sea did she tell us all three were on their way home, and she was awaiting a telegram announcing their arrival at Port Said. Upstairs, I saw the telegraph boy coming up the drive on his bicycle, heard the telegram being taken to Muriel in her study, heard Muriel say, 'Oh', and after a pause, 'No answer, thank you', and knew, as if it had been spoken that my father was dead.

We had always felt immensely proud of him and this last year had got to know him a little more. But how could we have feelings other than immense relief that our mother would now be permanently home?

*

Grace had endured a moving funeral service, the ship's engine halted, the coffin lowered slowly down a slipway into the Red Sea – that sea which has so often been the highway between India and home. It must have taken courage to meet this break in her life with calm composure as she and Avis came on home alone.

There were quite a few days before her arrival at Capel House, during which Muriel, with no doubt the best intentions, got on to a favourite theme.

In those days it was customary for the contents of a parental home to be left to the unmarried daughters, which Muriel's father had done. On her mother's death Muriel would inherit many more valuable heirlooms beside the Indian table and the mirrors, which, if sold, could have made her comfortably independent. If there was still a roof, however, it was generally accepted that such inheritance should remain under the roof. Thus our aunt considered herself to be penniless – a state which she almost seemed to relish – and now she could give full rein in lecturing us on the need for economy. Whether the lectures bore the intended fruit, I doubt, but they made me feel inferior, relegating us to a category apart, as if there was something wrong with us – or that is how it seemed to me.

Certainly the situation was grave; my father had died a few years short of retirement age, and Grace would receive a widow's pension, not of a civil servant but of an army Colonel. Moreover my father had not had time to pay the entirety of his life insurance, leaving Grace with three daughters to clothe, educate and ultimately house.

Meanwhile, in that interval while we waited for our mother and Avis, the faithful Maud was leaving us, and there was to be a farewell visit to the only cinema existing then in Guildford. It had a row of fire buckets under the screen, and a pianist who adjusted her repertoire to the subject, of which the audience had little advance knowledge but a fair certainty that all would come right in the end. However, on this occasion the theme was too near to the bone, embracing a worthy but impoverished woman carrying a child in her arms in the pouring rain, going from door to door seeking cheap lodging. Even Betty could not conceal her emotion and I came out shedding uncontrollable tears that even cream buns could barely stem.

The gloomy outlook, however, was soon dispelled with our mother's return, for she had an amazing faith not only in God but in things working out in the end, which is perhaps all part of the same thing. She and my aunt were perfect examples of optimist and pessimist, even to the definition of a pessimist being one who has lived with an optimist, for my mother in the following years was indeed sorely pressed and not in any sense calculating. The 'working out' sometimes poised on a knife-edge.

She now faced, from a distance, the disposal of their property in India; the sale into reliable hands of their horses, including her beloved mare, who had always recognized her step when she returned from home leave, and given a woman-to-woman neigh. Helped in all this by friends still in Lahore, she also found homes for their dogs, and a few treasured pieces of furniture were despatched to England.

With her return we were now allowed to use the whole house, could use the front stairs, and though our aunt's black moods and oppressive silences still persisted, they mattered less; and if the shouting and criticism still continued and our mother's silence gave a feeling of acquiescence, we could not know what was said in private. Anyhow, it had little effect. Nor was our mother's state as beggarly as described to us; Clem had patiently subscribed to the Indian Military Service Family Pension fund, which gave Grace a small boost towards our schooling, and gave us on coming of age £16 a quarter, to cease on marriage. At that time £16 was not insignificant.

Amid all the criticism of my aunt, let it be said in her favour that to her we owe our love of theatre. She made every endeavour to enlarge our minds, took us to current theatres in London, not only children's plays but to the enthralling spectacles at the Hippodrome, to the Follies, a pierrot troupe of song and nonsense that I found madly funny, and through her I can claim to have seen Herbert Beerbohm Tree in *Henry VIII*. I could accept Shakespeare better on the stage than in print.

The 1914–18 war saw my mother in sole charge at Capel House and gave my aunt her first opportunity of a career. Starting as a Quartermaster at a Guildford hospital, she later joined the Women's Auxiliary Army Corps, serving in different parts of the country until 1918, when German-speaking WAACs were asked to go and do office work in Germany with the Army of the Rhine. She joined a hand-picked company serving in Cologne, was

26

popular, made lasting friendships and gave noble assistance in a fearful motor accident when the driver went to sleep at the wheel. She was known by her fellow WAACs as 'Auntie' because she talked so much about her nieces.

1912–1922

SCHOOL CLOTHES TO OVERALLS

When we first went to Scole we were met at Diss station by horses, carriage and luggage cart, later by a chauffeur-driven Wolseley, and I remember sitting beside Wilby and daring him to drive at forty miles an hour. When the Wolseley company brought out a two-seater model, the Stellite, my uncle bought one of these to drive himself, chiefly on work for the farm.

The 1914 war robbed him of many of his farm-hands, also of Eric, now due for call-up, so he hoped to teach Betty to drive the Stellite, but Betty – never at ease with mechanical devices – drove him into the ditch. Then he tried me, though I was not yet old enough for a licence, but could be useful bringing sacks from the mill to Thorpe Parva farm, all within the estate. The Stellite had only three gears, two forward and a reverse, so the gear change was not easy, but my pride in driving it was prodigious. Its carburettor needed frequent adjustment, but with an engine so easily got at, and so visible, I quickly saw Wilby's methods of correction and started to do them myself – a further approach towards a future career.

Avis had a passion for animals, so her job was to feed the ferrets and exercise the dogs. I now built her a two-storey hutch for her rabbits, for the old carpenter had retired, but his bench and his tools still remained, as well as a pile of timber Eric had ordered and then done nothing about. Added to all this, my uncle now taught me to shoot, so that wartime Scole, I often felt, taught me more than the patient plodding at school. Here I was so positive, at school so negative.

There was rigid etiquette about guns in those days, and such severity about not shooting on Sundays that the woodpigeon, confident of their safety, sat on the gateposts within a few feet of us as we walked to church. It was the same when I slept out under the beech-tree; there they were, crooning in the branches above me, the farmer's worst enemy when they settled in flocks in the cornfield.

I started humbly with a single-bore rifle, but by the time I was promoted to a 16-bore gun I had become quite useful at harvest, particularly in a memorable bean field out of which, during cutting, the hares poured in such numbers that the gun got almost too hot to hold. It was anxious work, not to scare the horses drawing the binder, nor shoot the spectators, of whom far too many turned up, nor shoot the lurcher dogs that some brought to chase the hares that got away. However, without casualty I managed to supply many wartime meals for Britain, and in due course was eligible for the motor licence. I had also acquired the bicycle, but too late. The Stellite had stolen its glory.

I was now a pupil at Crofton Grange, following in Betty's wake. My mother had felt justified in the outlay while we were still living at Capel House, and Betty had been a rewarding pupil, but these conditions ceased to prevail during my term at the school. I was not at my ease in this cultured environment, the walls hung with Italian Renaissance prints, not because I was not interested – in fact I longed to know more, but felt I would never get to Florence or Rome. I was in a panic at the weekly dispersal of books from the library in case Miss Lyster discovered how few of the classics I had read. I also found reading them impossible with so much conversation going on around me, so handed them back eventually only half read, if read at all.

Miss Lyster attended to education, Miss Elizabeth to well-being. I was still small, with a figure like a beanpole, no feminine curves, and skirts had to be buttoned on or they would have fallen off. My hair was almost obliterated by the huge black bow tying it back, which was the fashion at the time. Through the Lysters' abundant generosity no deprivation through food rationing ever appeared to reach the pupils. The two sisters, Miss Elizabeth generally wearing a large straw hat, would sit at each end of a long table, each carving a massive joint, and the pupils thus had a choice of viands.

I suffered terrible chilblains through the bracing school conditions: dormitory windows open all the year round. The chilblains broke and had to be bandaged, but they released me from winter piano practice or playing in the drawing-room on Sunday nights. The war was then in full cry, with Zeppelin raids over London at night, but only if our local sirens gave warning were we brought down to the lower floor and shrouded in eiderdowns, looking like rows of sugar buns. Otherwise we remained upstairs, though some of the girls crept to the windows to watch the searchlights, and when one of them called out: 'There's one in the searchlight. It's on *fire!*', instantly everyone was out of bed, making for a door on to a balcony. Thus did I see a distant ball of fire, the Zeppelin coming down over Potters Bar.

Miss Lyster was imbued with a tremendous patriotism, fanned by the sound of the guns in France clearly audible at night. It was difficult to keep up with her high standard of emotion, and we were all asked to submit a list of our fighting relatives, which were pinned up in the big schoolroom. With my eight uncles, whose offspring were now in the late teens or twenties, I had the longest list but one, and rode on this glory for a time, but not for long.

29

With garden boys disappearing in recruitment, we were put on to sweeping leaves and rolling lawns; and a prodigious quantity of socks, scarves and balaclavas resulted from evening knitting sessions, while Miss Elizabeth read to us. Every now and again we gave a concert for the moveable wounded from a local hospital, and one wonders what they made of these innocent songsters, clad in white muslin, who were certainly not encouraged to ogle the male throng before them. Anyhow, there was always an abundant tea.

All this time, in the morning papers, poems were dripping off the pens of Newbolt and Kipling, and the casualty list made it all too obvious that 'the game is more than the player of the game, and the ship is more than the crew'. With what ecstasy Miss Lyster read out at breakfast from the *Morning Post* Kipling's poem on the minesweepers, 'Dawn off the Forcland', to a gathering of whom probably only a few could appreciate its poignancy.

In that year Granny died at Capel House as quietly as she had lived, starting her life in a horse-drawn vehicle across India, and in its last years witnessing a Zeppelin heading towards Guildford.

*

I was at home when my grandmother died and was deeply distressed over it, but it had never occurred to me that this would mean leaving Capel House. When this was revealed to me by letter at Crofton – where I suspect the kindly Misses Lyster had modified the terms to let me stay on – this was like a second bereavement. One's love for a place is not compounded of continual happiness there, but rather it is built up on the emotions, struggles and disappointments one has suffered along with enjoyment. Lying in bed at night my mind would now range over every corner of the house where I had lived so fully, for mine was a memory that stored detail to the exclusion of more important facts, and every inch of house and garden was connected with some special incident.

It now fell to Grace to provide a roof for her sister and children, a rented roof, perforce, and one less expensive than Capel House. With the war at its height this was a case of any port in a storm, and she was lucky to be offered a more modest domain, owned by the same landlord, for the remainder of the war, after which he intended selling.

This house, close to Guildford High Street, with a small garden round it, stood in a row of others like it, but as a resident staff was now beyond my mother's means it provided us with five bedrooms. On arrival home for Christmas, I found my mother loyally trying to fit into it her sister's heritage. The Indian table had been consigned to a furniture store, but the remaining mirror, its frame adjusted, had been squeezed into the drawing-room. Racing against blackout time, she was paring down curtains to fit the windows while I hung them for her; eventually she was forced to hang them, refitted or not.

For me this house had one great redeeming advantage: a small store-room, which my mother let me have as a carpenter's shop. Into its limited dimensions I compressed all my interests so it became at once workshop, studio, writing-room. Dolls and the *Jester* magazine had long since been abandoned; I was now making model war machines, and becoming the repairer of all minor breakdowns in the house in whatever medium. I longed to do munition work, and was honoured when an established carpenter asked me to help him in making crutch heads. He gave me the blocks and the pattern, and though I cannot say I despatched many to him in my holidays, he approved of their accuracy and finish.

A wildly different contribution to the war effort, however, I executed in a state of near rebellion. At various dancing classes I had learnt to use a slight body and a good sense of timing to become a graceful solo dancer. Now with innumerable concerts being got up for officers and men, I resented coming home to find I had been borrowed for these occasions when, with all my interests, holiday time was so precious. I would go off to rehearsals wearing an expression of thunder but, ever respectful of an audience, I never allowed rebellion to prejudice the final result.

Betty, on leaving Crofton, had complied with wartime urgency for schoolteachers and gone as a resident teacher to our former day school, now called Tormead. Avis had been sent to Nottinghill High School, whose excellent scholastic reputation culled pupils from interesting families, but she was not fond of the rather austere boarding-house for the long-distance pupils.

And what had I learnt at Crofton? From some aspects, not much. I was erratic at games; as a senior I found I had poor control over juniors, and scholastically I was still floundering, with bad spelling and a sorry ignorance of literature and history. I had wanted to go to school in France, to learn the language like a parrot and effectively mime the accent, all of which might have boosted my self-esteem, but the war had defeated me.

As it was, I staggered towards matriculation, at the end of my final year, with no confidence in any but mathematical subjects, and Matric was as vital for a professional career as the O and A levels of later years.

I erected a home-made tent in the garden at Scole, there to try and drive history into a head that could retain the incident but never the people whom the incident involved. There were yet ten months to go, but I felt I could do better studying alone than in class. The only abiding result of this is contained in a water-colour sketch, done by Betty, of the tent, with Avis standing at the open flap, not allowed entry, and me on the floor of the tent trying to concentrate – a sketch redolent of the frustration each character was suffering.

31

I never sat for Matric. The following year I fell victim to quinsy, followed by a horrendous attack of erysipelas in my head, resulting in soaring temperatures and a head so swollen and inflamed that anxiety about Matric was transferred to anxiety about survival. Yet again I defeated death, and the struggle wrought a vital change. So far the school had known me as an adolescent; I returned there a young woman. My hair, which again had to be cut, had retained its pale gold and now, bobbed after the fashion of the day, suited me very well. On my first sally out of doors I put on a black straw hat nobody seemed to claim, and saw in the looking-glass a surprisingly pleasing image. Many letters had reached me from Crofton, now into its last weeks of the summer term. No one could have rejoiced more than I did over having missed Matric, but I was amazed at the welcome I received, and to learn I had been much missed. I enjoyed those last weeks more than any before, and derived from Crofton two valuable legacies: a desire to go and learn for myself, and the discovery that I had a number of very good friends.

*

Every summer since the outbreak of war, on the Fourth of August, which was my Aunt Tinie's birthday, a fête in aid of the Red Cross had been held in the grounds of Scole Lodge. To this the countryside flocked gleefully at a time when there were few counter-entertainments, and only the house and the walled kitchen garden were closed to the public. Otherwise garden and grounds were given over to competitions, the sale of prize vegetables and livestock, while Mr Dak laid out his steam-driven, electrically lit roundabouts and swings in a meadow beyond the park. He did so well out of these occasions he invariably added a donation for the Red Cross on paying for the stance, and packing up at dawn next morning he and his machinery would vanish without trace.

By August 1918 there was a feeling that the war would not last much longer, and this seemed to add buoyancy to the occasion. Each member of the household was active in some measure towards its success. Betty and I were raffling the model of a Red Cross van I had made, which seemed to have a particular interest for some officers over from Pulham aerodrome, to whom, beyond securing the money, I assumed a total indifference. It was not unwelcome, however, to meet them again when, with Betty, Eric (then on leave) and other friends, we went down at dusk to the merry-go-rounds, and riding wooden horses seemed to make contact easier, so that finally, to the distant strains of Dak's music, we all finished up dancing on the lawn.

Thus it was I met Colin, a wartime Major of twenty-four years, seconded to the air force from the Lancashire regiment and not only very good-looking but keenly aware of good looks in others. By the time we

32

were dancing on the lawn it was evident that I was the object of his attention. I found it flattering but rather embarrassing, pretended to be ignorant of it, hoped nobody had noticed it. I certainly never expected to see him again.

Yet a few days later he and his Commanding Officer called on the Crawshays, inviting Eric and his two cousins to a dance at Pulham aerodrome. After that dance Colin came on a series of visits, and it seemed we were both of us falling in love. I resented it, kept telling myself this only happened to grown-ups, not appreciating I was now one myself. He arrived one day just as I was starting for the mill and I took him with me, hoping the sacks would be ready waiting and we could get them on the car without troubling the miller, but the miller was there. His jovial grin and his farewell expressed far more than I felt the occasion warranted. I had seen the same smile on Wilby's face, and had had to counter Uncle Dick's teasing, but my indifference to Colin's visits was belied by a sudden carefulness about my appearance.

What in fact made me vulnerable to Colin's advances was having been brought up in an aura of adverse criticism. It was balm to receive admiration, to be suddenly treasured and important. Compliments were so rare in the Boddam family that it seemed I was hungry for them, but didn't know quite how to handle them.

'Wasn't that a lovely trifle Aunt Tinie gave us for dinner last night?'

'Yes. Was it? I don't remember. You were looking so beautiful I couldn't take my eyes off you.'

Heady stuff. Small wonder I blossomed that summer, and in its warmth, lapped by those blissful surroundings, we both drifted into a state of ecstasy in which each failed to see the other clearly. It added to the intoxication that I was now an avid reader. During convalescence from erysipelas I had been mostly alone, and in bed started devouring Kipling, Dickens, Thackeray.... At Scole I had found, in volumes of the St Paul's magazine, *Off the Skellig*, telling in last-century prose, the adventures of a girl on board her father's merchant vessel and, dripping with sentimentality, her subsequent love affair, which at that moment suited my mood.

Marriage was never discussed between us; in fact, I don't think it was expected. I could not imagine the present bliss reaching beyond Scole. So when the occupants to whom our house was let asked for an extension, the rapturous autumn was prolonged, though it did bring a day fraught with anxiety. With October the pheasant shooting started. Colin's Commanding Officer, a keen shot, had been invited, and Colin was to follow the guns.

I was very aware of my limitations with driven birds on the wing and was in such a state of nerves I couldn't hit anything all morning, and Uncle Dick upbraided me for being too slow. But in the afternoon I justified not only my position in the line but also, I felt, in Colin's estimation, by bringing down in magnificent style a cock bird right overhead, and this seemed to restore my expertise.

Soon even October was ebbing towards its close, and also towards the inevitable collapse of Germany. Colin's leave was due in early November, when he must go north as he had heard that his mother's health was failing, but he suggested a short visit to Guildford first, followed by a day in town together before he had to leave. A tentative date was fixed, but back in Guildford this shining beacon on the horizon became another source of anxiety.

*

Our house, when we returned to it, was in scrupulous order, but cold as sin, with little coal in the cellar until the uncertain date of further delivery. Furtively I changed the eiderdown in the spare room for a warmer one. At Scole Colin would have had a fire in his bedroom. Shrouded in baize, the Georgian silver lay complete but tarnished and, always secretive about my deeper feelings, I waited until my mother was out before exerting a quite unnatural domesticity in cleaning it.

Yet, more alarming and less remedial was the fact that, having only just left school, I had no outfit suitable for autumnal London. Summer offered no problems as a rich friend of Grace's rejoiced in supplying her daughters with lovely summer and evening dresses, envied even at Crofton, where there was much competition. From Betty I knew I could borrow a passable three-quarter-length coat, but beneath it I had only my old school jacket and skirt, the latter worn so thin and baggy at the knees it was almost in a hole. This I felt wouldn't show under the coat.

It had not occurred to me then, nor did it till long afterwards, that I was a more desirable being against the background of Scole than in my own house. Equally defeating was the date for Colin's visit, which collided head-on with the Armistice, when there was neither sign nor word from him. Telephones were still scarce and there was none in our house, so in the mounting excitement and confusion I was not unduly surprised.

With other officers from Pulham, he reached London just after the Armistice, to find the city in a state of delirium, and since northerners look on London much as southerners look on Paris − a city of every enticement − his activities were the natural outcome of the occasion. The visit to Guildford got sandwiched into a single day and night, followed by a day together in London. The latter was sadly disorganized, with restaurants disrupted for lack of chinaware, and there was no time to go to a theatre, so we went to a cinema. Here I removed his hand exploring my knees, but he had found a hole in my skirt.

34

In the taxi to Waterloo there was a passionate farewell embrace. He was anxious about my getting home before dark, also about catching his train to Manchester. I was in a gloom whose despondency I could scarcely contain as we waited for my train, feeling this was the end of everything. Then he began suggesting a further meeting; could I not stay with him? He knew of a nice secluded hotel, no questions asked. As my train came in he pressed the idea further: I could pretend I was staying with one of my London friends.

I covered my feelings with the usual oblique answer: 'Well, perhaps. Thank you, Colin, it's been lovely.' I waved to a dwindling figure, glad he had no time to linger to see the devastation he had caused.

Later generations would wonder why I was shattered; what was so offending about it? If one aroused passion that is what one would expect. Yet we had only just got rid of the chaperon; the proposition put to me was the overriding sin. My precious independence was still balanced by a naïve innocence, and somehow this had spoilt everything.

Alone in the railway carriage, alone in my workshop, I tried to make out which of us was to blame. Had I given him wrong ideas? I never pondered the heady influence of Bacchanalian London, I never spoke to anyone of this bitter pill. I wrote Colin a long straggling letter, a mixture of accusation and self-mortification, to which his reply sounded truly contrite, and I think he probably was. We continued to be curious about each other, wrote at long intervals, but did not meet until he, a guest, and I, a bridesmaid, were present at Eric's wedding in London.

It would be hard to assess which did the greater damage to romance, the immoral proposal or the hole in the skirt. It was a milestone in the process of growing up.

*

My immediate reaction to what I viewed as tragedy was to disguise all feelings of grief and throw myself heartily into any surrounding entertainment that offered – and there was plenty. My mother and a friend well known in Guildford had been asked to organize and be hostesses at dances for the Canadian officers encamped nearby on Witley Common. The dances at Trinity Hall were a considerable success, and daughters of the hostesses' friends when pressed into service were not unwilling to attend. A number of attractive girls were mustered.

Most willingly I now attended and heartily enjoyed not only the dances but all the entertainments resulting. One of my followers, known as Red Tabs, was ADC to the Officer in Command, so it was with the General, his wife and Red Tabs that I was driven to London to watch the victory parade. For fully a year I enjoyed this sort of indulgence, but the lesson learnt through Colin made me sceptical of admiration and derisive of my own feelings if I tended to get carried away.

Grace, reared in the days when daughters stayed at home until they married, was prepared for her own to do so if they desired. We had to be of age before Indian Military would disperse bounty, and for me that was a wait of three years. In theory we were given pocket money, but it needed a less hospitable and more calculating character than my mother to stretch her income over all its obligations. Independence must inevitably derive from a job or a husband; the first needed a training, and the dearth of young men since the war and the abundance of unmarried women made it likely that girls with the best prospects would be chosen.

Thus, being a minor, I had no money, only a tremendous creative urge. I wanted to write, for writing was almost a disease in the Parsons family. Betty was the first to publish a short, beautifully written novel of penetrating observation, of which more later. I expressed myself in badly spelt, long profuse letters, in stories that never got published, sentimental verses, and thoughts committed to paper. I also used drawing and painting for expressing myself, even the piano, though daily practice at school had all but extinguished my enthusiasm. To the piano I told my sorrows and joys, for I had the house to myself for long periods, but on the intrusion of an audience I at once became self-conscious and stopped playing.

A further enthusiasm, kept secret in the workshop, was inspired by volumes of the *Country Gentlemen's Estate Book* found in the bookshelves at Scole. These gave architectural plans of buildings and even layouts of property, and under their instruction I designed house, stables and grounds of the sort of estate of which I hoped some day to be the chatelaine. I even made up a selection of families with which I might populate it, though of the husband there was no preconception. The planned estate had a strong resemblance to Scole.

This designing of houses left me with a strong urge to be an architect, but architecture had barely recovered from its stagnation during the war. It was doubtful at this stage that I could have been articled to an architectural firm, and in any case it was not the moment to seek financial help.

Betty had reached her majority with a twenty-first birthday party in London, and now, from the Indian Military, had £16 quarterly till marriage or death. Yet she would never make much out of teaching till she had a degree. Places at universities were filling rapidly in the wake of the war, and there would soon be none left. The family was already too occupied trying to find the means for sending Betty to college.

The means came, from a heroic and unexpected quarter. Muriel, now in Cologne, had arranged in the hour of departure that her small financial legacy from her father should be used for this purpose. Defrauded herself of a university career, she was determined her niece should not suffer the same

36

frustration. Thus Betty got a place at Bedford College, then in the sublime setting of Regent's Park in London, and obtained her degree in English before resuming a teaching career. Meanwhile, from a copy of the RIBA handbook I gleaned that the gateway to the profession was a five-year course at the London School of Architecture, plus living in London.

The odds seemed in favour of the husband.

*

Thus I continued my carefree life but with a feeling of excitement ahead, as if the spirit of adventure were in the offing and had brushed me with its wing. There were, after all, other irons in the fire: born into the age of the automobile, I had grown up with the automobile, had gathered from the Stellite the principle on which it worked though not how the power was conveyed to the road wheels. At the Guildford Technical School, then in the town, an evening session on the auto-cycle engine was about to be given, for which, at my behest, my mother paid a modest fee.

I was the only woman present, and possibly the best-educated of those attending the class. So, when it came to the examination, I was the best able to explain my meaning, and was very surprised to obtain a marking of 99 per cent.

Soon after, a paragraph appeared in *The Times* telling of a Women's Engineering Society that had been inaugurated under the auspices of Lady Parsons, wife of the inventor of the turbine, and Lady Shelley Rolls. The idea was to encourage an interest in engineering among women, and an address was given in London for anyone interested.

My mother and I went to a modest top-floor office, to find a young secretary, Caroline Haslett, no less. There were few indications then of the eminence this secretary would later attain. She described a technical college at Loughborough, in Leicestershire, which had trained and employed women in the war on munitions, and was still prepared to hold a few places open for women in their diploma courses starting in the autumn. The first year would be concentrated on general engineering and the following two years one could specialize in civil, electrical or automobile engineering according to choice. Classes would run concurrently with practical work in workshops, foundry and drawing-office.

I had been balked in doing munitions, I yearned to go through those workshops; what if I transferred my interest from building houses to building cars? Loughborough, at that time a technical college, appeared to require no certificate of entry, no matriculation; one started at shop-floor level, and having obtained the diploma one could surely secure promising employment. We knew, being distantly related to Sir Charles Parsons, that his daughter Rachel had trained as a nautical architect and had made a considerable contribution to the war effort in her father's firm. I saw myself designing car engines, car bodies.... Little I knew.

My going to a man's college created some stir among the family, and my mother confessed she didn't believe I would have been allowed to do this had my father been alive. However, I did not go alone. Among the Anglo-Indian families scattered around us was one very similar to our own. A widowed Mrs Travers, on the death of her husband in the Gurkhas, had come home to bear a third daughter in the house of her widowed mother, where she continued to live, not a mile from Capel House. Mrs Travers very much favoured her elder two daughters, but the youngest had none of their graces, was excessively shy, with all the awkwardness attendant, and she even surpassed me in bad spelling. Escape from her home to ours was a joy to Dorothea, if not always to me as I was maddened that everything I did was copied by her. Later we got on better, sharing many interests, particularly camping, when I might with benefit have copied Dorothea, who was a budding cook. There was no anxiety if we went camping on the Downs in those days, though I was often a disturbing element in the households of more cosseted friends, taking them long walks and failing to return till dark.

Mrs Travers appeared to have infinite faith in Grace, not only in sending her daughters to the same schools but, on hearing of the Loughborough scheme, agreeing to Dorothea going also. And Loughborough revealed the root cause of Dorothea's idiosyncrasies for, as we moved into the realms of higher mathematics, it was found that she was a brilliant mathematician.

*

We arrived at Loughborough in the autumn of 1919 to find another female student, Patience Erskine, intent on studying chemistry, and a pupil from Downe House, a school against which Crofton was wont to play lacrosse, generally getting beaten. It had been arranged that we three – known as lady engineers – should board with the local schoolmistress.

Shortly after, into hostels arranged for them, came a horde of young men, lately demobilized and eligible for a Government grant towards the study of engineering, though to many the grant was more interesting than the occupation. Of students, therefore, there were about three hundred men and three women, but more women were to join later.

Our trouser overalls excited much attention, but we were forced to wear terrible caps in the machine shops on account of the dangerous belting from the overhead drive. Few machines were then electrically driven. We also learnt there were pockets of antipathy against us for barging in on men's preserves, but there was no evidence of this when we met the dissenters. In fact we were at all times treated with the greatest respect.

If the students paid respect, not so the landladies; Loughborough was then a small parochial-minded town, and we were looked on with the utmost suspicion, thought to be abandoned even before we came. The schoolmistress soon found us too much, and fixed us up with a nice old body who fed and housed us generously, but a postcard sent to Patience by her mother: 'Darling, I can't bear to think of you pigging it in filthy lodgings in Loughborough', was not unnaturally our undoing. We were out on our ears before the end of the week, and suffered thereafter a painful series of short anchorages, until Patience took refuge with a friend she had made at the golf club, and I answered an advertisement and went to see a clergyman's widow who had rooms to let at reasonable price. Her greeting: 'I've heard all about you people' was not promising. The interview improved, however; she would take Dorothea and me on approval for a month, and in fact we stayed with Mrs Abbott for the rest of the time we were at college, and she proved a very kind friend. There was a piano in our sitting-room to which I told my secret heart, unaware that when I played, Mrs Abbott would sit on the stairs in the hall to listen. Had I known I could not have played a note, but this was not revealed till departure.

The college workshops were certainly more inspiring than the lectures, which were a sad contrast to those at the Guildford Technical School, which Dorothea and I had attended before coming to Loughborough, fearful of being behind the men students. In fact we found ourselves slightly ahead, and their carefree attitude towards homework was infectious. Our dedicated ardour began to wane, with time given to diversions: the college dramatic society, walking the country, Nottingham theatre, and I decided to teach myself to swim.

Swimming-baths had been mostly closed down in the war, so I had had little chance of learning an art to which far less importance was then given. The Loughborough swimming-bath was handy and almost deserted in the hours reserved for women, but I had barely taught myself breast-stroke when the college took over the baths for an afternoon gymkhana. As there were only two female entrants for a ladies' race, I was persuaded to enter, but on hearing I had only just learned to swim they gave me such an extravagant advantage that I won it. There was a good deal of laughter when I received a small silver cup.

There was no direct practical work on car engines at the college, only a large working model of a diesel engine. Among the students there was much tuning of motor cycle engines for the rallies we constantly attended. Dorothea had bought a motor cycle and side-car, which much facilitated our transport but failed dismally on test hills. Dorothea was to come in to her own, however, in Mathematics.

As taught in Guildford, Mathematics had seemed child's play, but at Loughborough we were all getting thoroughly bemused over Higher

Mathematics. The classroom in which we assembled was apt to be very warm and the tutor often came in, chalked up the problem on the board, gave us an outline of how to tackle it, and then walked out and left us to it. He had not been gone long before half the class followed suit, sitting outside smoking in the shade. One student said he had gone to the cinema. Dorothea remained, solving the problem, and in due course all returned and got from her various stages of the solution, but were wary enough not all to give the same answer.

I was lucky to get her coaching in Mathematics when it came to the exams, and in view of our many diversions we both had to do intensive last-minute study. It was crucial to get that diploma, and with greater attention I am sure we could have got firsts. As it was we eventually each got second-class diplomas, which in fact was all that was necessary.

*

It is fair to say that, whereas I had brought light into Dorothea's early life, the situation was now reversed. She was never financially cramped, as I was, and by 1920 had abandoned the motor cycle for an oil-cooled Morgan two-seater, in which one lay almost prone, not a yard from ground level and, since both of us had the same type of complexion, it burnt the skin off our noses as vehemently as had the unshielded motor cycle. In return it gave us a lot of useful knowledge.

By this time a car was no longer a sacred possession looked after and driven by a chauffeur, but Ford had not yet made cars available to the majority, so it was still a privileged minority who toured Britain at the wheel, an advantage I would not have enjoyed but for Dorothea. In the summer vacation we went on long camping tours.

True, not everyone set out to test themselves as rashly as we did. Until we learnt better, we viewed the hills and dales of the Lake District, for instance, on a par with the gentler slopes of Surrey, and when a sign proclaimed a route as impassable for motorists we invariably took it, and were luckier than we deserved. One such track started sloping steeply downward and disappeared in a spread of stones that began descending with us. We were in scree, and it was pure luck that the slope eased off before pitching down further, giving us an angle of escape.

Wrynose Pass, then a wet mountain track, gave us our first experience of wheel slip, and only by pushing our groundsheet under the wheels did we advance in spurts, the groundsheet being ejected downhill after each spurt. However, we reached Cockley Beck, then a lone farmhouse, where the occupants didn't know what to charge for the eggs and milk we bought from them. We little guessed we were the vanguard of a scourge which would later destroy large sections of that wild and lovely country; campers were then so few they were not looked on as an intrusion, and not charged for their welcome presence.

Those tours taught us to carry spare petrol, to mend punctures, to read maps and pack luggage intelligently; signposts were still confined to finger-posts right on the road junctions. Nearly all roads were now tarred for the impending motor traffic, which was as yet so sparse we could enjoy miles of empty roadway.

In fact, for the life I was presently to lead, these camping tours were more use to me than being taught Economics at the College, or how to measure the viscosity of oil. We learnt through our mistakes. Cars were then dependent on gravity feed, thus in country with steep gradients it was important to park a car so that petrol could flow to the carburettor. We learnt this one morning when there was not much petrol in the tank, and we had no spare.

Before going to Loughborough, I had never been north of London except to Norfolk or Scotland. Leicestershire I could see was ideal hunting country, but it compared ill, in my opinion, with the wooded hills of Surrey and Sussex. Now, having seen a far greater extent of England, I began to feel by taking up automobile engineering I had shut myself into the indus-trial areas, whereas I yearned for the architecture, the landscape and the way of life in the great beyond. Nevertheless it was Loughborough that was to bring me my first adventure, and to impress my later employers.

In our second year another 'lady engineer' joined us, her approach to her objective rather different from ours. Verena Holmes had gained a footing in the engineering world through munition work, and had clung on in the drawing office of the firm she had worked for, the only safe refuge from the unions intent on ousting all women munition workers. She was now seeking to gain a B.Sc. (Eng.), a singular honour at that time for a woman, and she had come to the College to get wider technical experience.

Her career was one of single-minded, indomitable purpose, leading even-tually to high honours and position, but we then knew her as a tall good-looking student who joined the existing female trio every day at lunch in a modest restaurant, and who occasionally joined Dorothea and me at our lodgings, along with some of the male students, all putting the world to rights. She was so young in spirit and so in tune with our ideas that we got the impression she was contemporary in age.

For me she became a lifelong friend, but it was not for a number of years that I confessed to her what I had done in her interest – so I had thought – in that year of 1920. A visit to a coalmine had been offered to our section, and those interested had to put down their names and their year of birth, though why the latter I cannot think unless the staff wanted to know the ages of their female students. When Dorothea, Patience and I came to sign, all born at the start of the century, we saw Verena's signature against 1888.

41

We were dumbfounded. Over *thirty*? One leg in the grave! She must have meant 1898. I adroitly altered it for her.

Summer 1922 we took our final exams, but the significance of the diploma seemed to have faded with the increasing shortage of engineering jobs. It was imperative to obtain it, however, but my mind was continually deflected by the shattering news earlier in the year of Uncle Dick's death. I knew he had not been well all winter, but I had never expected this.

I kept thinking of the previous summer when I had been given a house party for my twenty-first birthday, every spare bedroom at Scole Lodge, Thorpe Parva and the gate cottage filled with our guests, to whom we had given a home-made play, a tennis tournament and a dance. If this had troubled Uncle Dick he certainly had not shown it, out most of the day, sometimes watching the tennis and then seated at the end of the long dining-table – at that time in the hall, since the dining-room was then a ballroom. Soon after dancing began, he would slope off to his study and thereafter to bed.

He had been so anxious that I should get that diploma and now he would never know that I did. The news of his death bowled me over with grief and apprehension, and I was quite unable to attend the afternoon lecture. I wanted to be alone with my thoughts, shared only with Mrs Abbott's piano.

1919–1923

WILD GEESE

The venture of the *Wild Goose* emanated from the poor prospect of employment, and from the experience of a student, David Laurence David. In his teens he had sailed the southern seas in trading ships until the war landed him in fighting vessels, in one of which he was torpedoed in the North Sea. Rescued after some hours in the water, he recovered from pneumonia in hospital, where he managed to write a book which was later published.

This background had added considerable weight to his assurance that there was a profitable living to be obtained in the South Sea Islands in French possession, since the French granted settlement rights to people of any nationality who would clear and cultivate these islands. A dozen or so men, provided they had their own ship, could trade very handsomely with Tahiti or other islands, if independent of the French trading vessels which otherwise held down the market prices. He had made friends with such men and still got news of them.

David, son of a Welsh schoolmaster, was extremely well read. He was also an ardent Socialist, with Communist sympathies, the natural outcome of living in Merthyr Tydfil, in the proximity of the Rhondda Valley, and the Cyfarthfa Iron Works. Cyfarthfa's stagnant machinery was a memorial of the great strike, when the iron-master had closed down the whole works in revenge and starved out the valley. That ironmaster was a Crawshay, and Uncle Dick believed him to have been a distant relative.

David had grown up, therefore, in a climate of political argument and was extremely adroit at it, so it was inevitable before long that I would receive its full force, with my Empire background and disreputable connections. I, of course, had no expertise in defence.

Yet David was also a romantic, and in spite of his revulsion for all I stood for, he seemed to pursue my company. And how could I resist one who had sailed before the mast, who wrote *books* and got them published, and who, when not talking politics, had a nice sense of humour and a touch of the Welsh lilt in his speech? I had worked through a number of innocent friendships with the students, and this was equally innocent but seemed to arouse general interest, yet somehow I could never quite return the feelings that David appeared to have for me.

43

On his Norton motor cycle, a hot machine entered for all the rallies, he had visited me at Guildford, and got on surprisingly well with my mother – my aunt was conveniently absent. I too visited his family home, feeling rather overdressed for the part as a succession of train changes resulted in the carriages growing ever meaner on approach towards Merthyr. Moreover I had come from Scole and borrowed a suitcase from Eric, but not till I saw David's eye resting on the label did I realize it held the deadly word CRAWSHAY. We were both keyed up with anxiety until we reached his house, where there was complete relaxation. I loved his parents; theirs was a far more flexible socialism, and when I put on a more modest head-dress to go to church with them, 'You'll put on your pretty hat this morning,' said his beautiful little mother.

On that visit I witnessed history. Inevitably David took me to Cyfarthfa, where indeed I wanted to go, to see the valley filled with crumbling tenements that Crawshay had built for his workers, with a silent foundry where the ingots were awaiting the molten metal that was never poured, and machine shops with work centred in the lathes but never turned. All was now given over to rust and mould, where each faction had held fast until life had ebbed from the valley. On the hill was Crawshay's castle, his coach mouldering in the stable; on his tombstone was engraved 'God forgive me'.

I gather all this is now very different, but I feel Cyfarthfa should have been maintained as a historical museum. Doulais was now the leading ironworks, which we later saw, but was it much of an improvement? Components carried great distances had to be reheated, scrap metal lay about everywhere, and here too seemed to be a careless attitude towards human life. The Bessemer steel cauldrons at prescribed intervals made a quarter-turn on their pivots; belching flames, they leaned over to receive magnesium blocks, and these were fed into them by a man pushing a wheelbarrow up a rickety catwalk. With a cloth over nose and mouth, he tipped the blocks into the open furnace. Our guide admitted there had been a fatal accident through this procedure.

The sky over Merthyr glowed red at night as if on fire; the drinking-water was clear and invigorating, and out towards Brecon, beyond the limit of coalmines and mining towns, the country of Monmouthshire was beautiful.

Meanwhile at Loughborough, David's idea of the South Sea Islands had caught on, gathering strength when fishing vessels which had been converted to minesweepers in the war were sold off by the Government at greatly reduced prices. David and an adviser went north to view some of them. By summer 1922 a Pacific Settlement Company had been formed, and established as a limited liability company on the advice of a solicitor in Loughborough who took a fatherly interest in the venture. In the harbour of Buckie in the Moray Firth, an eighty-ton steam trawler with vertical

Kelvin engine, classed A1 and on offer at a modest price, was awaiting inspection by the Board of Trade, on whose verdict final purchase depended. Some repairs and a few adaptations would then be put in hand.

They were aiming at a company of twelve hand-picked men, and already by summer 1922 had eight of them, to whom one share each had been sold. That summer was to see the final exams, followed by dispersal, so it was important to make up the numbers while the students were still assembled, and it was in acquiring these in the time left that the ideal had to give way to circumstance. The remaining recruits were not driven by the same ardour, or indeed compulsion.

However, all shareholders went through a severe test on reaching Buckie the following year, when they started their first sea trials, little knowing that trawlers were apt to roll even on calm waters. Of their number, David was a qualified seaman, and there was a deck-hand and ship's engineer both with wartime experience, while the ship's original skipper, who lived in Buckie, volunteered to escort the ship as far as Corunna, where they hoped to coal for the Atlantic. This would give David an opportunity of occasional rest.

*

Dorothea and I became involved in the *Wild Goose* venture because, with a book on the subject and a sextant, Dorothea soon mastered the rules of navigation and was asked to give evening classes to prospective shareholders. Then when the press got wind of the project, and inaccurate reports on the venture appeared in the papers, David swiftly sold all rights to the *Western Mail*, and asked me to supply articles on the progress of the scheme. With this I gleefully complied. At last I had got into print, even though anonymously, and my rather cumbersome articles, printed in full, brought the company a surprising amount of money. They also brought stacks of mail from would-be passengers, impelled by poverty or the call of the wild.

At the time of purchase, the trawler was called the *Productive*, which I felt was calculated to invite doom. I suggested the *Wild Goose*, and strangely Lloyds Register of Shipping had *Wild* everything else but no *Wild Goose*, so thus she was named. My mother made a spectacular pennant for them – a wild goose in flight on a blue ground – and thereafter all concerned with the project were referred to as Wild Geese.

Shares for the company were open to women also, but the idea was that women would join later when trading had been established. I had no money for buying a share, nor for joining the company later and, charmed as I would be to help build houses on the island, I had no desire to live there for the rest of my life. Nevertheless Dorothea and I were invited to

45

Buckie to see them sail, which I felt would justify another article for the *Western Mail*. Indeed it did. The sailing date was intended for July, but on arrival in August we found crates being lowered into the hold, the sawmill had not arrived nor the rifles and ammunition – the Wild Geese had to live while clearing their island.

Dorothea and I were pressed into duties of which mine was painting SY *Wild Goose* in lieu of S.S. *Productive* on the lifeboat and all life-saving apparatus. The 'Y' was important as on a steam yacht one may drown without hindrance, whereas a steamship comes under Board of Trade regulations, which might mean suppression of the whole venture. I was on board doing this when they went out on trials, but it was a calm day. I had yet to learn I was one of the worst sailors on record. After several dashes to the ship's side I finished up lying prone at the bottom of the lifeboat I had been painting.

The company now consisted of eleven shareholders – one had had to resign on medical grounds – and an experienced ship's cook, unpaid and not a shareholder, but joining for the adventure. According to schedule the ship should now have been approaching the Cape Verde islands, but on the eighth of September they were leaving Buckie, whose every lodging-house had been stuffed with relatives, friends and spectators, the post office laden with mail. The *Wild Goose*, her load water-line well submerged, was at the quay, receiving last-minute gifts; speeches of gratitude and farewell were passing between ship and shore, then the house flag was hoisted amid cheers from onlookers, but in the excitement few seemed to have noticed that there were now considerable white horses beyond the harbour wall. As the ship came to the harbour mouth, a huge wave caught her broadside on and she heeled over at such an alarming angle that water came over the gunwales, sweeping packages into the sea and sending the crew sprawling, but she did not sink. It was a harrowing moment and silenced the cheering from the shore, but as the ship righted herself, the crew rescued some of the floating gifts, tried to look as if this was all in a day's work, and the *Wild Goose* followed a turbulent course along the Moray Firth to the entrance of the Canal at Inverness.

A trip down the Caledonian Canal had been offered to any friend or relative who cared to come, but they must bring their own bedding rolls. Only three had accepted: Dorothea, the sister of one of the Wild Geese and myself. In the horizontal, I found I was a better sailor than in the vertical, and I was determined to see the Canal. So I was in the lifeboat until the wind had dropped and the Firth had narrowed; and we entered the first lock just before sunset. We were not released till dawn of Monday; it was Saturday evening, and Scottish lock-keepers did not work on Sunday.

That enforced holiday was a bonus to all, not least David. Never had I admired him more: calm and decided, the whole weight of responsibility on

46

his shoulders, everyone referring to him as he quietly organized a massive undertaking. He had gallantly thanked Buckie for all their voluntary help at a farewell dinner given by the Wild Geese.

Now he had a tent rigged for us on the aft deck, within convenient distance of the 'wee hoose', as the Scots called the small white shanty overhanging the stern. There were spare bunks in a hold in the fo'c's'le, but one had to share this with a paraffin tank, and the deck was preferable, for we now had glorious weather for a blissful journey along the Canal. During that journey the deck-hands showed off their newly acquired talent in handling the craft and they took it in turns at the wheel. In the widest part of Loch Ness, it was reported, the old skipper had asked the helmsman, 'How's your head?' to be told, 'Very much better, thanks.' 'Not your head, laddie. The ship's head.'

Sunday papers in Inverness had revealed that there was a coal strike in Corunna, which meant coaling for the *Wild Goose* at Milford Haven instead, and at greater expense. Had we had normal sense, Dorothea and I would have stuck to our original plan of disembarking at Oban, where the other guest had a car waiting and could take us to Glasgow. The Canal had given me false ideas about my seaworthiness, however, and we chose to stay on till Milford Haven. Thus at the mouth of the Sound of Jura we got our first brush with the Atlantic, though I would not for anything have missed the colouring on the hills of that long, lonely coastline of the Sound.

All that night the *Wild Goose* struggled with the head wind, making little progress even in the lea of the Irish coast, so we ran for the shelter of Belfast harbour, where the harbour-master, baffled by our appearance, hoped we had no arms on board as the last ship to berth here was raided for arms and ammunition. The Sinn Fein trouble was then at its height. The Wild Geese denied any such cargo; their main urge was to go and get a good meal and then sleep.

On coming back to the ship replete, I saw the General Post Office was still open and felt compelled to send a reassuring telegram home. On entering, I found myself looking down the barrel of a revolver, and David who was with me was on the point of knocking down the holder of the revolver, when the holder said, 'Excuse me.' People had been lobbing bombs into post offices, it appeared, and a suspicious character, such as I must then have looked, was obliged to transact her business under cover of a weapon, though we all ended up on the best of terms. It speaks well for the times that a revolver pointed at me meant nothing, perhaps because the holder didn't look menacing, and bandits don't generally say 'Excuse me.'

We two remaining guests slept in the wheel-house, and some Wild Geese had rifles under their mattresses, but no raid occurred. During the day we lay prone on the engine-room casing, the only warm place on the deck. Dorothea was able to attend meals but I continued lying prone, nibbling a ship's biscuit. The *Wild Goose* was getting on down the Irish Sea, but approaching the Sound of Milford Haven we lost steam, and it took us all night and a good part of next day to reach the harbour. There was, however, one glorious distraction at the outset, when David called from the Bridge, 'Look out starboard!' We were so well trained we looked out starboard to see a four-masted schooner, all sails set, heading for the open sea. On the wind that was belabouring the *Wild Goose*, she was cutting through the water like a knife through butter, a graceful and enviable spectacle. And the *Wild Goose* had lost her motive power.

A convenient afternoon train bore the guests to London and home: it was nice to get out of one's clothes.

*

Moored in Milford harbour was a luxury yacht; we had all noticed her, and the owner had noticed the *Wild Goose*. Having learnt from the harbour-master something of *Wild Goose*'s history, the owner invited the whole crew to dinner at the Lord Nelson Hotel, with the idea of deflecting them from what seemed to him certain suicide. They had left it too late, he said; they would come in for the equinoctial gales. The Wild Geese remained adamant. They had reached their first objective, had gained experience, and for most of them there was no alternative.

The *Wild Goose* was coaling when the luxury yacht set sail, and the yachtsman was comfortably in Lisbon harbour when a monumental gale left wreckage all along the coast of the Channel and Bay of Biscay. The yachtsman tried to get news of the *Wild Goose* but failed, and it was some time later in the Lisbon Yacht Club, which commands a view of the river Tagus, that he was telling his cronies of the optimists that he felt must now all be drowned. At that moment a scruffy-looking vessel, lying low in the water, was seen to be struggling up the river. 'I'll eat my hat if that isn't the *Wild Goose!*'

It was. They were nearing Spain when the storm broke. Hove to all night, they had sprung a leak, and after this there was no rest for anyone for forty hours; those not on duty were bailing out an ever-increasing intake of water, and they had to make for Corunna after all. Corunna's repair was so inefficient that the leak started again and they had to make for Lisbon, where they were greeted by their former friend, and the yacht club granted them temporary membership while the *Wild Goose* was being repaired.

This led to the break-up of the company. Several Wild Geese listened readily to wealthy yachtsmen telling them there was no need to cross the Atlantic; they need only slip down the coast of Africa to Angola – then in Portuguese possession. It lay in the same latitude as the South Sea Islands, grew the same produce, was equally fertile and crying out for cultivation, hence excellent markets.

The company broke into two factions, one pointing out that the worst of the voyage was now behind them, and Angola was an unknown quantity where they would have no security; the other faction was in favour of sending two or three men to prospect; they could go deck-class on the mail-boat, need not spend much money or be away long. Meanwhile David wrote a letter to the solicitor in Loughborough asking how far could they legally bend the terms of the company if they went to Angola instead of the South Seas.

Until he had an answer, David refused all company funds for the Angola venture, but it made no difference as three of them had private means, so he sent with them one of the men from the other faction, but barely had his letter been sent, or the prospectors started, than a postal strike closed down all communication with Portugal from the outside world.

*

A limited liability company has to have a headquarters and someone responsible to deal with communications. The Wild Geese had asked Dorothea and me to be temporary directors in their absence, and Dorothea's home address was registered as the headquarters until one was established in the South Seas. My address was uncertain as we hoped soon to be leaving the Guildford house.

Thus before long Dorothea heard from the Loughborough solicitor, who had received David's letter and answered it at some length to say the alteration in plan would certainly be illegal, but had offered alternative suggestions. He then found that neither a letter nor telegram could reach Portugal, and he was asking could Dorothea possibly *take* his letter to them?

Mrs Travers would not contemplate Dorothea going out alone but, surprisingly, offered to pay my expenses if I would go with her. There was no hesitation. A visit to the passport office in Petty France was the first essential, so thither we went, but engineers though we may have been, we were still amazingly naïve and still looked incredibly young. When asked the purpose of our journey, we hoped to stress its importance by saying we were directors of the Pacific Settlement Company. This created havoc, and we knew no doctor or clergyman locally to whom to appeal. The clerk seemed to think he alone stood between us and the white slavers. Then I had a brainwave. I had an uncle at the War Office. Would he do?

He did very well. General Sir Harold Parsons stepped across to bail us out; he had not much time, but satisfied that our parents knew of this project – we did not stress the directorship – he was willing to sponsor us. Having thus obtained passports, we now moved on to Thomas Cook.

Mrs Travers had supplied Dorothea with an open cheque for all necessary tickets through to Lisbon, but on the counter of Cook's was an advertisement for the Handley Page Air Service to Paris. An open cheque, and the chance to fly! The extra cost was not prohibitive, and to salve our consciences we sacrificed the *rapide* service from Hendaye to Lisbon, for the *ordinaire*, or was it the *inférieur*, which more aptly described it? According to our calculations we would arrive in Lisbon in the morning instead of the evening before, so it would make little difference. Mrs Travers was quite satisfied with the price, though unaware of the details.

The Handley Page service flew between Croydon and Le Bourget, with transport into Paris. It was a biplane, carrying a limited number of passengers, and one signed a delicately worded agreement that the company took no responsibility for one's life or luggage. A woman passenger sitting knitting was, I suspect, an early form of air hostess, though no gesture betrayed her calling, and the more the plane was tossed about, the more compulsive her knitting. We were all issued with paper bags, but there was nowhere to lie and, flying low above the water, we got the full force of the blustery wind, the plane suddenly sinking or lifting to the discomfort of nearly all on board. Dorothea was afflicted, and I was so sick I could not stop even when we had landed, but there is always the compensation after a limited bout of seasickness, that one feels so well on recovery, and generally hungry.

Mrs Travers had thoughtfully provided, along with French money and letters of credit, a hamper of food for the train journey south of Hendaye. We started on that hamper on the *Chemin de Ceinture*, that convenient but now dismantled rail that took one round Paris, and now took us to the Gare de l'Ouest. Never belittle a first journey abroad, for it inspires a thrill that will rarely be captured again: everything so new, so surprising, even advertisements for Sunlight *Savon* enthralled us. Then there were the pillows in clean white covers, trundled along the platform, hired at modest price and pushed through the windows to us. We snuggled into these to the rhythm of the night train through France. In England it would have been saying *Nicodemus, Nicodemus*, but there is a Latin intonation in the continental beat.

After two nights of this, and the hamper long since empty, we began to grow apprehensive, as according to our schedule we should now be in Lisbon. However, an impressive character was found who spoke English, and he broke it to us that Lisbon was fourteen hours away. This prospect was indeed bleak.

We were also told that the postal strike was over; all post offices would be open the following morning. Later a small observation car was coupled to the back of the train, to which we and our luggage were escorted, and here we found plates of sandwiches. We had no Portuguese money to offer. Our gallant friend joined us towards evening, and asked had we friends in

Lisbon to whom to go? Yes, we had, but we were also booked in at the Avenida Palace Hotel, and since this hotel had not only kept our room, and was almost part of the station, we were escorted to its door, and our friend gave us his card in case we had trouble. The card revealed that he was the Postmaster General.

I had had a brief letter from David from Spain, so I knew the Wild Geese had survived the storm, but all further news had come from the solicitor, who advised application to the yacht club to find the Wild Geese, since poste restante would be closed. Even he was unaware that an Angola expedition had already started, or that those left in Lisbon had taken the now repaired *Wild Goose* some distance up the Tagus to escape harbour dues. It was now moored in the river near a small town Azambuja, with rail connection to Lisbon, and in fact our *inférieur* had stopped there on our way down.

It was after nine when Dorothea and I woke next morning, and were enjoying *petit déjeuner* in bed when the Cook's man was ushered into our bedroom. He had waited two days to get a signature to our safe arrival, and could not get on with life until this was achieved. We decided to go first to the now open poste restante, rather than the yacht club, to get news possibly of the Wild Geese. We arrived there just as David and two others came looking for letters from home, or possibly from Angola. It was then decided that we should go back with them to Azambuja until arrival of the next mail-boat, on which the Angola party was expected in a week's time. So after a merry day in Lisbon we went by train, and then on foot across marshy land, to board a very sorry-looking *Wild Goose*.

*

I had long suspected that David had hoped to create on a South Sea island a model socialist state, all members equal, all sharing alike, all shareholders limited to an equal number of shares. This had worked well at the beginning, when they were dependent on David's knowledge, and at sea, when they were most of them scared and he had the experience for getting them to safety. He was then their natural leader. Now it was only too evident that the *Wild Goose* was suffering from all men being equal, all too much of the same age, and that their leader could no longer control them.

They had, of course, no warning of our arrival, and as we climbed on board David apologized for the state of the ship, but he, the Captain, felt a bit tired of being the one to wash down the decks. His only ready assistants were the cook and a very amusing young member, Mettham, who was unfortunately lame. Oliver, a staunch supporter, had been sent with the Angola party, and there really weren't many Geese on board, as another supporter had taken a temporary job with a firm in Lisbon, and finally he kept it. The trained young deck-hand, rather sullen and mutinous, eventually got a job in Lisbon with a reputable shipping firm.

We slept that night in the wheel-house, but next morning *we* decided to clean up this ship, clear the decks of litter, wash them down, and scrub the white paint that had made the *Wild Goose* look so virginal among the other trawlers in Buckie harbour. We were assisted by David, the cook and Mettham, and when the ship again had self-esteem, we rigged the tent on the after deck and were guests for about a week.

Beautifully painted barges would glide past us on the river, their tall masts staggered back and always, we noticed, a complement of women on board; we would go to the markets in Azambuja and buy vegetables and cheese, and we visited Lisbon, at whose cabaret theatre enormous fisher-women, with laden baskets balanced on their heads, would pirouette on the lightest of feet to compelling music. Portugal was in a very disturbed state; impending revolutions would be announced like football matches, but were apt to lose impetus if it rained. There was no sign of the Angola party on the next mail-boat.

I was troubled that David was so glad to have me with him; it was on that enforced day of leisure on the Canal that he had first asked me if I would ever consider coming to join him in the South Seas, and I, at that time full of admiration, had been too lenient in my reply. I had also felt that my visit to Merthyr had been interpreted by his parents as recognition of a future engagement. Yet now, with all his plans crumbling, I hadn't the heart to be definite. I said, 'Let's see what happens', and on this we left for home.

Of the Angola party only Oliver eventually returned. The other three went directly back to England, one with a severe attack of malaria and another with a foot so poisoned with bilharzia that he was a serious hospital case. Thus the company disintegrated, and the *Wild Goose* was sold to the Tagus fishing fleet, and I believe depleted shares were paid back to some, but not to those failing to fulfil the purpose of the company.

Yet five Wild Geese did get to the South Seas, by amalgamation with some young Australians who came to Lisbon so broke, after visiting four continents, that they were planning to sell their craft and work their passage home. They were deflected from selling by the five remaining Geese, who stocked up the Australians' ship with stores from the *Wild Goose* and offered to finance the passage home if the Australians would sail via the French-owned Society Islands. This was agreed upon. So David, Mettham, the cook and two other Geese reached the South Seas.

It did not work out, however; they could not persuade the Australians to stay with them, and on their own were too few in number to obtain settlement rights. They worked for a time on a privately owned plantation in Tahiti, though what had never been sufficiently stressed was the tedium of clearing land of scrub. When only David and Mettham were left, they returned the following autumn, and it is a sad anticlimax to have to record that David finally ran a chicken farm. He had published more books, was eventually happily married, and said a chicken farm gave him opportunity to write.

1921–1925

THE SWEDISH VENTURE

Returning from Loughborough, with a diploma but little chance of employment, was not as distressing to me as perhaps it should have been; it gave me an honest excuse for seeking another job. Are they to be envied, the single-minded who certainly achieve their aims, or is it more exciting to be hampered by a diversity of leanings, ambitions and abilities, none of them perhaps amounting to much but leading to a colourful life such as mine turned out to be? People were always telling me what a good artist I was, of which I myself was doubtful, but certainly now my mind turned to art.

In the Guildford house I occupied a bedroom which was clearly intended for staff, and I had embellished its plain distempered walls with a colourful mural representing a fancy dress ball. Guests dressed as highwaymen, pierrots, ballet dancers and so on postured at intervals along the frieze; host and hostess, bewigged and crinolined, stood on the wainscoting to receive guests at the door, while over the door a sedan chair with flunkies awaiting departures.

I was rather pleased with all this and so were many who saw it, and a kind friend most painstakingly photographed it, which inspired me to take the photos to some imaginative firm like Heal's in London, to see if I could get a job doing murals. Art had been my best subject at school and I had continued to attend art classes at the Guildford Technical School, but still had no qualifications. The inexperienced, however, are generally the most adventurous and often have undeserved luck, and it never occurred to me to make advance arrangements for an interview, when probably I might not have met Ambrose Heal. He had not then attained his knighthood. Trying to look my best, I advanced on Tottenham Court Road, and a hostess in black silk came helpfully forward on my entering the shop, but cooled instantly on learning my mission. Had I an appointment? No. She was sorry but Mr Heal was at a meeting and not likely to be free for the rest of the afternoon. At that moment a door opened at the side of the entrance hall and the man himself appeared, looked at us enquiringly, the hostess retired, and I did the rest.

I finished up sitting on a high stool in his drawing-office, telling him the story of my life, which was luckily yet limited in years. He seemed rather amused, looked through the photographs and said he would come and see the room when next visiting his daughter, whose school was not far from Guildford, and this he did.

I was then a conspicuously late riser, rarely reaching the breakfast table before ten, and I was bedridden when a telegram was brought to me announcing Mr and Mrs Heal were arriving at 10 a.m. Never was a woman dressed, a bed made or a room tidied at greater speed, and the upshot of the visit was advice to go to a certain school of art for which Mr Heal would give me recommendation. Yet even while expressing gratitude for this gesture and for the trouble he had taken, I knew my lately acquired 'Indian Military' was not going to cover the cost. I could not ask my mother to finance a second training, least of all at this moment.

The moment was crucial because at long last we had found a house in which all were prepared to live. It was some miles from Guildford, in the village of Wonersh, which then consisted of little more than a street stretching between Grantley Manor and the Dower House, with the Grantley Arms a prominent centre. A few cottages and shops were spread around the adjacent common, and on the outflanks some stately homes. The Earls of Grantley had long since abandoned their handsome but dilapidated mansion – then called Wonersh Park – standing behind a high wall bordering the street. Some years back I had bicycled through this village and decided that here I would like to live, and from 1924 it became my home for the rest of my life.

*

The Old House bordered the street, a timber-framed jetty house formed by the joining together of four artisans' cottages, the two central ones dating from about 1600. Formerly a stream had flowed through the village and in times of flood had poured merrily into this central portion, whose floor was below street level. So at the beginning of this century, this central part, bound together by its timber framing, had been raised on jacks on to a stone sill above street level with oak block flooring superimposed. Cottages at east and west ends were then joined to it and given an outward dressing to blend. Various liberties had been taken with windows to let in more light, but some still had their original glass and fastenings, and this handsome mongrel my mother now bought.

Its most alluring feature was the ground floor of the central part, where the inner walls had been removed to form a long room of beautiful proportions, with a king post and a queen post supporting a massively beamed ceiling which was at a height to admit weavers' looms. Weaving had been an early industry in the village. Moreover, there was still an artisan in occupation, though not a weaver. Mr Brett, a shoemaker of some repute, was anxious to retain a business handed from father to son, and though he lived elsewhere, his shoemaker's shop opened on to the village street at the extreme west end of The Old House, and my mother was willing for him to remain.

What possibly had discouraged the sale of this house, and confined it to a relatively modest price, was that its eight upper-floor rooms, from east to west ends, led with few exceptions each into the next. However, by making one room into 'the girls' study' and carving a passage from the side of the bedroom allotted to me, occupants of west-end bedrooms could at least reach the staircase without encroaching on others' privacy. Even so, to reach the bathroom, they must either go downstairs and up a severely steep backstairs, or go through my mother's bedroom. It was years before we had the money to add more bathrooms.

Eight upper rooms for a family of five might seem excessive, but apart from an almost ceaseless flow of guests, my mother, encouraged by a successful experiment in Guildford, had come to look on paying guests as a means of support. Of these the happiest were the younger generation, some of whom became friends for life, such as Kika and Aileen Lindop, daughters of British parents based in the Argentine, who came to us in their holidays while at school in England. Older PGs were sometimes more of a strain; Muriel bullied them if they stayed too long, others appealed to my mother's benevolence to a point where the 'P' became an anomaly, whereas genuine guests often subscribed gifts of such generosity that they made the dividing line difficult to diagnose.

PGs were given the bedrooms at the east end, over a warm kitchen, next the bathroom and, as my mother was the earliest to rise and latest to bed, her bedroom was generally an open passageway. There was no heating other than the two open fireplaces at each end of the long room – invalids alone had fires in their bedrooms – and for two years there was no lighting other than candles upstairs and oil lamps below. All this was fairly normal at the time; electricity did not come to Wonersh till 1926, and when it came my mother, who had used the major portion of her capital to buy the house, used most of the remainder to wire it for electricity. We had found the house supplied with a telephone, which was a novelty.

The Old House firmly disposed of the remaining mirror; not only was it totally unsuitable but it couldn't be got into the house.

*

In spite of structural drawbacks, people seemed to like staying at The Old House, and when Grace declared she was going to do the cooking she little anticipated the load this was going to be. Happily, the mantle was lifted by one Dora West, brought to us by a notice in the window of the local shop.

She had early been trained at a stately mansion, and swept, scrubbed, polished and carried coal for us daily for close on thirty years. She also did most of the cooking, but not the housekeeping, in which bleak moments occurred – but always with a merciful reprieve, as when we set off for a picnic one afternoon, four adults and three teenagers, my mother murmuring, 'I don't know what I'm going to give you all for supper tonight.' Half an hour later we sat down to our picnic in a field almost white with mushrooms.

'How the Lord abets that woman,' said my elder sister.

In those days we could leave the window by the front door open all night for the early delivery of milk and bread; we could also leave the front door unlocked for latecomers from London or a dance. The London Army & Navy Stores delivered orders weekly, including a joint of meat, thereafter stored in a larder. There were convenient carrier services such as Avenal's, which came through the village daily, calling at any house that had an 'A' in the window, to deliver goods to Guildford or any other fairly local address.

There was no bus service, but an adjacent village, Bramley, had a country line conveniently close, with trains connecting with the fast service from Guildford to London. It was not long before the Hammond family of Wonersh started a bus service, so personal one could catch it at the door, even fling on a coat while they waited. It lasted for years, amalgamated with the Aldershot Bus service that carried one further.

The custom of calling on newcomers was still prevalent, and we got to know residents over a wide area. They generally called in their cars, my mother and aunt returning the calls on foot, though this was no hardship to them. So with London friends, Guildford friends and local ones, it was sometimes with sinking heart I heard my mother telling the departing guest to call any time they were passing. The long room could be a perfect trap for the younger generation if the older were ushered in; so, balancing my mother's hospitality, to ring our doorbell was to hear the sound of feet rapidly retreating upstairs.

Helen Alford, who had been at Bedford College with Betty, was a frequent weekender and also a long-distance walker. She and Betty blazed many a cross-country trail, goaded by a dangerous map marking rights of way. This had once carried them clean through a tennis party but, as no one protested, presumably they were within their rights. Helen was as good a mimic as I was, and her subtle imitation of one of our less desired PGs evoked from Betty the famous maxim: 'The guests that don't pay are not allowed to laugh at those who do.'

I need not say I was a frequent visitor to Brooklands race track, a few stations up the London line, and though my interest was in the cars and drivers, I often wagered a half-crown, the highest bet that Indian Military would allow. This had taught me that the reliability of the car was as important as the driver. In Weybridge lived one of my eight uncles, and he and his wife would lunch me beforehand with anyone I brought, but once when I came alone Uncle Durie said he would come along also, relying on me to advise him on whom to back.

There were eight races to go and in seven of them I was lucky in choice, by which time Uncle Durie was staking what seemed to me enormous sums, and even my half-crown had brought in a nice little nest egg. In the last race were only two cars, a twelve-cylinder Sunbeam and a hot-looking Isotta Frascini, and I advised the latter, the Sunbeam was notorious for speed but also for breaking down. Uncle Durie looked haggard on coming back from the Tote; everyone was backing the Sunbeam with enormous sums, and certainly it roared away, leaving the Isotta standing, the crowds cheering, and I dared not ask my uncle what he had staked. Yet at the far end of the track I saw the Sunbeam slow down and come to a halt, and the Isotta came romping in alone. Uncle Durie was all for dating me up for the next races, but other events intervening, I escaped trying to achieve what I could never do again.

*

Verena Holmes was another welcome weekender; she was marking time before going to find work in the States. I too was marking time trying to find some way of making a living, but there were no wage-earning jobs for the untrained young at that time, or had there been a VSO I would have leapt at it. The voluntary jobs then open entailed a good deal of personal expense. It was Verena who put me on to the job in Sweden; her sister had Swedish friends she often visited and had heard of a Swedish family, particularly the mother, wanting an English girl during the winter months, just to talk English with them and improve their accents. Above all, they would pay the passage out!

Had they said 'teach' I might have hesitated, but I could certainly talk English, so I sent a photo of myself, as required, told them my age, and agreed to winter in Sundsvall, some distance up the coast from Stockholm. Finally I went for an interview with their agent in the city, learnt from him that Mr Wikström was a timber merchant of some importance, that they lived in a beautiful house, and what was I meaning to charge? I couldn't see that, merely talking English and living in comfort, I could charge anything, but was advised to do so, and finally left it to the agent to decide. He arranged for £5 a month, exactly the amount I got from Indian Military, which left me intoxicated with my future wealth.

All this was settled early in the year but was not to take place until October. In the meantime, accompanied by the Lindops, we spent the summer as usual at Scole, unaware that this was the last time we should ever live there.

After a minimal period of married life, Eric's wife got a divorce. They had lived at Thorpe Parva, Eric ostensibly helping his father, but too many malpractices had come to light, and Eric was finally shipped to Australia, then the bourne for unstable characters. However, a daughter had been born to him, and in the interest of daughter-in-law and granddaughter, Aunt Tinie got Uncle Dick to revoke Eric's eventual inheritance of the Scole property, now hers for her lifetime. In due course she sold it to a neighbouring landlord, portioning the capital fairly to each claimant. Never a word had come from Eric and she had no idea of his whereabouts, but had assurance from an Australian bank that he drew his money and presumably letters. Aunt Tinie eventually went to live in London.

It was shortly before my departure for Sweden that I met a man I would gladly have married had he shown the slightest inclination towards marrying me. I was a 'pick-up'. Returning from a lunch date in London, I was wearing a sombrero I had bought in Portugal, which my aunt deplored as being far too striking. It seemed to lure a nice-looking man standing on the platform at Woking with a terrier at his heels. He got into my carriage and the terrier effected an introduction by jumping up on to the seat beside me. It was called to heel and an apology offered, but conversation was now loosed, and I learned that he was an army Major based at Aldershot and lately returned from Cologne. I asked if he had met any of the WAACs out there and mentioned my Aunt Muriel. 'Oh, of course I knew *Boddam*. Used to dance with her....'

When we parted at Guildford he said he would come and call on Boddam, and was told where to find her. He came soon after.

This was Esmond Morrison, whose friendship I was to enjoy for fifty-odd years, but he was having far too pleasant a life to be considering marriage. I deplored having to leave just on acquiring a new house and new friend, but both were still there on my return, and even before I left I put Esmond's friendship to the test.

When he had called on Boddam, we were at the Guildford house, where he came more than once, but we had now moved to Wonersh. Very soon I boarded a train for Bramley, never suspecting there might be a Bramley other than the one adjacent to our village, and with little in my purse, I found myself hurtling towards a Bramley in the heart of Hampshire. The prospect of a night in a cold waiting-room until a train got me home impelled me on arrival near 10 p.m. to ring Esmond in Aldershot. He was dining in the Mess, and in full Mess regalia came and rescued me. We reached home towards midnight to find my mother in her dressing-gown, her hair in a plait, writing an urgent letter she had forgotten. Delighted to greet Esmond, she showed him an, as yet, sparsely populated house. They made a bizarre couple, each with candle in hand, touring the rooms.

*

On board S.S. *Patricia*, in which I sailed to Sweden, was the Wikström's agent, so I had a royal introduction to the beautiful city of Stockholm, whose new Town Hall at the water's edge had only just been built. Not till I was seen off on the night train for Sundsvall did I get a feeling of adventure, though the Swedish job could hardly be described as such. It was a sojourn in gross comfort among benign natives who had come to love us since we had won the war, and where all the woolly underclothes I had bought were superfluous in houses far warmer than the average English homestead. My obstinate habit of leaving a chink of the double windows open – over an outsize radiator – caused the maids to wear coats for the bringing of early morning tea to a room far warmer than a Crofton dormitory.

I was fortunate in the family who had engaged me: Ando and Sigrid Wikström could not have been kinder, and if they had expected something more mature in a 24-year-old – as a Swede of that age would have been – they shared me out equally with the younger generation. Of these there was a seventeen-year-old daughter, in her last year at the local school, who much appreciated an 'English sister', having only younger brothers. There were three of these at Lundsberg, the Swedish Eton.

We lived in a large stone house halfway up a mountain overlooking Sundsvall harbour, its garden reaching down towards the sea. A cave dug in this garden, and stocked with ice blocks, formed a perfect refrigerator, and tapering cones, built of sawn logs, reaching to tree height supplied the winter fuel.

Within nearly every house was beautiful furniture, not least that made of birchwood, and fine coloured pictures; there would be bookshelves full of the classics of many countries: I had noticed in the Wikström's shelves *Djönggl Boken* and an English encyclopaedia. The country was then a patchwork of the dark green of the fir and the fiery gold of the birch-trees, and with the coming of snow the fir-trees became overdressed women in white, holding out fat gloved hands. The wooden houses – white, red, green – looked like toys under their canopies of snow.

As far north as Sundsvall the snow generally came before the frost, giving not much opportunity of skating, and skiing was mostly a utilitarian exercise acquired soon after learning to walk. That year the frost came first, making walking or driving very hazardous, but turning the Wikström's hard tennis court into a perfect ice-rink. This was a joy to Sigrid and me; Sigrid had been brought up in Stockholm, where there were ice-rinks, and when English weather had permitted it, I had patiently taught myself to skate.

For the Wikströms, with other means of transport, skiing was definitely a sport, and the Christmas holidays saw the younger generation putting on skis at the doorstep and wearing them against all hardship to reach their favoured slopes. When I joined them, an adult learner was a source of dismay, not to say merriment, and as they had learnt so young, they could give me little advice on how to begin. I was soon black and blue from falling on unforgiving ground and getting impaled on fir-trees and other obstacles, and only for the honour of England did I persevere. There were no what one might call amateur slopes for practising on, and I finished up with a loathing for the sport beyond description, and thanked God for the spring.

Another set-back was the discovery that the sea coast when it freezes does not necessarily lie flat. Horse-sleighing by moonlight was a popular sport, and the Wikströms had a big sleigh drawn by carriage horses, who galloped at speed along the coast to my instant delight, until a familiar symptom made me realize that even frozen, the ocean could make me sick. Luckily we had only limited time on that occasion and I held out. Thereafter I avoided the sport.

Barbro had her own little sleigh, a two-seater. One could drive either standing up behind the seats or, more comfortably, seated; armholes in the wolfskin rug permitted this, but buttoned up under our chins, the rug allowed little other voluntary movement. We went in the sleigh together one afternoon to fetch a book left at school but in Sundsvall High Street there were man-made grooves for the tramlines. It was into such a groove that the left sleigh runner now slipped, with the result that we advanced the whole length of a well-lit High Street more or less on my ear. The high-stepping pony was quite unrestrained by twisted reins, quite unaware of any irregularity but certain of destination, so we pulled up with a flourish at the door of the school. Here happened to be a member of staff, who put her foot on the upturned runner and, amid uncontrollable laughter, we resumed the natural position.

'Don't tell Papa,' said Barbro on our way home, but in a country far advanced in telephone communication, Papa had already heard.

After an abundant Christmas – I was given a complete skiing outfit – the barometer fell to eighteen degrees below zero. The black and white English setter, kennelled outdoors when I came, was now in the house, but a Lapp hound like a little black bear preferred to stay out in the yard.

I flatter myself I now set a fashion, for the men in winter wore tall grey lamb's-wool or black astrakhan caps, pressed in at the top like a Homburg. I bought a lamb's-wool one, pressed it down into a pork pie shape and wore it with effect. Barbro and her friends were horrified but admitted it looked well. By degrees quite a number were furtively being worn.

Aloof from war, Sweden still retained a number of old-world customs: it was pretty general for girls to give a bob curtsey to older women, but in the

61

conservative north I saw what looked like young widows coming out of school. They were wearing bereavement veils for a father. The head of the family was thanked by guests, wife and daughters not only for meals but drives in his car. In fact there was a veneration for the male sex by the female sex as something altogether superior, a feeling I could never quite share.

*

When school restarted after Christmas, Sigrid and Ando went with friends for a holiday to Biskra, but before leaving asked if I would stay on for the summer, to which I readily agreed. I was enjoying it, there was much more I hoped to see, and also I had now heard about Scole, and to stay on would fill the void of not going back there. To think of Scole was to hear the chime of the stable clock, or the crescendo and rallentando of the lawn-mower being drawn by the pony in padded shoes. One must not think about it.

Ando's mother, the dearest little grandmother, now took charge of Mar-ieberg. She lived in a country house outside the town and often came on visits. She had a beautiful singing voice untouched by age, and I have to confess that her tender rendering of Gounod's *Ave Maria* at this poignant moment reduced me to tears.

I had received gifts from friends on leaving England, but none so valu-able as the *Pocket Oxford Dictionary* given me by a far-seeing but pedantic friend in the Foreign Office. He had once sent me a list of my spelling mis-takes in a letter I had written him. Yet that dictionary was vital, and I could have done with an English grammar and a *Debrett*. Interest in the English Royal Family was intense, especially in the then Prince of Wales, while Bar-bro's history lessons covered a distressingly wide area. Who were the Lol-lards? I was thankful for that encyclopaedia I had seen in the bookshelves, but even that didn't give me rules for the behaviour of the English lan-guage. I may not have been much help to the Swedes, but this job improved my own spelling and taught me quite a lot of history.

Curiously, I learnt very little Swedish, chiefly because everyone used me to exploit their English. I learnt the odd sentence, and my early pronuncia-tion of *Sverige* – rather like porridge – when corrected, gave me the clue to the soft consonants, so the native name for Sweden became *Sfairia*. Yet lis-tening to Swedish being poured out around me gave me no idea of where a word began or ended, and my mind would wander off in its old-time habit of not concentrating. Yet my ears were drinking in the sound, the undula-tions and the lilting intonation, so that soon I was keeping Barbro and her friends in fits of laughter imitating them with those very sounds, and prob-ably here and there using actual words unknowingly.

When the snow began getting slushy, I took the setter for long walks and witnessed the havoc of spring. In the woodlands it behaved traditionally: small flowers pricking up through the snow, the gentle sound of melting and the sudden avalanche as a branch shrugged off its winter mantle. On man-made surfaces the spring wrought havoc, and areas had to be closed while chunks of roadway were retrieved, replaced, filled in and made to look as if nothing had happened. Slabs of the Wikströms' tennis court had to be renewed and repaired.

From the windows of Marieberg one looked down on Sundsvall's harbour, where strings of bright red Noah's Arks, towed by steamers, would be carrying cargo to the sailing-ships lying at anchor at the mouth of the harbour. Logs made up much of this cargo, logs conveniently brought down to the coast by the fast-flowing rivers, logs lying in the port for selection, looking like a stable platform but only the logmen had the agility to use them as such. To pause was to sink. I would stand galvanized watching the approach of these square-rigged sailing-ships. The first sign of them looked like a fault on the line of the horizon, a fault becoming a definite projection and soon recognizable as a square-rigged topsail emerging out of the ocean, followed by square sails increasing in size. If the ship had an iron rather than a wooden hull, the masts reached to an almost terrifying height. With enormous dignity the ship would approach to drop sails and anchor at the mouth of this sheltered harbour.

By June there were lilac-trees of varying shades of colour in the Wikströms' garden, and a galaxy of roses in their greenhouses that never got blown by the wind. They remained perfect in shape, bowls of them brought in to embellish the house.

When tennis began, the Wikströms' friends, male and female, came up to pit their strength against an English player. Luckily tennis was the one outdoor game which I was keen about, and in Guildford I had belonged to a good club. The odds were anyhow in my favour as there were few outdoor courts in Sundsvall, and most of my opponents were used only to indoor tennis. I had no difficulty in beating the women, but the men took it far more seriously, put up a better game and didn't at all like being beaten, and sometimes they weren't. The Wikströms' eldest son was frantic to beat me, and eventually he did. We often played till midnight, and could have gone on.

This Swedish venture wound up with a grand climax in Jämtland, some distance north, where Ando Wikström owned acres of forest, and where we would be three miles from a road or other habitation except for the Alströms, a forester and his wife who were also caretakers of Kullen, the Wikströms' house. Our food would be the yield of fishing-rod and gun, and I rather admired Ando, after the luxury of Marieberg, choosing the primitive life.

We migrated north, the whole family in two cars, which were left at a farm. We then walked through woodland or crossed lakes, the farm-hands carrying luggage and doing the rowing until the last and largest lake, where the Kullen motorboat awaited us and the farm-hands returned. At the far end of this lake could be seen distantly a high spit of land with a house on it. This was Kullen, neat as a dolls' house, with painted furniture, electric lighting, telephone and two bathrooms. The one for the men was the lake we had just crossed, the women's lay on higher ground at the far side of the spit of land. One thrust out into clear water warmed by the sun that had barely left it all night.

*

At Kullen one went to bed with the birds still singing, and the Alström's cock would start crowing soon after midnight. By day one heard the melancholy cry of the diver birds sunning themselves on the rocks, and for days there would be absolute stillness, then suddenly the wind would rise, lashing trees and water to fury, and to be caught out on the lake was to have a struggle to reach the shore.

The Alströms had a cottage in a clearing not far distant. Mrs Alström did our cooking, kept a cow and made delicious cheeses. Alström grew vegetables and, while we were here, fetched outdated newspapers and our letters from a distant post office. Though I had never been allowed to drive a car, I was, surprisingly, allowed to shoot, and even proudly added woodcock to the pot. Yet when I claimed to know nothing about fishing, I was told all English people fished, just as they loved dogs and went for long walks. The Alströms netted small fish near the shore but Ando rowed out towards the centre of his bathroom and put a rod into my hands with a dummy minnow on the end of the line, which I sloshed into the water not far from the boat and began reeling in, to find I had hooked a colossal salmon trout. It was almost impossible not to catch them. Eaten with Mrs Alström's cream mayonnaise, then her cheese, and for 'afters' the wild fruit growing everywhere – strawberries, raspberries, cloudberries – so much more fragrant than the cultured ones, we could not have fed better. One acquired a tremendous appetite out on the water; I revelled in this Eden, which could scarcely be called primitive living, and whose only flaw was the mosquitoes, but as mosquitoes like new blood I was certainly an asset here to the family. Only in the house one had peace, with netted windows and fly-flap doors.

I was the first foreigner Alström had ever met, and twenty-five years later when I went back, I was the second. Yet for all its remoteness, we once rowed to a distant lake where a solitary fishing hut used to be rented by an Englishman. He had papered its walls with pages from the *Illustrated London*

64

News and behold, pictures of Doulais, the firm I had despised at Merthyr, as the leading ironworks of the world.

After a tearful dinner in Stockholm we all dispersed in several directions and this gave me the chance to do what I had always hoped to do on my earnings. I bought two hundred miles of Norway which I could travel by coach, train or ship, whichever I chose or best suited the terrain. Some of the remoter hotels were still wooden constructions and my Swedish more useful than English as I pursued mountain and fjord of this beautiful country on a devious course from Trondheim to Oslo.

*

Though I think it valuable for everyone, at some period, to have difficulty in making both ends meet, yet if this is the norm, then a period of opulence is equally valuable, as that year in Sweden was for me. Besides the warm-hearted and lasting friendship of the family, their lifestyle had given me new boundaries, interests and knowledge, but there were times when I wondered guiltily, had I been so useful to them?

Now here I was back in the old rut: no fortune, no husband, no job, and a dozen things waiting at home for my attention, not least harvesting the Bramley Seedling apples from the colossal tree planted by the shoemaker's father and standing on what was now our lawn. I had brandished my Loughborough diploma round local garages, hoping to be taken on as assistant, to find them suffering a surfeit of applicants. By 1925 they were cutting down staff.

I found light relief in Avis, now assistant to a veterinary surgeon living on Wonersh common. My two sisters could not have been more different in character but I enjoyed them both. With Avis I played tennis, played the fool generally, and she supplied supporting casts for my mimicry.

Soon after my return I was invited to Camberlot, the Morrisons' place in Sussex, there meeting Esmond's parents, sister and brother. Mrs Morrison delighted in the young and I went there often, again getting a chance of shooting. It was not unlike Scole, but with a difference; horses bred at Scole were Suffolk Punches, here they were polo ponies. It was not really my environment, and I saw clearly that anyone marrying a Morrison would be marrying the whole family, whose decisions would be paramount for they were a very strong clique. Not that I was given a choice.

A boost to my career came from an unexpected quarter; Betty had met and got on well with a Mrs Gardiner of powerful character who had been intrigued to learn of Betty's sister training to be an engineer. Now an invitation had come for us both to stay at Thame Park, the colossal country estate where she lived on the borders of Oxford and Buckinghamshire. A house party weekend.

65

This was rather unsettling: did one tip the chauffeur sent with a car to fetch us, and was our clothing of a standard to be unpacked by maids, from whom no secrets are hid? I was very proud of the handsome leather bag I carried, but one had to keep it shut or its lining hung out in ribbons.

Mrs Gardiner had much on hand, so we found our own diversions, and I settled down to sketch the magnificent doorways of this Georgian mansion which managed to amalgamate perfectly with an Elizabethan wing. Later Florence Gardiner had time to lend an ear to my Loughborough training and tutoring through Stellite and Morgan, and up to that time I had not had much more. Mrs Gardiner clearly thought I needed more driving experience, and later bid me take over her massive Delaunay Bellville parked in Henley High Street, a challenge I dared not refuse. Cautious depression of the accelerator brought no result, so I pressed harder, whereon a considerable weight of power leapt into a happily empty street. There I was able to restrain it; nevertheless I later stalled the engine and Mrs Gardiner made no light task of having to get out and crank it. All passengers were relieved to get home.

Neither Betty nor I were aware that Mrs Gardiner and her husband were getting a divorce, and later she was to buy some acres of high ground overlooking the next village to Wonersh, and there build a house to which I often came. She was a very good friend to me, would let me drive any of her cars, of which she never had less than two, would ask me to fetch her friends from London, in fact gave me the experience I needed to open up wider possibilities.

Meanwhile with other distractions – I was invited to the Canary Islands and to Majorca – it was only too easy to let time slip by. I still had a mind to pursue art; but with the favourable exchange, it was cheaper to do this in the Quartier Latin than anywhere in England. Without further troubling Ambrose Heal, I meant to do this, improving my art as well as my French, but even so one needed money. Muriel, long since back from Cologne, made it clear I should be working or married or anyway out of the house.

Then Mrs Gardiner invited me to go with her to Venice, and this could not be denied. So I saw this city while the casas and palazzos were still privately owned, while the gondolas were still the main transport and motor boats had not yet penetrated the canals. There was still a king on the throne and it was an awesome spectacle when the Royal Mail came swinging down the Grand Canal, propelled by a team of liveried gondoliers with what looked like a monstrous jewel box on board with REGE POSTE written on it in gold. Though I was often to go back, how glad I was to have seen Venice then, for it was never the same again.

1924–1928

CHAUFFEUR-COMPANION

It was not until 1926 that I started applying to agencies, feeling now confident to offer myself as chauffeur-companion. Applications poured in from a London agency, persuading me that they were trying to get rid of the meanest jobs before offering the plums. Even driving and servicing the car was rated at less than £2 a week, and companionship involved household duties unspecified, and even a little gardening thrown in, jobs that I thought would and should be voluntary. I wondered what Wilby had been paid besides a free cottage.

I wrote a stern letter, which dried up the applications for some weeks but then brought a letter from a Mrs Robinson who had just bought a house in Southwold and a new Hillman car and wanted someone who could drive it and also be companion to her during the summer months. This sounded a promising 'starter', for I knew Southwold well, and Aunt Tinie, who happened to be staying with us at the time, knew and recommended Mrs Robinson, adding nostalgically that Eric used to play cricket with her sons.

So to Mrs Robinson I went; she was seventy and I was approaching twenty-seven, but these extremes can get on well together, as we seemed to do. She had engaged a raw little minion to come daily and cook and clean for us and, neither of us being domestic types, we combined in the office of training her. I supervised the cleaning and laying of tables – it was music to my ears to hear again the Norfolk-Suffolk accent – and Mrs Robinson took on admonishments over lumps in the bread sauce and such. Neither of us had anticipated that, on the occasion of a bridge party, when she had cleared away tea, the minion would put her head round the door and announce that one of the silver spoons was missing. Guests, being blameless, enjoyed the joke.

In fine weather Mrs Robinson would sit on the beach in the mornings, and I bathed. She liked picnics and exploring the country by car, and there were interesting tours with the local archaeological society. I had contemporary companions in her family and their friends at the weekends, and in bad weather, both of us avaricious readers, we were sublimely happy reading books from the local library. The only, and very light, drudgery was accompanying her on walks with her two Highland terriers.

A fast walker, and hungry for greater scope, I found it curiously tiring walking slowly.

In this job, of such contrast to the earlier applications, I was finding it hard to be worth my keep; I was just being a daughter, replacing Mrs Robinson's own, now married and living in Shrewsbury. The Hillman gave no trouble, even cleaning it was taken out of my hands if we went over to Mrs Robinson's normal home in Beccles, where William would emerge from the farm and, needed or not, wash and polish the car.

Roos Hall estate, in Beccles, belonged to the Nelson family, the Sucklings, but was let on a ninety-nine-year lease and the Robinsons were the occupants. Mr Robinson farmed a wide area and was responsible for introducing into England the black and white Friesian cattle. The Hall consisted of one wing of an Elizabethan mansion, of which the rest had never been built, and this three-storey building stood up tall and graceful on land at marsh level, with garden and portions of a moat at its feet, and a willow avenue stretching away to the river Waveney. Browsing in the parkland between the house and the Beccles–Bungay road, the cattle looked as if they had been chosen for their perfect blending with the backdrop, rather than their generous supply of milk. When a mist stole over the marshes and the house stood out in silhouette against it, the whole appeared more like a stage setting than reality.

Something of a sportsman in his youth, Mr Robinson's whole interest now was in the soil: in farming, and little else. Mrs Robinson's interests were in the mind, in reading, good conversation, collecting beautiful glass and furniture. She was an Australian of the family Gellibrand, had had a wide continental education and had travelled extensively.

Mr Robinson called on us one day to see the 'Southwold set-up'. In fact he wanted his wife's early return to be hostess as a man was coming to stay on business, so we left Southwold earlier than anticipated. Here it was soon evident there was less freedom, that the peaceful leisure Mrs Robinson filled so gracefully was apt to be bombarded by 'Fred'. We were sitting peacefully reading in the cool drawing-room one hot afternoon, the lazy hum of insects gyrating in the high ceiling, when Fred stormed in: 'Good gracious, how you women waste time! Lovely afternoon, best time of the day. ... Now *get* out!' Peace was shattered.

It was soon evident that social life at Roos had been warped by internal stress; fewer of the family came there and rarely any visitors of interest, though I do recall one who could not bear to be beaten at croquet, so we always had to let her win.

We went for marsh walks, we went to the Maddermarket Theatre in Norwich and to exhibitions, including the Colman collection of Cotman paintings, then housed in his own private gallery. Yet as winter advanced I longed for a break, but having stepped over the boundary, as it were, and as I still did not seem to offend Fred, I could be here for ever. I groped for an excuse weighty enough to balance the treachery of leaving my employer imprisoned without anyone even to drive her car. I decided to have my tonsils taken out.

*

Early in life I had had my tonsils removed, but by the old-fashioned method of cutting them off and leaving the roots. Subsequent sore throats and two bouts of quinsy in adult life were a sign that the roots must also be removed, but the opportunity never seemed to coincide with sufficient money for the operation. It was Betty who finally said she would pay, if I would settle a time for it to be done, and this seemed to me the ideal moment.

A few days in a nursing home and all was over, the roots despatched, but I was not intending to make so light of it and wrote to Beccles rather suggesting a rest had been advised, when a letter came from Mrs Robinson proving my solicitude on her behalf was not really necessary. She wrote from Bath, where she had gone with the friend who got irritable over croquet; her family was coming for Christmas. She hoped I would rejoin her in February.

I have to admit that in my gloomiest period at Roos I had leaned out of my window, looking on to the marshes and the willow avenue, and prayed to the Lord for something to relieve the monotony – I did not say 'adventure', but the Lord knew what was in my heart and gave liberally. Mrs Robinson's letter wound up: 'I'm afraid you must find it very dull at Roos. I was thinking we might take a short holiday in the spring, to the West Indies perhaps, or is there somewhere more interesting you want to visit?'

The *Sibijak*, tall and graceful, stood high on the water at Southampton, the latest thing in advanced technology, making her maiden voyage. Every shipping office had a golden booklet describing her as a home from home, with a special gyroscopic device to prevent rolling. Thus when Mrs Robinson and I were shown to our respective cabins we found, not berths, but brass bedsteads, all washing arrangements and sumptuous furniture, but no hooks on doors, barricades against flowing water, or restraints on moveable furniture. This was a floating hotel rather than a ship; the only reminder of the ocean was a discreet notice in three languages that in the event of trouble our lifeboat was No. 8.

The *Sibijak* was not going to the West Indies but to Java in the then Dutch East Indies, and Mrs Robinson and I were disembarking at Tangier...

Mary Smyth, a friend of Betty's and mine from Crofton, owned a villa in Tangier where she often wintered, and had written an article on

Morocco in the *Crofton Journal* which had aroused my interest and desire. I wrote to her asking for useful details and took both the article and her reply when I went to Roos. For I felt the West Indies had none of the spice or the element of risk of Morocco, and Mrs Robinson, who in all her travels had never visited an Arab country, was very willing to comply. The date of sailing just happened to coincide with that of the *Sibijak*.

We were still at Southampton at dinnertime, the dining-saloon resplendent and staffed by little Javanese servants, barefoot and carrying dishes on their shoulders. In true Dutch style we ate greengages with our meat. Everyone was in evening dress, and at the Captain's table was the director of the shipping company with his wife and daughter; many heads turned to look at them on entry. After dinner we listened to music in a vast lounge, where I noticed at least the grand piano was secured to the floor, but we were now leaving the home waters and I gauged it best to retire as I felt the first reminder that we were on open water, a reminder that became increasingly insistent.

Weather forecasts only reached a small proportion of the public at that time, so we were unprepared for a storm that night equal to the one which had greeted the *Wild Goose* setting out for the Atlantic, and creating equal devastation. The stabilizing apparatus of the ship was evidently not working, and we rolled so badly that my armchair became a menace, leaping at me from all quarters, while cupboard doors swung to and fro, drawers slid on to the floor and joined the contents from my dressing-table slewing round on the carpet. There was a crescendo of noise, starting with crashes and the sound of broken crockery below, then the ominous roll and crash of heavy objects colliding up on deck. I felt I should be at Mrs Robinson's bedside but was so sick I could hardly be an asset. It was Mrs Robinson who came to me.

I was by this time aware of an awful fact: my bed lay athwart the ship so that sometimes heels were above head or vice versa, and I now realized that heels had been uppermost for some time. The ship was no longer rolling, not righting itself, though heaving with the ocean. It was lying over to one side and there was no comfortable pulsating sound of engines. My stomach froze, which cured it at once of seasickness. Were we sinking?

Mrs Robinson, when she came, was fully clothed and said a ship's officer had told her to dress and go to the landing beside the lift. I also dressed in what I could get at, and in what I could least afford to lose, covering this *mélange* with a warm coat. I had to walk almost on the wainscoting of the corridor leading to the lift, and through its windows saw water swirling into the cabins on the lower side of the ship. Was this bath-water or ocean? I thanked Heaven that we were on the upper slope, but Lifeboat No. 8 must be hanging over the ship.

They had chosen glass for the lift shaft, encased in wrought ironwork on the separate floors, and the lift between floors lay drunkenly sideways. Clinging to the ironwork were a host of passengers variously dressed, Mrs Robinson among them, but not a ship's officer in sight.

From here one looked down through the central well of the ship, which pierced many decks to the dining-room where we had sedately dined what seemed like years ago. Tables, vases, tulips, violin stands and much more were huddled on the lower side until the *Sibijak*, which had taken on a flopping motion, with each flop sent this dissipated collection out a few yards, to retract immediately. A sort of freak lancers. I looked distastefully on this scene and felt I preferred the *Wild Goose*.

People were coming from their cabins now and going up on the deck, from which a chill and blustery wind was blowing down. A Dutchman emerged from a cabin with two little girls clad in mackintoshes, and Mrs Robinson appealed to him about whether we should go up. With tears pouring down his cheeks he said, 'Oh, *madame*, it is terrible. It is terrible...' and dashed upstairs.

I discouraged the idea of following them; an icy wind was blowing down from the upper landing and I felt there would be an official command if we were to take to the lifeboats, but if such were given I could clearly see there would be a rush for the nearest, regardless of numbering. Stories of heroism on the *Titanic* began floating into my mind. If there was a vacant seat left, I knew who must be helped into it, but an instinct told me that such heroism was not going to be demanded. The ship lay at a fearful angle, and she might indeed be shipping water, but she was not sinking as I had at first feared. Almost at that moment I heard again the ship's engines and presently she started rolling. Almost too soon, my stomach unfroze.

*

With a distinct list to port, and rather behind schedule, we reached Tangier. No official explanation for the ship's behaviour was ever given, but a young Dutchman also visiting Tangier and sharing our hotel assured us that the storm had overpowered the stabilizing mechanism, that cargo had shifted and, on the fore deck, a heavy derrick which had broken loose and hung out over the bulwarks had to be cut away for the ship to right herself. During this operation propulsion was damped down.

We had had to go a whole day without food, but once the splintered glass and crockery had been cleared, the barefooted Javanese became active and, as the weather improved, the ship became steadier; there was even after-dinner dancing. Moreover, the shared endurance had taken the starch out of the passengers; we all became immensely friendly, and those embarking at Tangier were received on arrival as heroes.

We stayed in Tangier with Mary Smyth in her villa on the Mount, but Mrs Robinson, a seasoned traveller, was also ready to range the whole of French Morocco by the excellent road and rail service the French had installed. We were warned not to look in through the open doors of mosques and to leave villages before sundown, when they closed their gates. There were still pockets of resistance by the Moors where we were not allowed to go. Only Marrakesh, infested with typhus, was denied us, and I had to wait forty years to reach it.

Once Mrs Robinson did rebel. We were in Fez, staying in a one-time sheikh's palace taken over by the Companie Transatlantique as a hotel. We were undoubtedly in the harem: small bedrooms overlooking an enclosed courtyard, and we had had our share of local colour from a night-watch-man prowling an adjacent street, calling the hours and finally rousing the slaves to prepare the pre-dawn breakfast, for it was Ramadan. Here I discovered we were close to Miss Dennison's surgery. Miss Dennison and her sister had cured bodies and redeemed souls in Morocco over a long period, so greatly esteemed that it was the Moors who had hidden and protected them during the massacre of the infidels early in the century.

I had an introduction to Miss Dennison, also a map showing how to reach her surgery, and we started down a muddy alleyway both steep and dark from the overhead creeper. Every now and again we had to pin ourselves to the walls to allow passage for donkey or camel, and Mrs Robinson refused to go further. At that moment I saw a familiar sight: LETTERS was written in Roman characters above a letter-box and a bell. We had arrived.

Miss Dennison showed us much, and it was a pleasure to walk around with her, she was so warmly greeted everywhere. She helped me in getting a *sulhamn* made for me. It hangs beautifully from the shoulders, made from a complete circle of material. The tailor's young apprentice, about five years old, was chained to the shop.

Seeing that I had a small camera, Miss Dennison asked if I would photograph the wives of a sheikh, who were keen to have photos of their fair skin, but this must be done in the absence of the sheikh, who might raise objection. So a few days later, entering by a plain door in a wall which adequately obscured the richness within, we were received by the sheikh, who told us the house was ours and all within it, and then went out, leaving us to his four wives for entertainment.

They were as intrigued to meet us as we were to visit them. They fingered our clothing saying *Roumi* – Roman, foreign – and each showed us proudly her own rather stark little room. Then, seated on floor cushions, we were given mint tea and edibles, and a neighbour came in with local gossip so potent, with gestures so graphic, that it was not difficult to construe. The wives received this gleefully but I could see Miss Dennison growing increasingly embarrassed until she finally broke out in remonstrance, when the little wives assumed expressions of shock and dis-approval, and the neighbour left. We were now rather an anticlimax, so I prepared hastily for the photography. Two of the wives were certainly fair-skinned, but no camera could depict the other two as anything but swarthy. I had to express my regret when eventually I sent the prints to Miss Dennison.

That holiday established me as chauffeur for Mrs Robinson's escapes: to Southwold, London, Scotland, Wales.... I was only asked to drive her at Roos if her relatives from Australia came there, but more often she joined the relatives in London. Then I would drive them around town and to and from theatres, but enjoying the theatre as well. Parking was no trouble, only the hostility of the taxi towards private cars awaiting specific clients. We went frequently to Bath, often taking tea at the Pump Room Hotel, where I was easily forty years younger than most of the company, who were all bonded together, on hearing of the death of Lily Langtry, with potent memories.

The break came when I was asked to go to Australia with Mrs Robinson in return for my fare and expenses; but, delighted as I would be to go there, it would not be *my* Australia.

The Gellibrands occupied high places. Too much garden-party hats and long kid gloves, and I had by now just enough money for Paris. Mrs Robinson took a niece and we parted regretfully. I gave her a book for the long journey and she gave me Priestley's *Good Companions*, which we had both read at Southwold and decided it was not his best work, but there was all the difference in this copy, for under its name on the title page she had written: 'To Claudia who is one of them'.

*

Before I left for Paris I attended a gathering that took place from time to time of Old Croftonians, and there I found a number who had been at school with me, including Elspeth Perrins. She had been the youngest in the school when I first went to Crofton, had little to recommend her visually, besides suffering the unpopularity of a gauche but strongly opinionated junior reputed never to wash. The two years which separated us would nor-mally also have segregated us, but during one term we were in the same bedroom, found we had interests in common, and liked each other, after which I was apt to stand up for her.

It was now ten years since we had met, and a finishing-school in Paris had done much to improve her appearance and establish her self-esteem. On hearing that I was shortly going over to Paris, she said she too was coming there later in the year and we agreed to meet. I little guessed the importance of this encounter.

73

Then I set out for France, admitting to no one, not even to myself, the courage needed for this plunge into the *Quartier Latin*, this bearding of the life class at the Grande Chaumière studio, whose students of many nationalities seemed bound into an affiliation that made the newcomer feel an outcast. The head student left one to find out for oneself where things were kept and what was the general procedure.

In Paris I made good use of its galleries, delighted in its flower markets and met some interesting students, but I strongly doubted I would ever keep myself on murals or even book illustrations, early inspired by Edmund Dulac's wonderful art. Prinet, of the artists who came to judge our work, brushed all this aside in favour of greater attendance at the life classes and study of anatomy, and of course he was right. Moreover, the *Quartier* had been eroded by the Americans as a cheap drinking ground now that the USA was dry. They were sending up the prices as well as denuding the area of its languages. The only people talking French, it seemed, were the Russian refugees who had poured in.

I was thus working through my money faster than I was gaining talent and I was further disturbed by what seemed like all my friends now flowing into Paris – the Wikströms, Mrs Gardiner, Avis, to name a few, and my pedantic friend Jock was posted to the British Embassy. Though I was generally the guest, there were thank-you gifts to buy and, once across the river, money melted like snow. I seemed permanently to be going to the Gare du Nord, though I have to admit I had pushed into my luggage evening clothing suitable for dining out or dancing at Le Peroquet.

By the time Avis arrived it was high summer and the studios were closing down in favour of sketching parties. I took some days off to show her around, but after Versailles and Fontainbleau we had barely enough money next morning to reach the Gare du Nord, and it was with feelings of yearning I saw her off, picturing tea under the apple-tree on the lawn at home.

I had put in for a sketching party under Delécluse in Brittany. It had a cheap hotel (*sans bains mais avec bassins*). There was always the sea. I called in at my bank on the way back to see if I could really afford it. It was going to be a close shave.

When I got back to my lodgings I found Elspeth Perrins had called to see me.

*

Elspeth for some years had been hostess for her father at his house in Malvern or at Ardross Castle in the north-west Highlands: a whole-time job as they put up the celebrities for the Malvern festival, housed tennis players for the tournament, and in Scotland there were the annual shooting parties. Now her father had remarried and Elspeth was free to lead a life of her own, which she had every intention of doing. Somewhat nervously, and for the first time, she had brought her car over to France, to go with a party of five in two carloads down to the Riviera.

In her car, Elspeth was taking an English couple living in Paris, and the driver of the other car was an American also living in Paris, Dolly Rodewald, a distant connection since Elspeth's brother had married into the Rodewald family. Dolly would be driving a girlfriend she had staying with her, Lib Parker, over from the States, and Elspeth was to have driven the English couple, whom she knew, but now they were unable to leave. Elspeth was asking me to take their place.

My heart leapt at the offer, but of course I could not begin to afford it. Elspeth said she meant me to be her guest, but that I felt I could not allow, and remained firm. As she left, Elspeth said, 'I can't think why you're being so obtuse. You know all about cars. You'd be a tremendous help.'

Left to brood over it, I saw I should be to Elspeth what I had been to Mrs Robinson, a chauffeuse-companion, and not even asking a wage. So what was I balking at? I was not being a *gigolo*. We were to meet, the whole party, that evening at Dolly's house in the Rue des Belles Feuilles, an environment far removed from that of the *Quartier*. Elspeth and I went together, and on the way I asked why she couldn't join the other two in their car, but on arrival I saw the sagacity of her reply: 'You lose your independence without your own car.'

Dolly Rodewald was slightly wary of me; no doubt she had been told of the engineering diploma, but her girlfriend, Lib, was immediately friendly and said she thought Elspeth wanted someone to go on into Italy with her, speaking of the fact as if I was already committed. I reminded her I had refused the offer, but Lib assured me Elspeth had taken no notice of that, news which I admit I greeted with tremendous relief. Of course in the end I agreed to go.

All down the length of France we picnicked under the shade of trees, enjoying time without pressure, the richness of country grass, the concert of the cicadas. At Voiron came the first breath of the mountains, at Castellane the first scent of the jasmine up at Grasse, then by the Route Napoléon we dropped down to the valley of the Var towards Nice, where we joined the Route Corniche. Ancient motor vehicles, horse and cart, slow-moving ox waggons, were all part of the traffic; women in the fields were wearing sunbonnets and in Nice the horses wore hats.

By this time we had all shaken down together; I had learnt that Lib was also being paid for and we termed ourselves the Parasites. Dolly had revealed herself as other than the rich Parisienne, producing excellent meals at the roadside, for which her normal life gave little opportunity. She seemed to know of subtle places to dine at throughout France, and her interest in the Riviera was more in friends there than in sunbathing.

The Route Corniche was then a simple main road along the shore of a fertile and beautiful coast. Towns and villages dispersed along it reflected the wealth and the needs of a largely visiting population seeking a temperate climate in winter, but since the 1914–18 war a summer season had developed, with migrants revelling in sunburn and bared flesh to the limits of French concession. Police with tape-measures were apt to go round ascertaining if bathing-dresses and trunks reached to the prescribed dimensions. Such legislation was now fading out under the increase of sunbathers and the consequent summer market; hotels and restaurants were opening up, but so far without detraction, and even Juan les Pins, where we finally rested, was still small and well wooded.

I had noted with regret in Paris that the smart set no longer had any use for the fair complexion, preferring now a sunburnt hue, rather greasy. This was a blow to my best asset and not easy to remedy as my skin blistered under immoderate exposure to sun. However, Elspeth had little use for sunbathing; she preferred exploring the coast, looking up old haunts, and often we drove up to the little medieval villages lying like pieces of unmelted snow in the heights of the Alpes Maritimes. Life there was simple and not yet ebbing to the towns. The main drain, an open torrent, flowed down the street at an angle that effectively cleared all refuse. '*Ville des débauchés!*' the inhabitants would say disdainfully on learning where we were staying.

Have they been tamed, and are they now tourist-ridden, the perilous Gorges de Daluis and the Gorges du Cians, routes that clung to the cliff sides, barely wider than the car, with passing places at infrequent intervals? Streamers here and there were stretched across the ravines, written on them: *Défense de Doubler* or *Danger de Mort*. But we felt, both cars, compelled to drive them, returning via Entrevaux with its genuine drawbridge and citadel. We dined at La Turbie, looking out over Monaco at a cerulean Mediterranean which changed through a kaleidoscope of colouring till dreaming in moonlight. A dramatic area of France.

Lib and I then had a further education in Sienna and Florence with Elspeth. Dolly, who knew Italy well, preferred to remain with her friends in France. For me this was an unbelievable experience: seeing the Leaning Tower looming up in the headlights as we arrived at dusk in Pisa, seeing in the original all those prints that had decorated the walls at Crofton and savouring them for a lifetime, so I thought, little guessing how frequently I would return. Elspeth let me do much of the driving and I found the brakes of her car needed frequent adjustment, an operation not difficult before the advent of hydraulic brakes. Far more difficult was it to find seclusion for the female form to creep under the car, which otherwise brought a Frenchman or an Italian eager to take over, when gallantry sometimes surpassed efficiency. In fact that holiday transformed a rather negative interlude into one both positive and instructive.

1931

COPING WITH THE BALKANS

At this point I must confess that for some years I had had a liaison with a tortured soul who believed himself to be a masochist, having found that to live with anyone for any length of time was to start bullying them, hating them, and he had decided never to marry. He had, however, all the masculine desire for the opposite sex and particularly for me. I was highly sceptical of all this, though not unwilling to be his dinner, theatre and dancing partner. He danced divinely and we excelled at the dances of the day, which included the waltz and the tango. The affair had gathered momentum when a teasing fate brought us together for a time and I became equally enamoured. Belonging to the Levant Consular service, his was a life I could happily have shared, but as Government service can brook no scandal, and as he was a non-marrying man, and as I was myself a bit of a loner and could understand his feelings, I decided to be a non-marrying wife, to meet and live with him whenever chance offered, as fairly often it did.

Such a chance offered not long after I had returned to England with Elspeth. Bernard had been in Jeddah, whose uncomfortable climate – not then air-conditioned – permitted short leave before being sent to Athens. I was asked could I meet him in Paris. I could, and I did. The driving jobs had accustomed my family to my going off at short notice, and the honeymoon was, as always, delightful but fleeting. What I always dreaded were the harrowing farewells.

This one was worse than most because I saw him off at the Gare de Lyons on the Orient Express to Athens, the very sight of which was enough to stir the imagination, its wagons-lit marked up with names like *Venice*, *Trieste*, *Belgrade*, *Salonika*. I sat in the carriage with him, on a sofa that while he was at dinner would be made up into a comfortable bed, and an attendant brought along the dinner menu, from which he ordered a mouthwatering meal. The longing to share this journey with him was overwhelming; if this was masochism it certainly was effective and I left before I need have done, in an effort to hide my feelings.

At Dolly's invitation I was spending the night at 22 Rue des Belles Feuilles and with trailing pinions I arrived there to a warm reception; but I

77

was in an absent-minded mood and, during dinner in all innocence, and not anticipating the reaction, I said: 'It's an extraordinary thing, but all my friends seem to have got themselves into the Balkan peninsular. I'd love to do a tour there. I seem to know someone in nearly every capital city.'

Dolly said: 'Let's do it.'

I felt this to be impossible. I knew little about the Balkans but was sure they would present a strong contrast to the cushioned life Dolly had always known. I said the roads would knock her car to bits, and no garage would have the spares for repairing it. A Ford might survive perhaps.... I did not mention another thought uppermost in my mind. Before I met Dolly, Elspeth had told me there was more to her than met the eye, and this I came to recognize on the Riviera tour. What met the eye, however, was a well-upholstered figure supported on the neatest little feet and legs, expensive clothing, a kittenish face with large kindly grey eyes, the whole appearance an invitation to every man she encountered. How could I get this exotic figure creditably across Europe, prevent her getting enmeshed with unsavoury characters? I knew her main desire was to replace the husband who had deserted her, I knew that under the light-hearted frivolity and the impulsive generosity there was basic common sense, but I was older than she was, would feel responsible on a tour of my seeking and was not even sure if it was possible. So I made no further allusion to it and went home without more thought of it. At the end of January I got a telegram: 'Have bought a Ford. Are you coming? Dolly.'

As with Elspeth's invitation, I could no longer resist.

There are occasions when the only way to discover is to go and find out, and this was one of them. The motoring clubs on either side of the Channel had scanty knowledge of the Balkans, local clubs had only local knowledge, and the Michelin office in Paris seemed pained at our daring. I had a good RAC map of Europe but it only reached to the further boundary of Hungary, and from the AA we had a written account of our route, growing ever scantier of information beyond Transylvania. Not till we reached Salonika did we find the large-scale Freytag and Bernt maps of Eastern Europe. The Balkan states, which had continued fighting for some time after the First World War, were at this time in their usual state of uneasy peace.

The Ford, a four-door saloon, was the A model which followed in the wake of the T model. On the advice of her garage, Dolly had obtained wheel chains, an extra petrol tank fixed to a running board, and a second spare wheel and tyre. She had also had the back seat removed to contain her several cases, plus a small cooking stove. To this I added my luggage, along with stout tyre levers and several tyre-repair outfits. When we left, thanks again to the co-operation of the garage every removable exterior object was padlocked to the car frame. Rose and Titine, two of Dolly's faithful staff, paid us a tearful farewell on the twenty-second of April 1931.

*

Our route lay mainly eastward: Germany, Austria, Hungary, Romania and since Dolly was ready to include Greece, we would then go south through Bulgaria to Athens. This covered most of my contacts; Dolly hoped to meet an Austrian Count she knew in Vienna, and later a Romanian engineer who, whilst studying in Paris, had stayed with Dolly and her husband in the house in the Rue des Belles Feuilles.

With so little helpful information, we had to learn through our mistakes, and at first did everything wrong. We started too early, encountering floods and swollen rivers, while the stacks of manure that the Alsatians used to keep under close supervision beside their front doorsteps, we found floating off down the streets. Germany and Austria were under deep snow and, of all dates, we arrived in Vienna on the first day of May. My introduction to this beautiful city was to find everything shut and the streets full of morbid processions, and we lunched at a soup kitchen for want of an open restaurant. Dolly's Viennese Count was away, and she learnt later he was getting remarried.

We joined the Danube at Linz, after which the road flirts with the river the whole way to Vienna and Budapest. Both cities, while espoused to Communism, still bore the hallmarks of Royalty, and Vienna covertly cherished memories of their last Queen. Whatever the feelings in the cities, however, the country appeared to remain independent. The sun shone after Vienna, the apple trees were in bloom, and we learnt to be cautious of religious processions, which were apt to kneel down in the road. It was Sunday and a feast-day, everyone wearing their finest clothing, even the policemen wore plumes in their helmets. In the village women sat on their doorsteps sewing, their menfolk in a separate group smoking their pipes, and the grandmothers, each with a long-handled brush, sweeping the chickens off the road on to the grass verge on our approach. This habit persisted all through the Balkans; sometimes piglets with curly coats also fed off the verge, and we little guessed what a formidable obstacle they would present, fully grown and independent, on our return. Hens were looked on as fair gain by motorists; we were never believed when we said we had not killed any.

We learnt to be wary of Gypsies. They advanced in clans, men and women in bright-coloured clothing, many of them very handsome, and always led by a young girl on a pony or a mule and busy stranding thread with her distaff. To draw up was to bring them swarming like bees round the car, and a gift of money once offered by Dolly packed them round so close and noisily that the only way to get free was to press gently ahead.

My contact in Budapest was away on leave, but a deputy conscientiously showed us round. We had stayed at a hotel on the Danube which was stiff with foreigners, but we were leaving the river to go eastward, as here the Danube flows south. As we turned to go inland we saw the Hotel Vadaz Kurt (Hunting Horn) from whose courtyard was emerging a carriage containing elegant Hungarians, and I envied Dolly being able to say, 'Next time I come, that's where I'm going to stay.' I little knew that I would be the one to return.

Crossing the great Hungarian Plain, tarmac gave way to gravel and the Ford assumed a comet-like aspect, a trail of dust flowing behind us. Here were small white farmsteads, each with a well distinguishable by a long pole resting on a fulcrum, a bucket on one end in the air and anything from a bunch of flat irons, a petrol drum or a birdcage on the lower end, to help lever the bucket out of the well. Here too the road was used as a training-ground: a mare being driven in the shafts would have her foal running loose alongside on the verge of the road, but on the approach of the Ford the foal would dash off in fright over the adjacent land. Then, on seeing its mother untroubled at meeting and passing the car, the foal would rejoin her and after a few more cars – they came at sparse intervals – the debutante would become inured.

We were now in an area, which continued all through the Balkan countryside, where a vehicle was considered eligible for any pedestrian going the same way, and, of course, where a woman driver was continually challenged for her licence. Dolly was far the more generous in giving lifts. I was all too aware that we were overloaded and punctures from horseshoe nails were taking toll of the inner tubes. Once when a soldier flagged me, I pulled up thinking it was official, and he hailed two friends and they all piled in somehow, their rifles tickling the backs of our necks. They just wanted a lift into town.

On the other hand a policeman, wanting to see my driving licence, asked where we were going, got into the back and directed us for miles till we reached a railway station. Here he said he could take a train back; he had come merely to show us the way. Where one could make contact, and French was still thinly the international language, we found a friendliness in all the countries we passed through, quite contrary to the predictions before we started.

*

Up to this point we had fed in wayside eating-houses or had picnics of food bought in markets but, as we approached the Romanian frontier, villages became an unsociable row of one-storey houses enclosed behind high wooden fences and gates. There was not a shop or market in sight, and no possibility of communication after sunset with all gates closed and the continual barking of dogs. The inference was that we too

80

should be off the road, but we had planned to be over the frontier and through customs before staying at Oradia, a fair-sized town over the border.

That we achieved this was something of a miracle, our progress hampered by the road turning into a muddy, grassy track, and then a long hunt in the dark for the customs house. One could understand the suspicions of the customs officer: two women driving a car fully laden, and arriving after dark, and but for his suspicions I think we might have been turned away. As it was, speaking good French but very aggressively, he ordered everything out of the car for inspection. When we made no move, he sent for two orderlies to achieve this, an operation that took nearly two hours of minute inspection. Certainly he maintained an official attitude, more than his orderlies did in this churning over of intimate garments along with cooking apparatus and tools. He finally sent an orderly with us to guide us into the town and to a hotel. Here we were bitten by bugs. Half a mile further on was one of the best hotels in Transylvania, but the orderly was either ignorant of it or unwilling to go further.

Now we were to learn that only in the larger towns would we find hotels, of which only the best would be clean. This caused us sometimes to abandon eating in the sheer struggle of getting from A to B before dark. Both A and B would have robust markets, so starvation taught us before setting out to buy food we could eat in transit, for the Balkan roads were either a series of hard ribs or a glut of potholes or plain bog. Bridges, if wooden, had rotting or missing struts, so one drove through the rivers, which generally had an adjacent ford; but all this, with punctures, reduced average speed, and towns with clean beds were a great distance apart. A to B averaged 200 miles.

We soon grew skilled at taking the ribs and the potholes and, like the local traffic, would drive along the edge of the adjacent fields, which was more sympathetic ground. We also learnt that if benighted we must call at the village police station, and accommodation would be found. Balkan armies had been restricted in size by international law, so a vast police force had been created instead.

I found Dolly able to stand up to all this far better than I had anticipated, but she was as adverse, as I had been in the bad old days, to early rising, and this of course was the secret of securing a comfortable bed the following night.

Meanwhile our noble Ford stood up well to the punishing roads, rather better than the tyres, which fell to our lot to repair. Blacksmiths were more prevalent than garages, though petrol was generally available on demand, even if not out of a pump. The only casualty was the bar across the front of the Ford, coupling the two front wings, on which the headlamps were mounted. It fractured, but we spliced it with a bough of a tree, roughly of the same curve, and a blacksmith with great competence welded a sleeve over the fracture.

To balance our tribulations, we were in a country growing increasingly lovely, with a background of snow-capped mountains, halcyon little villages ornamented with fruit trees, while shepherds, clad in a whole sheepskin, would be playing pipes to their flocks.

This was a bird-watcher's paradise: storks were returning to their summer nests, rollers were sitting on the telegraph wires, exposing their sky-blue chests, and there was every sort of bird of prey from falcons to eagles. Patrick Leigh Fermor remarks on the birds in *Between the Woods and the Water*, the second of his books describing his famous walk to Constantinople in 1933. Not confined to the road as we were, he must have seen far more of the bird and animal life of the country. Later we were to grow blasé about golden orioles and hoopoes.

At Sinaia, seat of Royalty, was a splendid garage, and the Ford arranged a puncture at its door, so thankfully we handed over repair, wash, servicing and change of oil. The garage proprietor told us a woman driving a Willys Knight car, all alone save for a big dog, had lately driven through on the same route as we were taking to Athens. 'But she was old,' he said, as if that counted her out, though I would have thought it added to her courage. We stayed in a lavish hotel among high society and free of bugs.

*

Well after dark we reached Bucharest along a smooth tree-lined avenue, then boulevards with lighted windows and a fluctuation of shiny saloon cars: the city as it was when Olivia Manning wrote her books centred on it, the city that called itself the Paris of Eastern Europe. We reached it on the eve of a spectacular event; flags and decorations had roused our suspicions, also finding every room booked at the Grand Hotel save an expensive suite overlooking the garden. Dolly booked it.

It was common knowledge that Prince Carol had renounced his right to succeed to the throne when he married Magda Lupescu in Paris in 1918 – a marriage later declared invalid. Yet he kept returning to Romania and on the death of his father was at once installed as King, an office he certainly appeared to hold in the procession we witnessed next day. Yet some in the crowds held that this was the inauguration of Prince Michael as King; as he was yet a minor, with Carol's younger brother as Prince Regent, they ruled the country during Carol's frequent absence. Certainly some years later Carol left his country for good with Lupescu, leaving Michael as King.

Of that procession I recollect Carol riding between lines of cheering citizens, his uniformed plastered with medals, and with a strong facial resemblance to the then Duke of Gloucester, our Prince Henry. They shared a great-grandmother in Queen Victoria. Another memory is of the beautiful hand-embroidered tunics and dresses of peasants and aristocrats alike in the crowds. The uniforms of the soldiers lining the streets were tawdry, but the national clothing had served generations, and some of it was weighty with gold.

We stayed some time in Bucharest as Dolly for some days had not been feeling well and here took to her bed, where she seemed blissfully happy languishing in a handsome dressing-gown with book and embroidery. Her Romanian friend, Marcellan Oliga, had soon found us and sat in an arm-chair by the bed looking like a dog confined to basket. I now followed up an introduction given me to an English bank manager with a daughter very keen on tennis.

This led to my being made a temporary member of the tennis club and there I met the French Chargé d'Affaires and his wife, also members and also adventurous motorists, who gave me information on how to repel bugs. From the bank manager I learnt of a doctor, who soon got Dolly back on her feet, and among the large colony of Americans installing a telephone system in Bucharest Dolly found some that she knew. Our sojourn ended with a farewell dinner given to us, which wound up with a gambling game that neither of us had ever played before. However, our ignorance seemed to be balanced with luck, for we walked off with most of the stakes.

Marcel saw us to Guirgu, where one crossed the Danube for Bulgaria. We were certainly grateful to him, for there was no car ferry and he arran-ged for a lighter to be spliced to the passenger ferry. He also found us somewhere to stay, for the only hotel was in Ruschuk on the far side of the river, and the family who put us up I am sure had made every effort for our comfort to the detriment of their own. No bugs, cheese pie supper, a jug of hot water in the morning and coffee, all for a pathetically small sum. There was, of course, no sanitation, only a place in the open air at the edge of a field, its locality betrayed by the smell.

It was mid-morning before ferry plus lighter arrived next day to take on the waiting Ford. Then I had my first exercise in reaching ship from shore by means of two planks sloping steeply upward and reversed on the more harrowing descent. I was to get used to this in later life.

Now came our farewell to the Danube, with which we had converged at intervals through three vast countries, from its early youth to its powerful adolescence. Across plains or through valleys it had flowed, sometimes in solitude, generally fringed with trees, sometimes enriched by castle, mon-astery or city on its banks. Often from village or cottage a pathway led down to its edge, where would be a water-wheel sawing logs, grinding corn, sharpening cutting tools. Always a friend to man, it would lend its strong current to floating rafts: logs tied together, a series of them floating down-stream. There would be a couple of men on the hindmost raft, each with a long oar to keep the procession in midstream, and each with his own small cabin. Dolly's early ambition, she told me, had been to marry a road-mender with a steamroller, to cook his dinner and live in his roadside hut. Now her ambition was transferred from a road-mender to a raftsman.

*

Each state we had passed through seemed to shun the word 'Balkan'. Romania assured us the Balkans started south of the Danube, and from their description of Bulgaria it was a land of cutthroats and thieves. This was scarcely borne out by a scene not ten miles into the country, where to the strains of a banjo a ring of young men and girls were dancing in a circle, holding hands, and all with wreaths of flowers on their heads.

In spite of phenomenal early rising, this first day in Bulgaria was an occasion of failing to reach B. Nor had we any transit food as Ruschuk had no market and we were deflected from Plevin, ninety miles on, by road-menders who sent us along an adjacent treeless and bumpy track in the heat of midday. This was in fact part of the original old Turkish route straight through from the Danube to Sofia. Our only nourishment was a shared bottle of Bulgarian fizzy water that the road-menders gladly exchanged for some of Dolly's cigarettes.

When at last we got back on the road, to trees and greenery, we lay on a bank in the shade to cool off. We were never going to reach Sofia that night, so we relaxed and came to some brilliant conclusions: what we needed was a van, rather than a car, one in which we could sleep, firmly locked in. And the occurrence of markets only in larger towns: could it be that where so little traffic plied, country people supported themselves, grew their own food, and instead of selling it they ate it?

At that moment a car actually approached and a German-speaking driver asked if we wanted help, told us of a farmhouse at Oranhi where they let a clean double room, and described how to find it. So instead of going to Oranhi police station, we went to the farmhouse, washed in a communal sink in a yard, endured a terrible lavatory, had an egg and cheese supper with the inevitable caraway seeds, and slept. Yet in spite of this undeserved gift from Heaven, it was a relief next day to reach bedroom and bathroom, reserved for us in Sofia at the Union Palace Hotel.

Sofia was more interesting on the return journey when the Minister was on leave and my friend Jock was Chargé d'Affaires. The same might well be said of Salonika, a 200-mile stretch onward from A to B with nowhere convenient to stay between. We had, however, some excellent transit food, also drinks preserved in ice and a pass through the frontier customs supplied by the faithful Jock.

When the road had an unstable foundation the Ford would take on the rolling gait of a ship at sea, and May had brought bouts of heat followed by thunderstorms, so bogs were inevitable. We had got skilled at negotiating them but in one, a long mud-bath right across the road, we inevitably sank; however, a man driving some bullocks harnessed two of them to the Ford and pulled us out. He did it so skilfully that we suspected he did it frequently, perhaps lived on it. Dolly certainly rewarded him liberally.

At ten at night we reached Salonika, which was crowded with sailors of every nationality. When they saw a woman driver they shouted '*Chaufette!*' At the Méditerranné was no garage, but parked outside the hotel the car was guarded like a mother by the night porter. In a huge bedroom we ate the remainder of our provisions and again slept. Morning brought sunlight and revealed a harbour with all types of sailing-ship and a steamer.

Salonika had everything: history, markets, a poste restante with letters for us and at last, at last, the maps we so dearly needed. Greece was a series of mountains and wide plains, of which we preferred the mountains. The plains were virtually bogs but often spanned by long wooden causeways, virtually bridges lying flat. Horses wore blue beads round their necks to keep off the evil eye. We put some round the Ford's radiator cap as fully deserving. People shuffled amber between their fingers, the Gypsies were migrating north along with the storks, and French was definitely the international language. I found it easier here to acquire French than in Paris.

Signposts in Cyrillic lettering had started far back in Bulgaria, but at Larissa was the first mention of 'Athinai' as being 281 kilometres distant, otherwise 175 miles. Here was a nice little hotel at which to stay, and a Ford repair garage where we left the car for inspection. Mount Olympus had formed the background of the day's journey and we even toyed with the idea of visiting the Vale of Tempé, for we believed that our troubles were over and we had reached the doorstep of Athens.

*

Yet each state we passed through had offered its special problems, and Greece was no exception. There broke in on our meditations a troubled hotel manager. Did we realize that the plain ahead was impassable for forty-five miles? There was a train on which one could put the car, but we must go now to book a truck before the station office closed.

Bernard in a letter had warned me of this plain which needed four days of sun to make it passable, and as on average only four hours separated the present storms, we decided to pocket our pride. Our Ford locked in the repair garage, we went to the station in a one-horse cab with the hotel manager and ordered a flat waggon, which aptly described what awaited us next morning. Another storm broke on our return to the hotel and the manager pulled the cab hood down over us so we arrived back in a sort of leather cocoon and felt resigned, possibly relieved, to abandon the Vale of Tempé.

In the dawn we set out with a parcel of food for the journey, with a Russian lad the proprietor recommended to help us at the station. Neither of us was in our element with goods trains, so we were thankful to have Boris to lift the heavy plank off the side of the flat waggon, which we reached from a ramp. He then roped the car wheels to the flooring; the reason was soon evident, with the bangs, knocks and jerks in making up a goods train. There followed a long hot journey, not made sweeter by a load of goats in the truck ahead, and we were thankful to find Boris still on the train as there was no other help at Lamia to get the car off the truck.

We spent the night at Lamia, and were eating our breakfast next morning when again Boris joined us. He had refused all payment for rail fare or hostelry, so we had no idea where he rode on the train or spent his nights. To my horror Dolly now handed him the keys to go and fetch the car from a lock-up garage some distance down the street. I pointed out to her she had handed him our entire property, but Dolly assured me she had an instinct about people; however, she was as relieved as I was when the Ford came promptly to the door.

We took him with us to Athens, clearly his objective. He was a refugee with no passport, no capital, and no ability to earn money since the recent law forbidding foreigners to be employed in Greece. He may have hoped Dolly would employ him as chauffeur, or, if not, some other wealthy visitor to Athens might take him on.

So for the rest of our journey we had a courier who laid out our picnic, brought cushions and washed up; but unfortunately the picnic food so far surpassed his normal diet he had a headache for the rest of the day. Meanwhile at the end of a long climb we looked down through trees at intensely blue water, and beside it stretched out like a map, the city of Athens.

We had made it. We had arrived.

The buoyancy of arrival, however, did not last long. Dolly left me and Bernard at the Consulate to gather letters from the poste restante before it closed. The desired letter was not there, only a letter from Titine telling her that her beloved but very ancient Brussels Griffon had died. She found the best quarters Bernard could book for us at short notice very dreary, and by the time I joined her, was hating Athens, hating Greece. How long was I wanting to stay? It looked as if we would barely stop the week-end. She spent next day hunting better quarters, and in a hotel next to the Consulate, where Bernard gave official dinners, booked a sitting-room, two bedrooms each with bathroom, suitable for the time we would be there.

A consul is not without training in diplomacy, however, and that evening Bernard invited us both out to dinner at Glyfadha and made up a fourth with a lonely American, Rowan, whose wife refused to leave home, and whose firm had a three-year contract with the Greek government. The result of this well-balanced foursome – two nationals from each side of the Atlantic – was that we stayed in Greece from the twenty-seventh of May to the twelfth of September, retaining the suite and leaving our luggage there while we explored this beautiful country, which no doubt contributed to the success of that sublime summer.

Bernard could do nothing for Boris; he was already harassed trying to fund British subjects who had lived and worked in Greece for years and now found themselves stranded. In a pedestrian alley-way not far from the Consulate the starving and penniless lay at night, and while there were British in this state he had no funds for other nationals. Boris soon found where we had gone and hung around Dolly, who would give him money at intervals for things she needed, on commission. This I felt would lead to his eventual absconding, which it did. Yet there was one brief interval when we looked down from the windows of our hotel to see Boris, an expression of seraphic bliss on his face, lying in a sports Buick drawn up at the kerb, guarding it for an owner who we fear did not make it a permanent job.

*

There have been many important excavations made in Greece since our visit in the early thirties, but I think they are outweighed by the solitude and pleasant informality in which one could then enjoy those that existed. To think that one could go up to see the Parthenon on moonlight nights and enjoy it in complete seclusion, and that the remaining Doric columns of the Temple of Poseidon still stood in glorious isolation at Sounion on that promontory rising perpendicularly from the sea. Can it be that the columns still stand in isolation, and there are no signatures on them other than Byron's preserved under glass? When we explored the Peloponnese, most visitors were still coming to Olympia by train, and among the fir-trees of its garden-like arena one found oneself rubbing shoulders, as it were, with the Hermes of Praxiteles. Corrosion was at work but not yet universally visible.

A more noticeable intrusion was the 'wireless'; every building in Athens was surmounted by a bevy of aerials and blared forth unrestrained sound, but our hotel was an exception, as was the Consulate, together forming a quiet corner. Our hotel windows looked out towards Mount Lycabetos, with its single cottage under a single fig-tree halfway up its steep ascent. One wondered which came first. Our hotel had mobile dining-rooms; there was one on the roof when we came, shielded by an awning, but it had to retreat back indoors when encroaching heat made the cutlery too hot to hold.

By that time restaurants were springing up like mushrooms on the cooler surrounding hills: wigwam shelters of interlaced boughs overhead to which cooking stove, water tank and ice chest were transported, and a clothes-line on which hung washed napery hardly dry before needed again. Menus were superfluous; one went straight to the ice chest to choose from giant prawns, squids, red mullet and other fish of the Mediterranean, while another ice chest contained the excellent beer and retsina. Lunch-time found many Athenians motoring up rough tracks to these cooler resorts, which are probably now established hotels. Our two escorts would take us up to them and also, on available evenings and weekends, to places of special interest, one of which particularly stands out in my memory.

We got a chance to join a fleet fishing with acetylene flares between the mainland and the island of Euboea. They formed a circle and we were taken aboard a small steamer that plied round them taking up the nets as they filled. It was a scene of quite fantastic colouring, the brilliant flares turning the water into a turquoise transparency through which one could see down to the seabed, and transforming the fishermen's overalls into a cerulean blue. Against this the deck of the steamer was silhouetted in darkness until a stream of glittering silver fish was poured into the hold.

The island of Euboea then belonged to an Englishman; no goats were allowed there so the island was generously wooded, and a small hotel in the south of the island was ideal in hot weather. We went there one weekend for respite from the heat and on the way were given a sharp lesson in the treachery of the Aegean Sea. We lunched at Chalkis, where the bridge joins island with mainland. Not a cloud in the sky, not a breath of wind. We sat on the shady side of the quay, close to one of the inevitable hatstands supplied in all restaurants, for Greeks were then partial to stiff boaters, and hatstands would be laden with them, and one wondered how anyone recognized his own.

Halfway through lunch I noticed a gentle swaying among yachts moored nearby that had formerly stood rigid, and within minutes of that observation the sky was darkening, the wind had risen, and soon we were clutching at tablecloths, glasses, cutlery, while boaters were blowing like autumn leaves into what had been a quiet channel and was now a race lashed to fury. We finished our meal indoors, where the electricity had failed but lightning was providing a substitute, and the staff, so used to this kind of behaviour, carried on undisturbed.

The heat was now considerable but Greeks seemed impervious to heat or cold and made little effort to contend with either. Withered now were the wild flowers that had graced our journey; only the courageous oleanders remained defiant. We kept the windows of the Ford severely closed in transit, and always carried a load of melons – their juice remained cool whatever the temperature. The melon season was at its height; we would pass plantations where the owner sat perched in a tree with a gun, guarding his crop from the seasonal poachers.

88

Dolly and I went for some days into the Peloponnese, where the Spartan plain was living up to reputation, but the interior of ancient Byzantine churches was positively chilly, so stout were their walls. We passed through some delightfully rural areas where towards evening a carcass was turning on a spit to feed the surrounding population. Hotel-keepers looked on us as their special responsibility, one of them coming down the road on a donkey to look for us as darkness approached. An arid spot, bare of all greenery, we crossed approaching Taygetos mountains and on the roadside was the then familiar sight of women breaking stones. This always enraged Dolly; there was machinery for this, why wasn't it used? The answer was clearly that women cost less and were no doubt glad of the money. Sitting by the roadside, they were able to have a nice chat, and Spartan women were used to the heat. A couple of male overseers were seeing they did not slacken, but there was a seven-mile walk to and from Sparta.

On our return from Mycenae the women were just knocking off for the day and hailed us, against the wishes of the overseers, who anticipated disaster. They were large women, but without the car seat and all melons now consumed, we got five of them on the floor in the back, where I also sat, and two in the front beside Dolly, who was driving. Their wrinkled skin was without blemish, they smelled not of sweat but dust. They hailed with joy anyone we passed on the road, and rewarded us with smacking kisses.

*

I wound up this expedition visiting Corfu from the port of Patras. Dolly left me there – she had a date in Athens – and Bernard came and fetched me from the port some days later. Inclined to be hazy about transport when travelling by other means than by car, I watched the steamer on which I was booked leave the harbour, and caught a later one, a cattle boat calling at Cephalonia and Ithaca and despatching cattle at these ports by the simple means of tipping them into the sea. We followed in the path of Ulysses, and my ticket secured me a comfortable cabin on board, but I arrived so late next evening at my hotel in Corfu that I had difficulty in prising it open.

Next day all bedrooms were booked by members of the British Air Force who had been promoting the sale of British planes by doing aerobatics over Athens. They were now enjoying a weekend of leave. I enjoyed it with them and saw the beauties of this lovely island as their guest.

September was now approaching. The hot weather persisted but it was getting chilly at sundown, and Dolly felt we could no longer tour on the wages of her staff in Paris, who had been left with only three months of advance pay. So we must soon take leave of Bernard, Rowan and the hotel staff who had been so good to us, but beyond that we knew no one, such had been the discretion. Bernard had certainly organized our membership of the Glyfadha swimming club, but we had seldom gone there, finding more halcyon bathing elsewhere. I had felt piqued when Bernard had given a duty dinner party at our hotel, seeing the table laid out in the courtyard with flowers, with Bernard's own candlesticks and the hotel's best linen. I felt the seat opposite his belonged to me. What havoc I could wreak if I put on evening dress and turned up at the reception. Instead Dolly and I dined out in the square under the pepper trees.

How far off the mark I had been in thinking I must steer Dolly from indiscretions. Many men had made passes at her – at both of us for that matter – and she would dismiss them with disdain but saw them always in the light of a compliment, always had to look back. The prize occasion had been when we were sitting out at the pavement café and a man selling lottery tickets was walking up and down the street. A stout Greek passed by, quizzed Dolly, took a chair not far distant and began buying lottery tickets. When he had reached a fair sum he held them out to Dolly, who turned her back on him but began to giggle. He bought more tickets and again held these up, but we never learnt what was his limit as we now paid the bill and made for the Ford across the street – that ever-attendant chaperon. Dolly waved to the man from the safety of the car as we departed.

When it came, the journey home was not without adventure.

We set off via Delphi, where we stayed a day or two before rejoining our downward route some miles short of Lamia. The heat had dried up all the bogs, and Dolly had acquired new tyres, two of them free on complaint to the makers of the original ones. Thus we had few punctures. Also, she had shipped home all her superfluous luggage and had sold the cooking stove. We now drove across the plain we had travelled by rail, and found it hard as a rock and alive with road-builders and their transport – donkeys, with their foals scampering and leaping in the air like kittens.

We raced the length of Greece, anxious to stop a night again in Salonika and wondering, would we get the same bedroom? We dallied at Kozani, an attractive little town where a shop contained hand-made musical instruments. One of them like a small, slim violin the craftsman played for me, and I bought it, knowing it would fascinate Avis. Dolly meanwhile was studying a notice we had seen once or twice on our road. We had picked up quite a few phrases and words in Greek and could use them with good result, but beyond the word 'Thessalonica' she could make little of the rest. It was not till we were nearing Salonika itself that she wondered, was there something special going on there?

There was. A National Fair was taking place; all hotels and boarding-houses were crammed to capacity, and the doorman at the Méditerranée, who recognized us, wrung his hands at the impossibility of our finding rooms. While we consulted the management he guarded our radiator cap, which had no lock and was a prime object of theft. The management told us to go to the police station; they alone knew all sources of refuge, but I felt sorry for the policeman allotted to us, with all the chaff he got having to bed out two unaccompanied women.

There followed an abortive search and finally, after telephoning for some time, he took us to a handsome bungalow in an opulant quarter along the coast. Here a man-servant answered the door and the policeman left us thankfully. We were shown a large bedroom, oriental in style with a vast canopied double bed. The servant, not a Greek, sounded as if he was referring to food, which we certainly needed, and he then left us.

Dolly was deeply suspicious of the place, pulled back the curtains to find shuttered windows, and then lifted the bed-covering to find a pair of men's pyjamas.

'Here, I'm getting out of this!' she exclaimed, and went to tell the man-servant, but her call remained unanswered. I went to a staircase which led down from the hall, suggesting kitchen quarters beneath, but was arrested by an ominous growl from a vicious-sounding dog. Dolly meanwhile had found the front door locked but had managed to open a window next to it and was climbing out of it, bidding me to follow. It was now dark, but she jumped and found only a slight drop to the ground beneath.

I was no more anxious than she was to sleep in that bed, but thought it probable the man had gone to buy food and had locked the door for safety. The pyjamas were not so easy to explain. We had so far left our night handbags in the Ford and were barely back in it when a shadowy figure approached up the drive and shied into the bushes on seeing two women he had left locked in the house now making their retreat. Dolly, now confident we had narrowly escaped a harem or the white slavers, did not pause in her haste to get back to the police station. Here a younger, French-speaking policeman took us in charge, and after another telephone call – this time I gather recommending us as esteemed clients – directed us to the house of I should think his aunt, where amid a refinement of crocheted doilies, table-mats and net curtains we had dinner and bedded down. The policeman on delivering us had assured us the Ford would be safe in the street outside, as extra police were on duty.

'So we don't have to sit up all night watching the radiator cap' were Dolly's last words.

*

Our reception in Sofia was in strong contrast. The road was still harsh but all bogs had dried up, and I had been able to notify Jock of the time we hoped to arrive. This resulted in the Legation car waiting at the frontier with a hamper of food, an excessively handsome chauffeur talking immaculate

91

French – a Russian emigré secure in a post such as I feared our poor Boris would never attain. There was also a second driver who could take over the Ford so that we could rest in the Austin for the remainder of the journey.

We certainly approved of the edibles and drink but were neither of us keen to hand over the Ford, so we drove ahead of the Austin and, skilled by this time on any surface, we did not long trouble the Austin with our dust and reached Sofia an hour ahead of it.

There followed a programme of carefully thought-out entertainment, and though Dolly had formerly giggled at Jock's old-maidish precision, this red carpet reception suggested to her that I would do well to marry him. I admitted I owed much to him, a kind friend, not to mention my improvement in spelling. On visits to London for the day, when Jock was at the Foreign Office, I was allowed to borrow his car parked on the grass beyond Downing Street. Driving that smooth Lagonda had worked on my feelings but I was saved from the brink – if such really existed – by meeting Bernard.

From Sofia our route diverged from the outward one: we were going back over the Dragoman Pass through Yugoslavia to Belgrade. In Yugoslavia we seemed to slip back to earlier times; women wore embroidered country clothing and, on the approach of the Ford, veiled themselves, assuming that a man was driving. I had hoped for a direct road from Sofia to Sarajevo, a town more interesting than Belgrade. There was certainly a road to it from Belgrade, but to go there now would take us far off course, and though the map showed a bridge across the wide river Drina, that was no guarantee of the bridge being intact, and the Yugoslav motoring club had no information about it. A taxi-driver outside the club said there was a large iron bridge. Dolly was eager to go there, felt she could legitimately use another week of Rose and Titine's wages, so we careered off to Sarajevo.

We had, of course, no weather report, nor anticipation of two outstanding features of that year: a revolt in the British Navy which presaged Britain for a time going off the gold standard and, after an exceptionally hot summer, a sudden cold which caught the swallows and other birds migrating, so that hundreds of them perished and planes were eventually sent to pick up those still living and carry them to warmer climes.

We saw these birds huddled on the lintels of windows and doors, trying to keep warm, but thought this was their natural behaviour, unaware of their plight. Soon we ourselves were feeling much like the swallows, for it was wet and chilly when we left Belgrade, and our so-called main road was very lonely; horses shied at the car and we met wild-looking peasants. In the villages the accumulated dust on the cobblestones had turned to slippery mud, and the Ford was apt to take on a crab-like approach if the brake was not skilfully used.

92

The Drina certainly had a noble bridge crossing it but by the time we reached Zvornik on the far side, rain had turned to fine snow. However, an excellent schnitzel with onions and rice cheered our spirits in an inn with such a steep roof it resembled a beehive, and packed with a chattering crowd. Our maps gave no contours; we were unaware a mountain pass lay between us and our goal, and the snow was now settling while women, shrouded more against male presence than climate, were walking about in it barefoot.

*

The innkeeper was receiving reports on the mountain road, widely divergent apparently, but he seemed an authority and warned us to start now rather than wait to put on chains. So we left by a road that at first clung to the side of a ravine, though luckily we were on the inside. It was not so good when log men appeared with enormous drays, but always ringing a great bell to warn of their approach, which we thought most sensible. The horses were apt to shy at the car, one pair nearly going over the edge, but the drayman had a strong brake and pulled the horses back, with much cursing and lashing. At this point the snow on our windshield broke the wiper, and the one of us not driving had to hang out keeping the screen clear. The snow began to ease off at the top of the climb.

Here we reached a snow-covered tableland where there was no other indication of the road than the wheel tracks made by the drays, and the sight of water emerging through the snow on our flank made me aware of how dependent we were on these tracks. By the time we had crossed the plain, not only were we down to a single track but darkness was falling. Here we reached a road junction, and we knew we must take the right-hand road, which to our relief started a downhill course with high forest on our right, while on the left the ground fell away steeply. At least the road was well demarcated, or should have been had not a snow mist now descended.

We crawled down that road, our headlamps not really helpful even when the snow had melted off the glass. Enormous trees were faintly visible on the roadside and I wondered vaguely if there were wild animals among them, but we were more concerned with the dwindling petrol. We had plenty in the spare tank on the running-board, but that was under a mountain of fine snow. We dared not switch off the engine and drive on the brakes for fear of the Ford becoming a toboggan. An awkward wind was piling drifts against the bank side.

It seemed hours before we saw lights in the valley, or before Sarajevo emerged like a stage set, with domes, minarets and steeples covered in

93

snow. Our faithful Ford snuffed out on the last drop of petrol in the yard of the Europa Hotel.

Next morning we badly needed local currency as we were on the door-step of a weekend, but as nothing would get Dolly out of bed, I went to cash English pounds, and had them spurned. I was told of a 'rebellion' in England, but seeing my blatant disbelief I was told an English lady was shortly coming to the bureau and she would explain. Quite as surprising as a rebellion was the fact that when she came I knew her quite well. Margaret Macleod and I had shared the same dancing class years ago. She was staying in Sarajevo with a Russian woman who lived there. I explained my presence, and Dolly and I were invited to lunch. When I got back to the hotel I found Dolly having no difficulty exchanging her French money at the reception desk.

Our Russian hostess was particularly interested in our drive from Belgrade and at what time we had arrived. Hearing it was about ten at night she was horror-struck. Didn't we realize it was always at this time of year, with the first snow, that the wolves came down from the mountains: one always knew when they were about as the woodmen started ringing their bells. Wolves were afraid of noise; that was the origin of the sleigh-bells. Had we a loud horn? (I did not reveal that our horn was choked with snow.) There were known to be bears in those woods we had come through, and tales followed of the foolhardy and their bones being found...

There seem to be different theories concerning wolves, some saying there is no concrete evidence of their ever having killed or consumed humans; but I agree there is no point in offering one's body for the test, and I think it is possible we might have had trouble had we been forced to get at the spare petrol.

Meanwhile we enjoyed this city of polyglot population: tarboosh and turban alongside tall-hatted priests and Jews with side-curls. Through its centre flowed the river spanned by the bridge, the site of an assassination that sparked off the 1914–1918 war. The snow melted and the sun again shone as we drove to Zagreb; corn-cobs were ripening under the eaves of the houses and tobacco leaves were drying on sunny walls, a further stage of the industry we had first witnessed when women walked along trenched fields, making a hole in the earth at intervals and planting a single seed.

In Austria we now found it difficult to stay on the road; one had to get inured to the smooth tarmac, and the Ford, formerly such an object of interest, had to get used to being unremarkable save for a few blue beads. Yet indeed there was something strangely moving when we came into Paris at evening, driving up the Champs-Elysées towards the lighted Arc de Triomphe, just under 8,000 miles, five months and eleven days since we had travelled down.

1931–1936

FAREWELL LOVE, HAIL *BRIGHTER BONDAGE*

The Balkan tour landed me quite unexpectedly in a career as a chauffeur-courier. I had no anticipation of this on coming home in my usual state of penury, with pastoral objects dispersed in my luggage: a shepherd's crook, two small oval wooden barrels made for me in Corfu and the Kozani 'violin' from which now emanated, in distant corners of the Old House, Scottish airs imposed on its Hellenic soul. A strong believer in starting at the top, I sent an account of the tour to *Blackwood's* magazine. It soon returned, but a shorter version sent to the *Crofton Journal* with no gainful aspirations brought an immediate demand from Kathleen Chilton, a fellow Croftonian, asking would I, the following year, drive her to Prague, Vienna and Budapest.

This tour was in course of preparation when Elspeth came for a weekend. She had abstained from joining the Balkan tour in favour of finding and furnishing a suitable London dwelling, and this she had now done, wondering if she was going to be lonely. I told her no one with a spare bedroom in London would ever feel lonely, and proved abundantly right. She in turn assured me I must *sell* the experience I had now gained in motoring, not give it away.

By this time 'Chilly', as she was called at Crofton, was booking seats for the Vienna opera week, and best bedrooms in the house of a Viennese Countess reduced to taking in paying guests, clearly too late a stage at which to demand a wage. So it was purely as a fellow Croftonian that I reached beautiful Prague and saw Vienna in happier mood – though it put on a mild revolution during our stay this did nothing to disturb opera, Spanish Riding School and the like. And where else in Budapest would we stay but in the Hotel Vadaz Kurt (or Jägerhorn), which was like theatre in the evening when dining out in the courtyard, with the variety of uniforms worn by the men and the flounced dresses of the much chaperoned young girls. I may not have been so carried away as Chilly by a week of Wagner, but I was certainly moved by the true Gypsy music, both here and at Spolarich in the eastern quarter of Pest.

I came home rather in agreement with Elspeth's suggestion: Chilly's car had given trouble the whole way and, like most English cars at the time, unused to long climbs, ascending the High Tatra and the Dolomites it boiled. I would get into lower gear and drive slowly, like walking a horse up a hill, but still it boiled.

The prospect of advertising or going again to the agencies was very depressing, but I found it wasn't necessary. Work flowed to me. Elspeth had an elderly aunt, Mrs Seddon, living in London and driven around by a needy friend, but one tied to London. In early spring Mrs Seddon was hoping to drive a friend to Buxton for treatment and I found Elspeth had all but signed me up for the job. I must ask a decent price, she insisted. It was Mrs Seddon who named the price and it was liberal, so I drove her to Buxton, and for many years after that drove her abroad in spring and autumn. I drove my cousins and I drove local friends.

Sadly, Mrs Robinson, since her return from Australia, had been an invalid, and died at about this time. I had met her sister-in-law at Roos; she was wont at intervals to order a new Rover to await her at Rootes in Piccadilly when she arrived from Tasmania. Grace Nicholas, as she now was, would arrange for me to drive her in London and on the continent, then return the car to Rootes, who freighted it back to Tasmania on the same ship with Grace.

So on it went: two if not three clients a year. Certainly I was dependent on the Old House in the intervals, but could now afford to be liberal at home and fulfil jobs that were always waiting.

Thus in the course of time, pre-war and postwar, there were few interesting parts of Europe I had not explored, and just in time. The Salzkammergut was not yet overrun with tourists, the White Horse Inn still an inn, and though I drove to it, the inn was still fed by the little steam train from Salzburg and the two steamers, *Franz Josef* and *Elizabet*, which crossed the lake to meet the train.

As a personal friend, I got treated to seats for opera, ballet and Oberammergau, and shared a window in Siena for the *Palio*. The same tours were often repeated but I would vary the approach, including some place I particularly wanted to see. Clients got tetchy with too much packing up and moving on, so I arranged an itinerary to reach somewhere interesting every three days for a stopover. Elspeth was right: there were many people happy to pay for someone to do all the paperwork and bookings, and look after the car. We never booked rooms in advance in course of transit; there was far less travel congestion abroad than in England, and even in England one could still draw up at a destination and park there. We would finish the day's run soon after five, choose a hotel, and I would go in and inspect rooms, sometimes getting a bathroom thrown in if we were a party of four or five. For myself I took a cheap room probably on another floor, but often it was the quietest room of the lot. Michelin was already a most useful hotel and restaurant guide, but confined only to France.

And what if the car broke down? I could deal with the simpler things which mainly spring from a few main causes, though on the road clients often urged me to apply for help at filling-station or garage. Loughborough gave people the impression that I knew everything about a car, but all the time car design was changing, with increasing mechanism being shoved under the bonnet, making it take longer to locate a fault and get at it to repair.

For major trouble I admit I was glad of 'the man who always comes'. Driving Chilly on a remote and very bad road near Lake Balaton in Hungary, a copper pipe from the petrol tank sheared off at the nipple where it joined the carburettor, and the car depended on gravity feed. The only hope was to reverse the pipe so that the sheared end would be held by a firm anchorage under the tank, and the intact end could be relocated to the carburettor. Yet getting the pipe free looked rather as if I were gutting the car of its entrails, with Chilly standing in a state of nerves beside me. So when a helpful-looking man in a Bugatti drew up and asked if I would like help, I said 'yes'. He approved of my scheme but I was thankful to have his moral and physical support.

What astonishes me now is the modest price of travel at that time, even accepting that the pound was of greater value and enjoyed a higher rate of exchange. I was often asked how much money a client should take and would say two pounds a head a day for every day on the itinerary. This would cover everything, I explained, from accommodation, food and petrol to presents and entertainment. They never believed me and took a furtive supplement, which they found they did not need. Less moneyed clients could do it, without deprivation, on one pound ten shillings a head a day.

*

I shall not describe these tours, but some of the situations, one might say antics, attendant on driving Mrs Seddon seem worth recording. They left me impressed with the considerable influence of a widow's veil.

On one of the spring tours she had bought a new car, delivered to her only a day before I joined her, and out on the open road a powerful smell of hot rubber made it necessary to adjust the brakes. This made us late for the boat, but nearing Dover we caught up with a large black car which I had a feeling was also making for the ferry. Though the dock gates were closed on our arrival, at the sight of the black car they opened, and the band of the Black Watch sprang into action, playing a suitable lament as the black car entered, followed closely by Mrs Seddon's car, her widow's veil suggesting – and none dared question – that we were part of the cortège. This was the young King Farouk of Egypt being brought home from Eton on the death of his father. While courtly speeches were being made we quietly got ourselves and our car on board.

The first year I took Mrs Seddon abroad was a great occasion: a celebration of the Oberammergau play, when we proceeded in two carloads to the Villa Daheim, the home of the Anton Langs, great friends of Mrs Seddon's; Anton was playing the part of Christ. I drove Mrs Seddon and two of her daughters, and Elspeth brought her car with further members of the family. The visitors' book at the villa was weighty with celebrated names, but I enjoyed it as much on a later visit with Mrs Seddon, in early spring, when the village was under snow and the inhabitants were not players but housewives and craftsmen leading their normal lives.

On the occasion of the play, we were joined at the villa by three Dominican fathers from Hawkesyard Priory in England, who came and returned by train, all save Father Austin, who remained with us for the rest of his leave. I learnt Dominicans were granted yearly leave but were expected to give up the first week of it to a noble cause.

Mrs Seddon was a just but exacting employer, really what I needed. She taught me punctuality and never to encroach on the hostess's preserves. My head bitten off, I took it to heart. She was a powerful matriarch, and what she considered her duty she relentlessly pursued. Halfway through life she had gone over to the Catholic faith in spite of the turmoil this created in her family; her husband was a much-loved and respected Church of England clergyman. The Dominican held responsible for this was Father Austin, who had been a student in Palestine when the Seddons and friends arrived in several carriages and he was despatched as their guide. Later he visited them in Painswick and there fell ill, and long discussions during his convalescence were thought to have led to the eventual conversion, though Father Austin was horrified, holding family life sacred.

When I joined Mrs Seddon she had long been widowed and all bitterness had abated, Father Austin remaining a friend of the family. It now became a habit, towards the end of August, to get me to drive her and one or two members of her family to some delectable place on the continent, there to be joined in September by Father Austin, and when the others had drifted back to school, college or husband, we would continue touring, getting the Father back to Hawkesyard on time.

Mrs Seddon's ardour for holy relics landed us in some quaint situations. The Father remained wholly sceptical but, with a ripe sense of humour, he enjoyed – as I did – the remote places and pinnacles at which they were found. Hunting one of them saddled us with climbing the Katchberg, the steepest road in Austria until modified, and highly deceptive since the stiffest gradient was right at the top, reached by a wide, innocent-looking gravel road.

We were near the top when, in lowest gear, the engine started failing and I asked Father Austin if he would mind walking the rest of the way, and he complied. Soon it began failing again; I could not ask Mrs Seddon to walk, but there was sufficient width of road for me to swing the car round and go up in reverse, the lowest gear of all. No one could have been more delighted to arrive backwards than Mrs Seddon, who relished achieving the impossible. Nor could she have been happier later when we saw the entrance of the Gross-Glockner Pass, the road over the summit just then completed, its entrance cut off by a few empty tar barrels until the official opening. These were removed for us by a road-worker, and we drove in to inspect and in fact reached the top, replacing the tar barrels on our return. It was remarkable in Austria and southern Bavaria the privileges conceded, the customs lifted and the *Eingang Verboten* signs whisked away at sight of the widow's veil and the Dominican habit.

Father Austin, widely read, used to read to us of an evening after dinner. He was a great diarist and I, like my mother before me, was also a diarist, and Mrs Seddon, who always wanted us to read out our diaries for the day, could see no cause for reluctance. It never seemed to occur to her either that, for a man of his calling, it was unnatural for Father Austin to be mewed up in a car next to a youngish woman for days on end. I was aware of his feelings but thankful he maintained a stern discipline throughout, dispersing all problems.

There are two conversations of this period worth recording. One was on returning through Switzerland from a spring tour with Mrs Seddon, who had discovered her sister – widow of a Church of England Bishop – was staying not far distant, and she had invited the sister to tea. They had not met for some years, and Mrs Seddon seemed in an unnatural state of anxiety, adding extra cakes and wondering if Gertie's feet were holding out. (Mrs Seddon's were her one weakness.) So when a large chauffeur-driven car drove up, from which Gertie leapt out and sprang up the hotel steps, followed by a pale companion, whom it seemed right that I should take on, Gertie was left to her sister. After family affairs, what did these two, both approaching eighty, choose to discuss but which of the highest passes each had been over.

'Have you been over the Stelvio, Isabel? It's the highest pass in Europe.'

'Have we been over the Stelvio, Claudia?'

'No, I'm afraid we haven't.' But aware that I must keep up the side I added, 'But the Stelvio's easy. It's been graded. Nothing to the Katchberg. That's the steepest pass, I believe, in Europe.'

'Have you been over the Katchberg, Gertie?'

Gertie hadn't.

The other conversation was at home with my aunt Muriel, to whom all Catholics were perverts, and she strongly disapproved of my cavorting around with Father Austin. When at Christmas he sent me a copy of Helen Waddell's *Beasts and Saints,* of all innocent gifts, my aunt asked sternly how he could do this, having taken the vow of poverty? I had no idea. I knew he was librarian at Hawkesyard, but that didn't improve matters unless they had unwanted copies. 'Well, I just don't know. I only know Mrs Seddon used to give him ten shillings at intervals for glasses of beer. And I do know Dominicans can send Christmas cards.'

'Oh well,' said my aunt, 'he couldn't pinch all those.'

*

It is possible I could have worked up the chauffeur-courier business into quite a profitable concern, employing assistants, but not only did I prefer the personal link with my employers but there were always those conflicting interests seeking attention. A compulsive writer of letters, articles, stories, my first incentive on returning from the Balkans was to get into print on the back of knowledge gained. *Blackwood's* had seen promise, but the standard of English was not good enough; however, the sting of rebuttal had been softened by my information being useful elsewhere. The Riley team, starting from Athens in the Monte Carlo rally the following winter, were more than grateful for the road reports I sent them at the request of the AA. I signed them 'C. Parsons', feeling they might carry more weight if sex was indeterminate, and when the team came second, C. Parsons sent a note of congratulations, to receive an enthusiastic reply. They thought I ought to have the congratulations for the only reports, of many, either accurate or useful. They had, of course, benefited from frozen conditions sealing the bogs, but the surface of the great plain was so slippery they had to have special tyres and thick rope bound round the car wheels. They too found it treacherous getting back on the smooth roads and had skidded off into a snowdrift. The letter wound up with an invitation to lunch if I was ever in Coventry, and I felt sorry the chance never occurred.

In 1929 Betty had written a charming short novel in beautiful English, with only a slight plot but keen observation. *The Dove Pursues* was taken by Chatto & Windus, the leading publisher of the time. They said it was not expected to make much money but she must write a follow-up. This she did, but it was not taken. To be a successful writer one has also to be a dogged pusher, but Betty merely put the manuscript in a drawer and resumed her normal and chosen occupation, that of teaching.

My trouble was having too many occupations. I had signed up for driving Mrs Seddon in April but the previous month I had happened to read one of Angela Thirkull's light-hearted novels, *Turnip Tops*, and felt sure I could write a book of that style. Almost at once the form came tumbling into my brain and I was recounting the experiences of a young widow left in reduced circumstances taking up a series of jobs for which she had no training or competence, only the knack of serene survival. I used my own experiences in Sweden, on the *Sibÿjak*, in the Latin Quarter; and one of Betty's jobs, reading Shakespeare with Americans. I was careful to make all characters fictitious for, though I was certain the manuscript would be returned to me, if it should get taken my employers would read it, and though they might identify me with the widow I made certain they would not see themselves mirrored in any way.

There had to be love interest, so I introduced a heart's desire, but with no resemblance to Bernard save an occasional similarity in our conversation and his pursuit of good food. I looked forward to reading it to him when he came on leave, knowing he would see the reflection of my own follies, and the situations would make him laugh.

Once I had started the book I could not stop; I took it with me to Buxton and wrote it at night, also while sitting in the car outside the Hydro. Mrs Seddon and her friend were both anxious to assist the Muse. Then Mrs Seddon asked me to drive her in Austria from the seventh of August for a solid six weeks of absence, and I realized the harmonious combination of chauffeur, writer and temporary wife was going to raise difficulties. Bernard was now in Addis Ababa, sending me interesting descriptions of it, but due this year for leave, and I wrote at once asking if he could synchronize his leave either before or after Mrs Seddon's dates. I was back in Wonersh when I heard he could not arrange his leave for any other time than the sixth of July, which meant barely a month together and cramped at that, as I had been pushed into giving a dance at the Old House at the end of July. It would be some recompense if he came to it.

So I went on writing the book and by July had reached all but the ending, on which I was not decided, but I never read it to Bernard, in fact never saw him again. No letter came telling me his plans until July, when he wrote from Paris saying he was sorry not to be able to attend the dance, for I would be surprised to hear he was getting married. No details, only a hope that I would let him know what this meant to me.

So the non-marrying man was getting married, and the non-married woman was left feeling a considerable fool. I told him this, but added that, though the news had been like a sledgehammer blow, I knew it was the best thing that could happen. It was folly my going on arranging my life to join him when chance offered, but I had seemed unable to break away. I ended by wishing him happiness. What else could I do? I sent the letter off quickly before bitterness set in. It set in soon enough. Seven years this had gone on, and now silence.

*

I had Betty's bosom on which to weep, for she was home that weekend. She knew all about my double life, but I had never betrayed it to Avis, who by now had given up veterinary work for the bright lights of London. She had a job in the gift department of Harrods, coming home at weekends, and it was she who had instigated this dance. Two local friends, both working in London, had sunk their salaries in renting a London flat and were going to get married at a registry office, with a future of living close to the bone. The wife was a great friend of Avis's, and this dance was to give them at least some sort of celebration.

There seemed every likelihood of it being a flop. By the time I could give my mind to it every jazz band within reach was already booked and I had to hire a lone pianist. Then a spirited hurdy-gurdy playing in Wonersh inspired me to vary the pianist with a barrel organ. I hired one with a repertoire of Strauss waltzes and a polka. Then I had cold feet about not enough refreshment and hired a barrel of beer. Three loads of guests came from London, the rest were local friends, and the long room could only take up to seventeen couples. Neighbours walked down the street looking in at the windows, both barrels – organ and beer – were rarely idle, and Heaven subscribed a warm moonlight night so chairs and refreshments were out of doors. This dance, for which I had little appetite, was a tremendous success.

For me it was saved by the arrival of Esmond Morrison, whom I had hesitated to invite. Home on sick leave with broken ribs, he probably would not feel equal to it, but Esmond was the only other person who knew of the Bernard liaison. At length I could no longer contain my feelings and spread them over several pages, telling him also of the dance he need not attend. He came, not to dance but to support me, and whisked me off next day to Camberlot, where, though I felt the whole family must have been briefed, they were the model of discretion. Esmond argued the case both for and against Bernard, and even the abruptness he refused to accept in a hostile light. Bernard was having to do a very difficult thing, which he hated doing, and even brevity was probably wisest. I had to admit I was never coerced, my meeting him never taken for granted, but much enjoyed, and we were now almost like husband and wife. I certainly felt better after this thrashing-out of the matter, and it was just as well that within two days of getting home I was starting for Oberammergau.

I had no interest in my novel after receiving Bernard's letter; it lay about unfinished and untouched, for I seemed to have no confidence in writing, the *joie de vivre* drained from my pen. On my return from Oberammergau, Betty was away on her summer holiday, but I found she had read the book and left a note with it saying it hadn't a hope of publication as it was, but she thought it well worth working on, and when she got back would go through it with me. This set me at once to write a suitable ending, and since my personal story had wound up in sorrow I felt it essential the book should end happily. It was not till the winter holidays, however, that Betty had time to give to it, and grammar was now presented to me, not as a series of rules, but as common sense.

I was shown the reason why statements were incoherent, where noun and subject had got hopelessly entangled, changing horses in mid-stream, as Betty described it. I was induced to refer to the dictionary not merely for spelling of words but for their derivation and meaning, which could reveal when the wrong word was chosen. The dictionary became my best friend. I would not say I was Betty's best pupil but she left me alert to the common errors, and also with a manuscript so fraught with corrections it had to be retyped.

Even the fair copy needed adjustments, but Esmond now read it, and when I told him I would love to dedicate it 'to my husband' but feared that would arouse too much curiosity, he suggested I should dedicate it 'to my husbands', since the one I killed off featured in the early pages. I took his advice.

The novel was not sent to Chatto & Windus until February the following year. Later I heard they were charmed with it and would be delighted to publish it in spring or early summer. The news reduced me to tears. I was having an early breakfast, catching a train to London. I took the letter with me and went to the gift department at Harrods that seemed to be a focal point for all Avis's friends. When I showed Avis the letter tears also came into her eyes. It seemed to be the general reaction.

Authors were then a more exclusive crowd; there were not so many on the ground. I held my head high when I went for an interview with Harold Raymond, a senior partner of the publishing firm who from henceforth guided my progress as an author. I was allowed to design my own dust-cover for the book, and *Brighter Bondage* came out in the spring of 1935 and was into its second edition by autumn, with flattering reviews.

I sent a copy to Bernard; a letter with it wasn't necessary. The whole book was written to him, and I knew he took *The Spectator*, which had given it a particularly favourable review. I was with Mrs Seddon, her daughter, grandson and Father Austin at the lovely old Abbaye Hotel at Talloires on the Lake of Annecy when two letters arrived for me, posted in quick succession by Foreign Office bag and forwarded from home. They disclosed that both Bernard and his wife had laughed a lot over *Brighter Bondage*; Bernard was particularly enthusiastic, urging me to keep on writing, but he had not realized his wife had already written to me and hoped she had said nothing to upset me. On the contrary, her letter had revealed that much anxiety had preceded their engagement, that all conversation had seemed to end up talking about *me*.

Thus I learnt that Esmond's assessment had been accurate; I had not been lightly tossed aside, and they had evidence, in the book itself, that my life had not been blighted. A warmth of feeling seemed to emanate from those letters, for which I wrote to both thanking them, but there was no ground for continuing the correspondence so that was the end.

The Italian menace hanging over Abyssinia soon broke into open conflict and Hitler, observing that no active opposition resulted, stepped up his own aggression. Over the following years I was to see photos of Bernard in *The Illustrated London News* with the Legation staff, or meeting Churchill in Morocco, but where was I that I never saw any announcement, or read any account of Bernard's death in a motor accident on the Cairo–Alexandria road some time after the world war? I did not learn of this till years later, nor did I ever know if Bernard found happiness in married life.

May 1937–April 1938

A PASSAGE TO INDIA

It was an unnatural sensation to have money flowing into my account: a generous sum on publication and royalties steadily piling up. *Brighter Bondage* was now being translated into the Scandinavian languages, and I had had a request from *The Bystander* for short, light-hearted stories. These were well paid but, much restricted in length, were not easy to write. However, I threaded them in between the chauffer-courier jobs which went on unabated.

Wealth took time to accumulate and I left it untouched until I knew what I was going to do with it. The only incursion was to reward Betty, whose far worthier novel had been rudely eclipsed, and but for her help mine would never have been published. I knew two things she wanted; Betty nearly swooned on being asked which she like best: a good watch or a handsome mothproof chest of drawers.

In the winter of 1936 I met a neighbour, Mrs Shadbolt, who told me she and her daughter were contemplating a coach tour across America; would I like to join them? I certainly wanted to explore beyond Europe, but felt a coach tour would be too restricting. What about buying a car in the States and selling it on the West Coast? Mrs Shadbolt was doubtful. I would have to be responsible for the car.

This initial suggestion was made over the meat counter of a Guildford shop; at a later meeting we had a better idea of the mileage and time required, and a shadowy estimate of costs in what was reputed to be an expensive country. My bank manager seemed profoundly troubled, having an old-world indifference to anything so new as the West, but with abiding trust in my family, he offered to arrange for loans, if needed, at reputable banks on the West Coast of the States, in case I ran out of money with which to get home.

To assess how much, he rang for his currency expert, an elderly man in a green Eton jacket, who retired to work it out. Then I asked for a banker's letter that I must take for my interview with the American consul. Another bell when rung brought in the same man in the same jacket. Yet I must be ever grateful for their combined efforts, which enabled me, when I reached the West Coast, to go on following the sun.

I wrote to the AAA of New York asking could they arrange for a second-hand 30 h.p. Ford for us to purchase, giving the date of arrival. They replied saying they thought I must be referring to the sixty-five h.p. sedan model, and were applying to a reliable garage. I must expect to pay £60 to £70.

We planned to take about six weeks along a southerly route, from the East Coast south of Washington to Los Angeles, and then up the Pacific Highway to San Francisco and Seattle, about seven thousand miles. Here we hoped to sell the car and go over to Vancouver Island, where Canadian-born Mrs Shadbolt had relatives and I had an introduction to Elspeth's cousin, who ran a dairy farm and was always glad of someone to do the milk rounds. So I could be milkman until returning by cargo boat through panama, before the Atlantic got impossible. The hand shook that wrote a cheque for close on £107 for $430 worth of traveller's cheques, the pound then being worth just on $4.

At home there was a general feeling of departure; Avis had lately married Deric French, a Captain in the Royal Engineers, one of a family we had long known in Norfolk. They were starting for India with luggage labelled WANTED ON VOYAGE mingling with my more modest containers labelled STATEROOM NO. 8. The terminology was misleading. I had paid £16 for a third-class bunk on the same ship on which the Shadbolts were travelling second-class. Their class was to be stiff with Germans fleeing an impossible country. I was to find it hard to live up to the respectability of my English cabinmates.

I found Elspeth quite ready to drive Mrs Seddon that year, after which Mrs Seddon was joining a daughter in South Africa. Avis considered Vancouver Island halfway round the world, so I could quite easily slip across to Calcutta. I held out no hopes but deep in my heart I knew this was going to be not only the USA. It was going to be the world, but I did not go rejoicing. In spite of my love of exploration I had a deep affection and feeling of protection for my home. We left in May 1937.

We did not know then how generous was the USA to the needy traveller, that YWCA hostels, at which we always stayed in cities, would be like serviceable hotels. We were also to discover the auto-camps for motorists spread across America, groups of bungalows supplied with every need, and a shop, if not a restaurant, at the camp entrance. They ranged from single cabins to family ones, far preferable to the postwar motels.

On arrival in New York the traffic had looked terrifying – we were not yet tuned in to the one-way street – yet once behind the driving-wheel one found traffic control far better than in London, and signposting also clearer on the high road. America had in fact a happy mastery over material things, which brought iced drinks and fresh salads to the deserts, and comfortable beds universally distributed, which they certainly weren't at home. 'Dry ice' – carbon dioxide in cartons – was used with a current of air to

106

cool their cars and the auto-camp bungalows, an early form of air-conditioning. Pre-war America was still touchingly bashful about its youth compared with 'the old country', and British visitors were still rare enough, away from the cities, for the locals, describing themselves as full-blooded British, to come far down the street to shake the hands of the even fuller-blooded.

*

I make no claim that this venture was exceptional; many people have done the same on less money and found equally interesting jobs, but have failed to publish an account. I started writing mine between the Munich crisis and the first air raids in London. I had to cut it down to meet the paper rationing on the occupation of Norway, our suppliers. I had to agree to only one further edition allowed, and it came out under the title of *Vagabondage* in 1941. After the war, people were advertising for it, offering a price exceeding the original, but Chatto's were naturally not interested in republishing a travel book by then seven years out of date. Some of it I am now using again.

I am taking from this book selections only, describing places that have greatly changed or that leave me with a special memory. For of course we explored all the great features of the states we passed through – Italian reservations, Grand Canyon and National Parks – attended country rodeos, and relished to the full the sociability of the people. And I derived a special joy, once across the James river and into Virginia, in the re-creation of East Anglia. Fields began narrowing to similar dimensions, bordered with hedgerows and trees, and the estate of Upper Brandon, starting with the bootjacks outside the garden door, was almost a replica of Scole Lodge. This estate, where we stayed a weekend, had been owned for many generations by the family Bird, who were friends of Mrs Shadbolt. The only difference was an umbrella on the tractor, to shield the driver from the sun.

A further special memory is waking in the dawn in the Mohave desert. The state of Utah had given us our first taste of heat, so we stayed in the cool of an auto-camp in Las Vegas in order to cross the desert at night. On coming to it at night it was merely a circle of light on a roadway, giving no idea of the limitless extent on either side. By 2.00 a.m. we were chilled to the bone, so pulled into the side, snuggled down and slept. All too soon we were woken by early light, to find we were not in a desert at all but in an exotic garden surrounded by flowering cacti and the silver plumes of the yuccas, like puffs of smoke joined to the earth by slender stalks. The spring flowering was in session, the whole earth covered with a myriad of tiny ground plants luxuriating in the dew.

107

The YWCA of Seattle attended to our every need, and we tossed all but the clothes we were wearing into their efficient laundry service, yet no one took any notice of our advertisement for selling the Ford. I had, however, good friends in Seattle, and Major Cowan swiftly sold it for us for a hundred dollars more than we gave for it on the East Coast.

Landing in Vancouver Island was like returning to Britain. I stayed several days at the YWCA in Victoria, very much a country hostel compared with its counterpart in Seattle, but nevertheless with a heart of gold. They had no room in which to write but they made one for me, and I accomplished a story for *The Bystander* that had been floating in my mind. And I made a round of the travel bureaux, for I had money over from the USA journey, and money also from the car, so with all this wealth I was not going home, but going on. I judged there was time before a war broke out for further adventure, but the Shadbolts deemed it to be imminent and as soon as possible went home by Panama. Whilst waiting they hired a car and I went with them far up the East Coast of the island beyond the road, and camped on the sandy track between woodland and shore. We had camped remotely under the great redwoods of the USA, but this camp remains always in my mind: the great silence broken only by the lapping of wavelets and, so near, those gigantic mountains across the straits on mainland Canada.

Eventually I booked a second-class ticket for London on the *Hikawa Maro* for £76, leaving Vancouver on the fourteenth of August. (The clerk kept his thumb over the price of the third-class tickets.) I intended to stop off at Yokohama, at Shanghai and Penang, in each case picking up a later ship of this line. Then I wrote home asking for all letters for me to be sent to the shipping office in Singapore, where we would be calling. I then went up the island to find that being a farm-hand was also loaded with social activity such as I have never anticipated.

*

When I boarded the *Hikawa Maro* I was anticipating hardship, and the boat was small for an ocean-going liner, but I found every comfort: excellent European food, or Japanese if preferred, and delightful menu cards which one could retain; the only drawback was the day we sailed from Vancouver the Japanese first shelled Shanghai. The first-class passengers almost to a man got off the ship; the seconds stayed on because they could not do otherwise.

The passengers – students, teachers and missionaries – were bound together by friendship, facing a future unknown. Nearly all were American or Canadian; I was the only one from Britain and was generally known as God Save the King. I had a missionary in my cabin going to convert the

Chinese, not just to God but to God from a particular angle, and she practised meanwhile on me. God, however, came to my rescue by rocking the boat, when preacher and subject fell sick. Conversion was postponed, never to regain its former impetus.

At table I sat next to an older and gentler missionary who had seen Japan through earthquake, fire and religious wars. Anxious on my behalf, she rehearsed me in a useful vocabulary with which to reach the YWCA in Tokyo from the harbour of Yokohama by rail and taxi.

I found also on the ship a tall humorist, member of a family of humorists, one Lucia Runyon. She was what I called head mistress and she called principal of a school in San Francisco, and combined this with being a rancher from the hinterland of California. As we neared Japan the climate grew hot and sticky, and I was walking the decks with Lucia when there emerged out of the mist a skyline at a steep angle rushing up into the sky and again descending, covered with a soft coating of fir-trees, its feet obscured in haze. It was the exact pattern seen on a lacquer tray.

I went to my cabin, and there found the daily bulletin shoved under my door, telling of a rain of *Chinese* bombs on the international city of Shanghai. 'Every one of the four thousand Americans in that bleeding international community was in grave danger.' We were to grow used to the propaganda lies in the following years.

Taxis comprised the major portion of the Tokyo traffic: shiny saloon cars, they plied in droves, wheeling and turning in unison like a flock of starlings, and with astonishing dexterity. Somehow they did not collide nor appeared ever to have done so. There were no street names in Roman characters and very few directions, but luckily the YWCA had maps of Tokyo in English, showing the tramlines and their numbers, and I used these to find my whereabouts in the city as much as for catching the required tram. People waiting for transport sometimes sat on their haunches, a restful habit which, however, denuded the city of seats, and I often regretted the loss of this squatting talent in early life.

Lucia joined me at the YWCA, having learnt that her exchange school in China had closed, and she was now advertising for teaching in Japan. While she was unemployed we explored and attended just about everything, including the homesteads producing the Japanese umbrellas and lanterns. They were like working parties: men and girls, some seated on the floor, but all combined in exquisite and highly accurate handwork at prices which precluded the introduction of machinery. I have a fear that metal and plastic have now usurped the place of these far lovelier creations, and I fear the same pains and finish no longer go into the tying of parcels in the shops.

I particularly enjoyed excursions with Lucia into the country: a patchwork in shades of green with myriad butterflies and flowers. Only once did

I floor Lucia in asking the name of a plant; her subject was botany. Indeed I often felt I was myself one of the specimens she put in a box with holes in the lid to study on return home. For Lucia had never before had sustained acquaintance with a 'Britisher', and as such I provided amazement. 'My! Just say that again' and a notebook would be produced in which we entered 'box' for trunk or suitcase, 'face-flannel' for wash-cloth.

'And it isn't even made of flannel.'

'No, but it probably was once.'

'Well, for Heaven's sakes!'

Accompanying someone of six foot, in a country where the average height was less than five, was to enjoy merriment of the funfair variety, but not so amusing for the person who could never walk upright through a door or lie in a bed at full stretch. New buildings catered for extremes, but not the buses or trams – our usual form of transport – and I retain a memory of Lucia suffering 'standing room only', her head in the ventilator in the roof of a bus and the tickets being collected from way below her hips.

However, finding our present quarters rather beyond our means, we soon became lodgers in a Japanese house owned by an English woman, a Miss Vesey, who advertised rooms and demi-pension at the equivalent of £5 a month. In a very Japanese quarter, it was a house of sliding panels and heavy overhanging roof, in a street only wide enough for bicycles and rickshaws: the *Ryudocho*, (The Dragon Hole). Here tin baths and hot water were brought to our rooms, also meals, and our bedding was made up on the floor, which solved Lucia's problem as it needed only the addition of an extra floor mattress to match her length. I am glad to say we had European pillows; from my window I could see a little family next door lying out like a row of fish on their mattresses, their heads supported on porcelain neck rests.

We had not been here long before Lucia took over a small school of American and English children in Yokohama, where accommodation was also provided. So she left, and we saw each other rarely. But we were to correspond over the years, and Lucia supplied our family with wonderful food parcels from America in the final war years. She made one rare visit to England, when she came to the Old House.

Meanwhile I too had contracted work through a most useful and kindly contact, work I could happily fulfil in The Dragon Hole.

*

My contact was with Masuko Uno, a Japanese girl who had come to an English school, gone on to Bedford College and finally acquired a degree in English when Betty had been her coach. This was very exceptional for a Japanese woman at that time, and she could never have returned to Japan without that degree. She was staying at the Old House when she heard the welcome news, and had expressed her gratitude in offering help to any member of our family who might come to Japan. I was the one to benefit.

She was now working at the Foreign Office in Tokyo, involved in the reception of English-speaking VIPs, but also overburdened with office work and suffering a good deal of conservative prejudice. Her outlook was entirely Westernised, strongly disapproving of this war with China, which at this stage was not singular, even in Japan.

We got on well together and she gave many evenings to introducing me to Tokyo, and was sometimes able to weave me into VIP expeditions. Yet I was always conscious of adding to her obligations and, as foreign relationships began to deteriorate, felt she ought not to be seen too often in my company. She had realized my need to economize and had negotiated for me to write articles for the *Japan Times*, for modest pay certainly, but that would go far in a country like Japan. Or so I thought; but a cheap country lures one into financial indiscretions far more than an expensive one, and there was so much of beauty to buy – some of it not cheap at all. Three of my articles had appeared in print, but I had had no money.

Meanwhile, where could I write better than in The Dragon Hole with its background noises coming distantly through the open panel? On sunny days there was the chorus of the cicadas in the ginkgo trees, on wet days the *clop-clop* of the wooden pattens on the muddy cobbles. After school came the twittering of children's voices silenced by the low voice of the storyteller, and there would be spasms of gossip on the doorstep of a fan shop, whose owners made fans all winter and sold them all summer. At evening one heard urgent prayers from the courtyard of the adjacent Shinto temple, and the rattle of coins being thrown into an open box.

The *Japan Times* brought other relief, however, with an advertisement offering good prices for European clothing, which I speedily answered. It brought to the door a stout body in a kimono who sat on the floor looking like the God of Plenty, and to whom I got rid of all my party clothing, save my best evening dress. There was no interest, perhaps luckily, in my garden party hat, worn so frequently during my time at the dairy farm. The final offer was so far above expectation, I now tossed in an old pair of riding boots, which added a lot more. So on this, and what I had left in hand, I decided to go and visit other parts of Japan, and booked a berth on a liner arriving at the port of Kobe in three weeks' time.

I took a final article to the *Japan Times*, complaining of the inconvenience of waiting for the money owed, which seemed to arouse deep concern. They would contact the finance department and, as I had no fixed address between now and departure, it was arranged that all fees, including the one for this last article, if accepted, should be sent by cheque to the shipping office at Kobe. Now there remained only two more nights in The Dragon

111

Hole, during the first of which I was to experience Tokyo's first air-raid practice, for which there had been a certain amount of preparation during the preceding week.

Miss Vesey's maid was now a 'fire-bucket-handler', her status inscribed in Japanese characters on a sash worn over one shoulder and looked on as a direct message from the Emperor. It was donned whenever a siren sounded, when she joined others of the same calling and they stood in line passing imaginary buckets to each other till the all-clear. They little realized that fire would ripple through these wooden houses, their leaden roofs descending on the ashes, whereon the trusting bucket-handlers would either have run away screaming or have died nobly at the bidding of their Emperor. The chances were even.

The first full air-raid rehearsal was to see Tokyo blacked out for an hour, but at least it was timed for the night of the full moon, only this moon failed to co-operate. An almost carnival spirit greeted the occasion in spite of the many streets bordered by deep culverts, in spite of bicycles being as numerous as taxis and the cyclists invariably carrying tea trays or other burdens at shoulder height. Everyone poured into the streets, and though I doubt casualties or accidents were ever published, even from The Dragon Hole one heard crashes. However, the ordeal lasted only half an hour.

The failure of the full moon was the result of a typhoon which caught the southern isles of Japan. This brought resulting gales and rain as I set forth for Numazu, on Masuko Uno's recommendation, and spoilt the visit to Lake Hakone. Nevertheless as I waited for a train I was granted a rare spectacle, for out of the clouds huddled like a cloak on her shoulder, a snow-clad Fuji rose magnificently and granted me full vision of a mountain that enjoys almost as much seclusion and veneration as the Emperor. She stood right out of the clouds during my journey to Hammatsu, the head-stone of a scene so Japanese I felt I was crossing a colour print or again a lacquer tray. Trains were so punctual that a small book was issued to passengers which told by the clock one's position on the line, a habit I believe borrowed from the USA. Here, in addition, small trays of tea were brought to passengers by attendants who also brushed the floor. Many times I looked back at Fuji and thanked her for her generosity. The straight simplicity of her form made me feel the Japanese had themselves designed her, or that she was the inspiration of their subtle taste.

Foreigners were now rapidly leaving Japan; those remaining were not yet suffering the face-slapping of later date, but there was a feeling in towns though not yet in the country, that foreigners and their property no longer mattered – an indifference quite contrary to my first impression of welcome, of careful handling of property and careful assignment to the owner.

In the short interval left to me in Japan, I was to have a face-to-face encounter with a burglar, and be arrested.

*

In Kyoto I revelled in the massive wooden architecture of its seventeenth-century temples and palaces, particularly that of the Nijo detached palace; permission to view it was growing ever more difficult, but I finally succeeded. I could have done with the maple-wood flooring of the Chion-in Monastery – boards that whined as you walked on them – in my bedroom of the Japanese inn where I stayed. This hotel had been recommended to me, and over soya-bean cakes I discussed prices with the proprietor, ordered the first bath of the morning from the bath boy, and indulged that night in my acquired liking for sleeping on the floor. Here, beside the luxury of the cushion mattresses, was furniture to scale: a low table, reading lamp and the lacquered stand on which my clothes were folded by a little geisha who seemed to find me a fund of amusement.

The room was enclosed like a box. When the geisha left, I found the panels that gave on to my balcony were locked, but I drew back the curtain an inch or two, preferring to wake in daylight. Can it be that eyes were watching while I wrote my diary, pushed my handbag under the table by my bed and put out the light? Some time long after, I was woken by a movement beside me, and saw not a yard from my face a man's head. I sprang up, shouting, and pursued the man to a panel he had pulled back in the passage and from which he now escaped. From the light in the passage he had found my bag. Keys, passport, steamer ticket, and traveller's cheques were all taken.

I rang my bell, shouted, banged on panels. Before me stretched an endless vista of trouble and thwarted plans, of wasted time at consulate and shipping office. . . This sort of thing doesn't happen to me, I wailed inwardly, reproaching my Guardian Angel, who evidently could no longer bear my agony. I walked over to my suitcase, which I could not open without my keys, but kicked something on the floor. It was the compact out of my handbag, and close by lay keys, passport, ticket, cheques and account book. They lay in a little pile near the open panel, a heap the thief was going to pick up, having replaced my empty bag.

Some time later, back in the eiderdowns on the floor, I received the whole management, and described the attempted theft. They were distressed, puzzled, confident the thief came from outside – of which I was not so sure – and two of them sat up keeping watch for the rest of the night. A clerk came on his knees while I was having my breakfast and spoke firmly to the little geisha, who was reading my Japanese phrase book. When plainly I wanted to know what he had said, she found a sentence of which the translation was 'I leave here today.'

I was indignant. On leaving the place I pleaded her cause, though dismissal had not seemed to trouble her. The manager said she had left a panel unlocked downstairs, but in any case the whole interview was redolent of accusation, as I was asked to describe what I had seen of the thief and, anxious as I was to avoid it, I seem to have painted a description not only of the manager but of the whole male staff.

My arrest took place as I was leaving Miyajima, an island of the Inland Sea, connected by ferry to the mainland. It was a forest-covered hill with a small village at the landing stage. There were no roads or wheeled traffic but it had a temple whose lovely torii gate stood with its feet in the water. Further inland was a modest hotel whose porter came down to the ferry to carry my rucksack. Schoolchildren meeting me bowed from the waist; sampans lay at anchor in the fishing harbour, and nets were being dried and mended on the beach. On the outgoing tide women dug for shellfish, and one of them thrust a trowel in my hand for me to dig also. So I helped to collect their evening meal and kept them merry with my attempts at Japanese.

I had now come to have a great respect for Japanese women; years of inconsideration had left them unembittered but with a patient warmth and helpfulness. Upper-class women still retained the national dress, which lent such colour to the city streets, while their menfolk wore European suits, which they retained through the hottest season, when Europeans were inclined to don the kimono. Increasingly the Japanese male was now seen in uniform, which seemed to imbue him with an attitude of aggression, and no doubt those conscripted from the country were suffering agony, their feet for the first time shod in boots.

Miyajima was rich in butterflies, and maple trees now turning brilliant red. It was in a sensitive zone; the blinds had been pulled down in the train that brought me to the ferry, and I was told I could take photos anywhere on the island but not out to sea and, except for the torii gate close to the shore, there was no reason for so doing. Another occupant of the hotel, however, who wore a magenta suit, seemed to be very rash with his camera.

When I left, I took a photo of the island from the ferry. I had to wait till I could get a fair portion of it in the finder, but even so this was hardly looking out to sea. The moment I had taken it, however, 'Magenta', who was also on the ferry and evidently a detective, came over and demanded my camera. He wound the film off and asked for my address; he said he would send me the other photos but must resign the last to the police. He seemed, I thought, heartily glad that after his long vigil I had infringed the law.

The hotel porter who was accompanying me to the train was afraid I would be in for a lot of trouble, and I was certainly a marked character as soon as I boarded the *Terukini Maru*. This was my home during the three days it was in Kobe harbour, where an impressive inquest took place in the first-class saloon.

114

It was difficult for the purser, instructed through Masuko Uno to give me every attention and now learning I was a spy about to be interrogated. I think he kept a nice balance. Magenta had retained my last two photos; we pored over these two rather poor efforts as if they were naval plans. Beer was brought for the police but nothing for the prisoner. There was a list of questions that had to be answered, and I could see they were anxious not to seem foolish in my eyes. Where was I at school? Government school? A private school had no meaning, and I think was classed as a charitable institution. Where did I get money? We got in a terrible tangle over this; I hardly liked to reveal the barter in second-hand clothing, but said that I wrote – this had to be described – and that I had a Government pension. This was very significant, but disappointing as earned through my father.

It was my camera that got me off the hook; an ancient pocket Kodak given me by one of the Canadians returning home after the 1914 war. Retained for its excellent lens, by Japanese standards it was deplorable; their shops were filled with magnificent up-to-date models. Surely the British Government would have furnished me with something better. The interview ended with my writing an apology, and we all bowed to one another and retired. All photos were now in my possession, and the last revealed what I had not noticed at the time of taking, that among the sampans in Miyajima harbour was lying a submarine.

Free now to leave the ship, I rushed to the shipping office, but on the way saw a shop sign: 'Good prices for European clothing'. I rushed back and prised some more items from my wardrobe, and this covered my immediate demands, leaving me a few yen in hand.

No cheque ever came from the *Japan Times*.

*

I had not been the only prisoner on board the *Terukini Maru*; I had found there two ridiculous but attractive American youths who had jeered at a parade of Japanese soldiery, had been chased and caught, and had spent the previous night in gaol. They were now confined to deck-class aft, but surfaced to second-class meals and were to be landed in Hong Kong. I gathered they looked on this as promotion, usually travelling as stowaways, and they discussed prisons as if they were hotels. 'How are your prisons in England? The one here in Kobe was lousy.'

The *Terukini* kept well aloof from all ports along the Chinese coast until Hong Kong, where notices appealed to travellers not to enter China unless on urgent business. 'Oh well, some other time,' I said to myself, not realizing I would have to wait forty-two years. In Hong Kong harbour the casualties strewn around were not due to war but to the recent typhoon. A tramp steamer with bows stove in lay on the waterfront, and the largest

115

liner of our shipping company stood along the coast, stranded but upright, on a spine of rocks which had pierced her hull but held her securely. She was like a ship in a bottle, all in order but misplaced.

I had found great merit in travelling alone; no concessions were needed to other people's desires, one could do as one pleased and change one's mind. My diary was my companion. But in fact the term travelling alone has no meaning. One is never alone. I had to learn also that in a ship gossip spreads like unleashed quicksilver, and the fact that I had only three yen when we sailed from Kobe seemed to arouse greater concern in my fellow travellers then it did in me. Once on board I could reach Singapore empty-handed, even London for that matter, but I had hopes that money awaited me in Singapore.

Nevertheless, my penury brought the offer of a silk shirt from a shy, serious-minded fellow passenger who had bought a dozen in Kobe and would not hear of payment for it in Singapore. I could see he dearly hoped I would accept, and since deck tennis, along with my depleted wardrobe, meant continual laundering, I expressed genuine gratitude. I had not anticipated that it would wrap round me with a yard to spare, thus I put it, so to speak, in my bottom drawer.

My benefactor belonged to a society that sent a car to meet liners and take passengers sightseeing rather than let them fall to the temptations of the port. So it was from a rescue coach I was to see the then garden-like beauty of Singapore, to drink in the abundant fragrance of its flowers and flowering trees, to look at lush green lawns and every form of luxuriant shrub and creeper. There was a golf-course like one in Paradise. Why had I never heard of this beauty, surpassing other more vaunted rivieras?

In the morning I had taken a rickshaw into town and, among multicoloured houses, tall, narrow, of irregular height like an untidy bookshelf, had found the shipping office. Here was the money my pen had earned, and a touching little cheque from my mother to help me get to Calcutta. Having restocked with traveller's cheques, I sat in the garden of the Raffles Hotel and read abundant letters. Those reaching me in Los Angeles and Victoria had been like tiny voices growing fainter with distance, but here we were on the airmail route, with home only a few days distant. It was almost like talking to each other, and there was one very adjacent voice. Avis was hoping I would join them for Christmas. In the bookstalls of Singapore was *The Bystander* containing the story that I had written in Vancouver.

Happily solvent, I now went to a most helpful travel agent and, much elated, rejoined the ship as far as Penang to fulfil an ambition long dormant in my mind.

I had seen it first at the Paris Exhibition in 1931, a pavilion built of concrete created to look like weathered stone, the outstanding feature of the exhibition. I had never heard then of Angkor Wat, thought this pavilion was just a flight of fancy, not a copy of a temple long existent in the jungle of what was then French Indo-China. Within I had found photos and descriptions of the real Angkor and had formed a vow: Some day . . . somehow . . .

I had kept it in my mind all through this journey, but so far with discouragement rather than assistance in getting there. Victoria had advised me against going alone. However, Singapore treated it lightly and booked a second-class rail journey from Penang to Bangkok and then to the frontier of French Indo-China (Cambodia). From there a bi-weekly coach service would take me to Angkor Seamreap.

Thus at dawn I took the ferry from Penang across to Prai, meeting-place of land and water, and just inland the train to Bangkok was waiting in the station. Sahibs in neatly pressed linen suits were standing at the doors of the first-class coach, whom I passed on my way to second-class. This astonished them to the point of coming along at later stations to look at me in my compartment as at something in a cage. Perhaps I was breaking a convention, but second-class was well arranged, its occupants friendly, and only their luggage might be termed awkward; large wicker baskets with market produce sticking out, a hen or two with closed eyes and tied feet. We had not gone far before an official took me to an empty carriage that I suspected of being first-class, but I was glad to have a table on which to write.

Green, green was Malaya – as it was then called – with rubber plantations, coconut groves, and here and there the glint of a bright-coloured sarong. This was the dry season, but spasmodic showers pelted the train, freshening the atmosphere, and then the sun would appear and steam would rise from the drenched back and clothing of buffalo and man together ploughing the land for next year's rice. All day, all night, we advanced through this water-logged country that was now plain jungle, all building supplanted by structures of palm leaf and bamboo raised high off the ground, and not without reason.

We were now some way into Siam, and when I came back from dinner in the first-class dining-car – for want of any other – there seemed to have been some muddle about my sleeper and I was given a first-class sleeper in exchange. I revelled in my good fortune. I could wash and sleep in comfort, but for a long time I lay with the blind up, looking out at the jungle and the moonlight and, as it always does, the train sang to me, its rhythm beating out measure for measure the continual silhouette of trees and creeper, the future becoming the present then falling away into the unforgiving past.

A strange country, but who was I to call it strange? Was I not the stranger? This jungle and its creatures belonged here, but this train, this lighted phantom stealing through the jungle with its headlamp, its all-seeing eye, was the real eccentricity. I had come to have a great admiration for it, con-

117

tinuing in faltering just above the water-level where was no other stable foundation than this line, its embankment and its rare stations.

I did not then know it was the work of the British, nor did I know that it was an extension of this line, westward beyond Bangkok, that was to become the Death Railway.

*

I stayed in Bangkok a couple of days, exploring a city whose highways were then mostly canals linking the main river with the markets, but I understand that many of these canals are now roads. Of roads then existing, only one reached beyond the perimeter of the city, which was otherwise enclosed at a distance by the jungle. The city had a fine assortment of pagodas, Buddhist temples and a Royal Palace from which visitors could be denied access if legs were bare of stockings or arms bare of sleeves. Water taxis were few, but one could arrange to visit the early morning market on a market boat, the owner glad of the additional payment. Thus, the sun barely risen and mist still on the water, I joined a little family whose flat-bottomed boat, roofed with a palm-leaf awning and propelled by an outboard motor, was laden with baskets of sweet potatoes. We started along the main river, which was fringed with wooden shacks standing clear of the water on stilts, the occupants washing their teeth and their bodies at the water's edge, deftly covering nakedness with the sarong. Even a buffalo was receiving ablution.

We then turned inland by one of the canals that reached to the markets, from which came a babble of voices, and there was a congestion of shipping most skilfully handled. The markets were rich in fruit and vegetables: prawns the size of crayfish, pomelo, durian, coconuts, gourds. . . . Anxiety visibly lifted as the baskets of sweet potatoes were exchanged for desired goods, and we came back by what was virtually a leafy lane of water beneath overhanging trees, where the family pulled into the side to eat their breakfast.

I reached the border of Cambodia by a country train whose stations were written up in Chinese, Japanese and Roman lettering. At the frontier was a money exchange and I cashed a traveller's cheque for what I deemed to be sufficient for a week in French territory, but I had small cheques to bolster the sum if necessary. It had not occurred to me that there are no banks in the jungle. A German who was offering me a lift in the car he was hiring might have reminded me of this. I, however, preferred independence, and rejoiced in a well-driven coach journeying along a smooth road bordered with signs such as *Tenir votre droite* and *Ralentir*, making me feel I was back in France.

At first it was open country with long flat bridges across marshy land that was interesting to vultures, kites, herons, storks and here and there king-

118

fishers. Towards evening mynahs squatted in the dust beside the road and one or two cicadas had flown into the bus, so we carried our own music. The jungle which all this time had been creeping closer now enveloped us, and at the first and only road junction where we halted there was a small village, obscured in darkness save for fires burning to discourage evil spirits and wild animals. The fires did not exclude the intrusion of this bus, more likely to influence the lives of the villagers than any spirit.

Angkor Seamreap was a native village to which had been added a residency, a post office and a couple of hotels, the larger one having a zoo. These were on one side of the Seamreap river, which had been, and still was, the high street of a village, but now a road was added. On the far bank was native life, and a wooden water-wheel like a ship's paddle-wheel was ready to do manual labour. It was a beautiful village of traditional dwellings, and to flow down the river or take the road was to reach the great lake, the Tonle Sap, and eventually join the mighty Mekong flowing into Saigon. I walked to the Tonle Sap.

On our arrival I went to the smaller hotel, facsimile of a hundred such in France, with notices of *Bhrrh Vin Tonique* and *Pernod Fils*. The *patron* was so impressed that I meant to stay a week – three days is generally given to Angkor – he agreed to my *en-pension* terms for that period. Not till next day did I discover there was no bank, and though hotels were prepared, indeed delighted, to cash cheques, it was at an exchange that made it just not worth while to do the 120-mile bus journey into the bank at Pnom Penh. I was determined not to overspend what I had cashed at the frontier.

The city of Angkor Thom was less than two miles distant along an open track cut through the jungle. One could walk or take a bicycle rickshaw or one's car. Rickshaw boys were not keen to wait for their clients at evening as the jungle was full of wild game. Notices in the hotels warned visitors that they visited the temples at their own risk, which covered falling masonry and wild animals, though my only encounter was a huge snake across the doorstep of a temple from which I was emerging, whereon I retired, and so did the snake. I heard from others of more alarming encounters.

Angkor Thom had once been a splendid city, squarely enclosed by seven miles of wall embraced by a moat; bridges and ornamental gateways gave access to it in the centre of each side. Within were many temples, monasteries and religious ornaments in various states of preservation, but the largest, finest and best preserved was the temple of Angkor Wat.

Until the mid-nineteenth century it had been a legendary city, based on reports of missionaries and the writings of a Chinese envoy of the thirteenth century, and as one walked along the track to it the first hint of its existence were the towers of Angkor Wat. One wondered if this was the view that broke on Mouhot, a French naturalist journeying here in 1861, who wrote

119

in his diary that the possibility of a city existing here grew ever more absurd. The next day he saw the towers. There followed explorers travelling in the grand manner, on elephants or by water, and sleeping in the precincts of Angkor Wat, but when I came this was a commercial proposition – with a kiosk at the entrance.

One could not resent this for the task of preservation is enormous. Angkor Wat was the best preserved through local people continuing to worship here, including the Buddhist monks. But of those temples left sleeping, giant trees had grown over and into them, banyans had thrust their tentacles like serpents between the stones, as if resenting the presence of a city here built of stone imported from mountains twenty-five miles distant.

The city of Angkor Thom was built by the Khmer kings between the ninth and thirteenth centuries. The Khmers were descended from immigrants from West India who overran the peninsula, thus Hindu mythology is depicted in the bas-reliefs. It is also quite noticeable that the present Cambodians resemble the faces in the carvings and the colossal faces pointing to the four points of the compass in the Bayon, another temple within the city. Then the Siamese overran and occupied Cambodia and for four centuries the city lay sleeping, the jungle with slow delight reclaiming its own. I have often wondered what has been the jungle destruction during the recent long years of warfare.

Angkor Wat is superb architecture; terrace by terrace the galleries rise to the supreme height. I explored it in every phase of day and in moonlight, and my last evening I watched the sunset from the topmost shrine. Facing westward, one looks out over the descending galleries and a long causeway that leads to the jungle, a vista cut in line with it to the foot of the setting sun. Away and away the jungle stretches over flat country, but the sun has uninterrupted view of the temple until it sinks into a green ocean, and Angkor Wat is then suffused in blood-red light.

I had been listening to the sound of chanting; priests in their yellow robes gathered here always of an evening, and repeated intoning would accompany the setting sun. Now all was silence as I lingered in the afterglow, thinking of the long road home. Could it possible be as enthralling as the outward journey? Would I be granted yet another secret ambition? I little knew that a powerful factor towards its attainment was close at hand.

*

With Avis and Deric I lived in unsurpassed security. Fort William, stronghold of Empire, overlooked the Hoogli river – an offshoot of the Ganges – also the Maidan, open green park land at the more British end of Calcutta. A circular fort, completed about 1771 and not much altered since, Fort William bristled with old-world cannons on the top of the ramparts, while officers billeted here lived in what had been storage holds for powder magazines. Skilfully adapted, these were most acceptable bungalows, protected from heat by their thick outer walls and opening on to an enshrouded green lawn which enjoyed the pleasantest and coolest aspect of the city. Distantly it looked on to Chowringhee, the main road where the British did their shopping, containing Firpo's restaurant, the club, the Great Eastern Hotel and branches of London firms including, inevitably, the Army & Navy Stores.

Here life was on a plane rather higher than that of my late travels, but it was not long before my past caught up with me. Fort William contained Warren Hasting's banqueting hall and other such relics, and Alison and Moriarty came here as tourists.

Moriarty had travelled deck-class on the *Terukini Maru*; we had met in the dining-salon and at deck tennis, and I had watched him disembark at Singapore with a small haversack of champion limit for travelling the world. When I returned to Penang from Angkor, there he was again deck-class on the boat for Calcutta, which stopped four days in Rangoon on its way, and I had taken him on a visit to my elderly cousin in the Commission, stationed far up the Irrawaddy.

In Rangoon I rang my cousin to ask if we would be welcome, but did not mention we would be travelling third-class. This was Moriarty's normal level, and I was equally obliged to be frugal with what money I had, if I was to attain my further ambition. Consequently my cousin, who had driven some miles to meet us at dawn, was waiting at the wrong end of the platform, and it took him some time to adjust to the shock as the third-class loosed its rabble. He had not yet had his breakfast, and thought we ought to have a bath before we had ours. His Irish wife took it more calmly.

I had no idea that I had a 'fan' living not far distant. The Director of the Burma oilfields had been so entertained with *Brighter Bondage* he had said that if ever I visited my cousin he hoped to meet me, and would take me over the oilfields. So, though I probably fell below expectation, at least the oilfields were a great success both for me and for Moriarty, who had never before seen wooden derricks, or found people so ready to divulge at what depth they struck oil. Here, alongside scientific drilling and extraction, was the spade-and-bucket method of Burmans owning oil-bearing land but preferring this method to having oil extracted for them.

We could not have enjoyed greater hospitality during that visit and were finally given first-class tickets on the Irrawaddy steamer, and first-class sleepers where we joined the train. There was to be no more 'third-class nonsense'. Back in Rangoon we found Alison had joined the Calcutta steamer; a trained nurse, she was using her hard-earned gains to fulfil a comprehensive list of sightseeing, which included Fort William. I introduced both friends to Avis and Deric, who met me at the ship's side, so their arrival at the Fort was not unexpected, and greatly enhanced by Avis giving them lunch.

As lunch guests their view of the Fort was more intimate than that of the average tourist, and I doubt if the banqueting hall left so deep an impression as the sanitary arrangements prevailing at the Fort. Lucia's notebook would certainly have been produced had she been there. Most of this area of Calcutta had long ago gone over to main drainage, but the Fort persisted in the earlier method: instead of pulling a plug one unbolted a door leading to the outside world whereon an 'untouchable' came in to empty the slops. A year later, I learnt, the Fort was almost pulled to pieces while modern plumbing was installed.

We laughed heartily at Alison's list of compulsory visits, which included 'sunrise over Everest', a spectacle not vouchsafed to many. Nevertheless I was with her, Moriarty and about sixty others clustered on Tiger Hill a few miles out of Darjeeling, in the cold pre-dawn. It was like waiting for a prima donna uncertain if she would appear, a long wait with the jackals howling, until light began to filter in from behind us, throwing the earth into exaggerated relief. There was now a slight silvering of the Tibetan snows and the pinnacles of the Kinchinjunga range, which looked like the breaking crest of a wave, and far away there was no denying a presence: a distant silver cap growing ever more luminous. Yes, it was Everest, and when the first rays of sun were flung across the skies they would touch none save that distant peak, when the true monarch would be revealed to whom Kinchinjunga and all that starry retinue would be but courtiers.

This we never saw. With the stage set for the supreme happening, mists rising from below hid Everest from sight as if, growing bored with entertaining a bunch of onlookers, Everest had pulled the bedclothes over a sleepy head and left Kinchinjunga to do the honours.

And what a deputy! The sun now with a golden finger touched the heights in order of superiority and Kinchinjunga, who enjoys playing to the gallery, came forward to take her bow, the whole front of the range a golden red rising from deep blue and purple in the valley.

It was fantastic; it fully compensated for our having failed in our objectives, made it worth the overcrowding of the interclass – same as third – on the Darjeeling to Siliguri railway, where, however, Alison and I had had reprieve. We had found a coach with a woman's head painted on the door, a coach empty save for two little Indian wives, and had slept stretched out sublimely. When the husbands brought water in the morning for the wives to wash, Alison's handbag, which met every emergency, supplied a face-cleaning lotion, raising us to similar standard. One could get dirtier travelling the Indian trains of those days than by going down a coalmine.

I wonder if it still plies, the small light-gauge railway that completed the journey from Siliguri to the heights of Darjeeling, a marvel of engineering skill since it climbed at an angle almost equal to that of the road. Road and rail frequently crossed each other, but rail was already menaced by road and a cheaper bus service. The sahibs made a point of going by rail.

*

After this there was no further 'third-class nonsense'; I was in fact pitched into the Viceregal season: Lord Linlithgow arrived, heralded by a salute of guns and followed by the Navy – battle-cruisers hung with bunting docking impressively outside the Fort. Bugles sounded instructions within the Fort, loudspeakers voiced them on board the cruisers.

The social activities resulting from these visits were not really convenient for one who had sold most of her wardrobe. Luckily, I had retained a handsome evening dress, and was thankful of the garden-party hat I had failed to sell in Japan. Avis and I were much the same size so I could at times ring the changes in borrowed outfits. She also gave me a pair of discarded white kid gloves that had gone spotty on the underside, a blemish which could be concealed. I defy anyone to have known that was a vagabond in all that jewelled and uniformed society.

In spite of a desire to see India independent, I cannot pretend I did not enjoy the pageantry of it; the Governor's mounted bodyguard, the dignified Rajputs attendant at race meetings and polo, the Viceroy's impressive entry down the length of the ballroom at the Belvedere Palace on the night of the ball, his retinue of officers in full dress uniform eclipsed, nevertheless, by the colour and jewellery in the bays by the dance floor marked *Ruling Princes*.

Nor will I ever again see such polo as the final match between the teams of the Rajah of Jaipur and the Rajah of Phobal. The *pugri* was the only head protection for a contest so sublimely graceful it resembled ballet rather than the high-speed dangerous game that it was. Twice the time had to be extended to determine the winning team, and a last-minute goal, wrested by Jaipur, scarcely established superiority. Avis gave a dinner party that evening at which all guests had been spectators, and the match was gone over detail by detail. No one then realized the sun was about to set on this expensive standard of excellence, that the polo surviving the war would never again be the same.

There arrived in Calcutta that Christmas a Baroness von Blixen Finecke who had driven alone from London in a specially fitted Ford car. I learnt the Baroness was looking for someone to drive back with her. My secret ambition, my long-cherished dream, was to drive from India to England overland.

While staying at The Ramparts I had met the editor of the *Calcutta Times*, who had not only suggested but published (and paid for) an article I had written about my impressions on arriving in India. He had also told me that

123

a party of four people already owning a car needed only £60 a head for the running and living costs of the journey to England. This brought the venture within my scope, so I went to the Automobile Association to hand in my name as a possible useful addition, if any car owner happened to be seeking passengers to share this journey.

The secretary was not one to encourage adventure. 'Madness to start now with rivers all swelling with melting snows, bridges washed away. . . .' All this I knew only too well, but I felt I could not lean on Avis and Deric till Easter; so I met the Baroness (the Baron's second wife, not the author of *Out of Africa*), saw the lovely job that had been done on the Ford, and said I would be ready to go with her but could only raise £60. She seemed very ready to take me on, but obviously needed more money and was generally vague about everything else. Soon after I withdrew my offer.

There were a number of reasons for my withdrawal, but the most conclusive was the arrival of a letter I have never expected, offering me an interesting job in Malaya that would neatly tide me over till nearer April. This letter came a few days before Avis and I were setting out to join Deric, now in camp at Gopalpur some hundred miles along the coast south of Calcutta. It was quite an attractive place where many wives joined their husbands, but generally by train. I would accompany Avis and then take train and boat to Malaya.

The secretary at the AA was once more flung into depression when I went to get details of the route to Gopalpur. He had in fact grounds for anxiety, though the route was not difficult in normal weather, or with a car whose speedometer was not always failing, or in a country where sixteen miles out of Calcutta the bearer could not understand the local dialect. We were deeply dependent on an interpreter as, with the speedometer out of action, and hence no mileage record, and of course no place names written up, we could not tell our position on the map.

There had been a look of foreboding on the bearer's face when told he was to accompany us, and not without cause. Storms broke unaccountably upon us, hailstones battered on the windows, the roof of the car leaked on to the bearer and the dachshund puppies in the back. We suffered engine failure, when I would bend over the dead machine, the bearer holding the bonnet flap over my head much as parasols are held over Viceroys and Governors. Finally, we reached the river Sanke – never more rightly named – which we had to cross by ford, but in the confusion of storms and dialect we crossed at the wrong point. It took sixteen strongly built locals and five hours to pull us out of that river, only to find that here the road ended and the village on the opposite bank was the wrong village. I think I can safely say we were where no car had ever been before. This adventure, illogically and indirectly, led to my driving to England.

We slept that night in the car a discreet distance from the village, which was celebrating a Hindu festival with dancing and the beating of drums. The bearer curled up outside the car like a parcel left under a tree; most of the night the puppies barked and the rain fell steadily. There seemed little chance of getting back across a swelling river, little chance of catching a boat for Malaya in five days' time, for on getting that letter I had wired Singapore that I was coming, and booked a berth on the next boat. Madurai, our faithful bearer, however, saw no cause for despair.

Next morning he organized helpers to carry the car across the river, a sixteen-horsepower saloon car balanced on saplings cut down for the purpose, through water above our knees when we ourselves forded it. Avis rewarded our helpers, who throughout had shown no signs of grievance.

Madurai was in fact the chief sufferer, wearing the expression of one whose darkest fears have been realized. He disliked us to be in any way connected with the running of the car beyond a majestic position at the wheel. Moreover, I had tried to discipline the puppies; I stopped them barking during the night, congratulating myself on the peace which followed, unaware they had found my overcoat and were happily chewing a hole in it. By morning there was virtually no back to it left, and when inclement weather compelled me to wear what was left of it, exposed to the world, this added to Madurai's misery.

At Gopalpur I made a present of my coat to the puppies, and in spite of what I had called them on discovery, my insurance, which disclaimed payment on clothing eaten by vermin, eventually gave recompense. Nor had our gallant struggle been in vain. Whilst in Malaya I wrote an account of that journey for the *Calcutta Times* and received handsome reward. Also it brought to the door of the Dak bungalow where we stayed, a young Scotsman encamped at Gopalpur.

'I say, if you can get a car here in this weather, I believe you could get mine to England. My wife and I have always wanted to make that journey.'

'What's your car?'

'A Chevrolet. I've had it some years.'

'When are you thinking of going?'

'My leave starts in April. We'd need a fourth person.'

'April! That's settled. I'll find someone. *I'll be there!*'

I took the train back to Calcutta and cashed in my steamer ticket to London. It had to be returned to the office in Victoria that sold it before I could be reimbursed. I left the garden-party hat as a present for Avis, who had rather envied it, and tried to recompense Madurai for all the agony I had caused him, and then caught the steamer for Singapore.

*

To account for this job in Malaya I must go back to a dawn departure from Angkor, in a bus far inferior to the coach which had brought me here and in which I was seated at the back among the mailbags. On one of these was lying what looked like John the Baptist in a much worn linen suit.

The reason for my lowly position on the bus was due to a sordid scene the previous evening when, having kept so severely within my limited means, I believed I had saved enough to have a beer with my meal, and asked for my hotel bill before dinner to know how far I could relax. I was soon drinking plain water. I had miscalculated; it was not a week I had been here *en pension* but eight days. I was not a piastre in hand but six piastres short, and met the debt, to the proprietor's fury, with Siamese coins but at such a high rate of exchange it left me once again penniless. I told the small porter he had better let me carry my own case to the bus. He smiled and put it on a seat in the vagabond enclosure.

Darkness had barely turned to day before the prophet among the sacks woke and asked me what nationality I was, a southern American accent at once betraying his own. From that stage we advanced rapidly to religion, youthful repressions, personality conflicts and dreams being the expression of one's ego. I was handed a card which looked as if the last time his linen suit was washed the card had been in the pocket. It read: *Kilton R. Stewart: Psychoanalyst.*

I had never met one before, knew nothing of Otto Rank in Paris, of whom Stewart was a disciple, but was interested hearing of his life shared between public institutions and solitary expeditions, when he carried out research among such as the hairy Ainus of northern Japan, the head-hunters of Formosa and the Negritos of the Philippines. Talking to Stewart, one learnt that the answers to many present-day problems were to be found in the study of primitive cultures.

This type of conversation went on with only slight pause for a frontier which was no obstacle to the vagabonds, the one having no money to change, the other no luggage. It continued while we shared my packet of lunch owed to me on the *en-pension* terms from the Seamreap hotel, a lunch I had offered to sacrifice in trying to meet my bill. Very rightly, the proprietor had said it was not worth six piastres; it was certainly inadequate to feed two people, one of whom, with faultless white teeth, had also a voracious appetite. Sadly I watched a second orange being skinned, but it was being skinned for me.

'When did you last see food?' I asked.

'Oh, a day or two ago, I guess. I didn't have much time at Angkor this time.'

'Angkor! Where did you stay?'

'Why, at the temple.' This was said in a voice of one asking, where else?

126

Three times in his life, I now learnt, he had visited Angkor, getting a rickshaw boy to bring him out food; this last time he had only got there the previous night. Pilgrims of the old school were evidently not extinct.

I now learnt he was going to Bangkok to find his luggage, which had got carried on by mistake to Saigon. He seemed in the habit of losing it, but this time it had been lost over some days. 'I haven't even got a clean shirt!' he protested.

Ah! What had inspired me to bring that gift shirt with me to Angkor? I got it out now and showed it to him; we agreed to meet for dinner when we would both have been to a bank. 'And you'll know if the shirt fits you,' I added.

'All second-hand clothes fit me,' he said. He wore it at dinner.

Payment for the shirt helped me over the remaining night and day in Bangkok, and I certainly had a more penetrating view of the city, exploring it with Kilton Stewart. We climbed a many-tiered stupa from whose dome a flexible wire ladder reached to the top of a tall pinnacle rising from the dome. No doubt to climb this ladder to the top was a penitential exercise for erring Buddhists to expatiate sin. It hung outwards in a dangerous curve over the abyss below, yet Stewart had to climb it. He had done it before and wished to prove he could do it again, but twice during the climb it turned over, so that he was hanging under rather than breasting it, while I realized I knew nothing of his address or family contacts should there be a tragedy. A crowd had gathered below. He got to the top.

Less dangerously, we explored Chinese second-hand stores selling hot-water bottles, ironmongery and oil stoves, but at the back of these shops were rare pieces of Chinese porcelain, and I learnt that amongst his lost luggage Stewart had valuable carved ivory, jade and Oriental knives. The steamer bringing his luggage, he had discovered, had run aground on an island in the river and he was bound to stay in Bangkok until the tide had lifted it. Otherwise he would have come on the night train I was catching back to Penang, and got off at Taiping. There he was joining Pat Noone, the Government ethnologist in Malaya, and they were going on an expedition into the jungle, studying an interesting group of aborigines. Maybe if I cared to wait he could get me on to it; it would surely be useful for a writer seeking copy.

I thought so too, but doubted the Government ethnologist would hire me solely on the strength of having a typewriter, moreover one so old that it had been forgotten in the USA that made it. 'That's a cute little machine you have,' Americans would say. I told Stewart of my date in Calcutta that I could not at any price relinquish, and added that from there I hoped to motor home. Stewart sat pulling at his beard. 'Well, that's the way I'll make for home, if I go at all. But I never make promises.' Thus we sat scheming with I think not more than £18 between us.

Stewart saw me to my third-class sleeper on the train, and in the moment of departure I was asked my address in Calcutta. Twenty-seven, The Ramparts, Fort William. I had no expectation of hearing from him; something else or someone else would soon be diverting this attractive rogue, whom I saw only as a showman, womanizer and bold adventurer but nevertheless interesting companion. Open-handed and full of good will as he was, I would not at that time have put much reliance on him. Mrs Seddon had enjoyed defeating the impossible; Stewart simply did not recognize it.

As the doors began slamming and whistles sounding, Stewart moved down the corridor murmuring, 'Twenty-seven the Ram's Parts, Fort William.'

*

The letter from Stewart that came to The Ramparts told me the jungle expedition had been postponed as he and Noone were attending an archaeological conference in Singapore. No salary could be offered, but if, for experience, I cared to give secretarial help, Noone would be glad of it, and I would have no expenses once I had joined the expedition.

In this letter I traced the influence of Pat Noone, whom I had heard about but never met. He was the Government ethnologist in Malaya and had become more or less the Member of Parliament for the aborigines, the only white man to speak their langauge. With Noone's backing I was ready to take ship to Singapore.

They had been there for some time. Stewart had walked into a nest of people wanting to be psychoanalysed and was now getting free of his patients, the Rankian method being quicker than the Freudian. The work was delaying him yet a week, so Noone had gone ahead to prepare for the expedition and I did some preparatory study at the Raffles museum. We were staying with the curator of the museum and his family.

Thus Stewart, whose finances had been at low ebb when I met him, was now rich. Wealth came to him as easily as it left him, and whether absent or present was unimportant to him. Since people are rich or poor, not according to their means but to their anxiety in spending, Stewart was one of the richest men in the world. He obeyed to the letter 'Take no heed for the morrow . . .', which may be very creditable but was sometimes inconvenient for fellow travellers. Stewart made a further revelation at a cocktail party at the Tanglin Club swimming-pool to which we were all invited: that he was an elder of the Mormon Church.

This was a crowning discovery. I had learnt something of Mormon history while in America: of their being ousted from one place to another across the States till they made their last stand in the deserts of Utah, turning them into habitable country. As a descendant of two families prominent in this history, Stewart had a hundred and thirty-four first cousins, and a grandfather who went to Mexico rather than give up his four wives when Utah was joined to the States and became monogamous. America now rather esteemed these law-abiding citizens, but Stewart in a life of roaming appeared to have violated most of the Mormon abstentions, and it was now a supreme jest that in his early years he had gone on the foreign mission that establishes an elder. Yet in the following months I was to be in his company, I had time to discover this often exasperating companion was genuinely Christian.

I told Kilton of the nearly completed road party setting out in April for England, and he was keen to join us so, rather wondering how he would integrate with the Scottish couple – who might themselves have found a fourth passenger by now – I wrote them the news before we disappeared into the jungle.

Pat had chosen a not too remote village of Temiar Senoi, the group they were studying, to work on a treatise with the subject-matter right there before them. The village stood in a small cultivated clearing, and two minutes' walk brought one to the Korbu river, our bathroom and our swimming-pool. The jungle formed a barrier between us and the world, a barrier through which we had come on elephants. In this village, elephant-driving was a talent common to all, learnt at the age at which one learns to bicycle. Elephants and their mahouts were as cheap then to hire as a taxi. We had three, all females and wonderfully considerate. Left to play about outside, as they were, they would pull down a branch from a tree and fan themselves like Victorian dowagers, but never disturbed, or ate, the roof of a house.

The Temiar houses stood high off the ground, neat structures of inter-laced rattan thatching with a flooring of split bamboo. They could be built in a day, and one was built now, adding to a small colony outside the village, to be used by Pat. The one I occupied had an upstairs bedroom with a balcony, and below at ground level were a plank table and seat – in fact our office and dining-room. It had been there some time, and only rocked when an elephant scratched its shoulders against the balcony. For six weeks we lived here within sight of that Temiar down-river group; for six weeks time was only indicated by night and day, by hunger or fatigue, and only my faithful reporting in my diary showed us the progress of the year.

Jungle life was not what I had expected. I had visualized tents, semi-darkness, boiled water to drink and little chance of washing till April. Instead, hot water and early morning tea were brought me each day by Puteh, Pat's Malay servant, while beer, ginger beer, tongue, curries and a gorgonzola cheese were amongst supplies carried on the elephants' backs to sustain us.

Our days were largely spent collecting and sorting data while I typed to the dictations of Kilton and Pat. Kilton seemed to work best in the horizontal; lying flat on the bench, he gave dissertations containing words like *physiological palaeolithic* and *schizothymic*, words often outside the scope of my dictionary, and I was glad of that barrier of jungle which prevented me from being sacked.

Pat generally wrote his treaties in longhand and then dictated it to me; in his reading aloud was a quality that reminded me of Father Austin. His treatise showed the relationship, in this Temiar group, between dreams, dance and philosophy. They had a certain dance to expiate anxiety, which seemed to me a good way of dealing with this generally unhelpful emotion. They gave us nightly opportunity to study all their dancing.

When the petrol lamps had been lit in our own camp (and immediately swathed in moths), flares would be seen in a long empty house in the village – the village hall. Then the drum would start beating, the villagers would arrive, the women mostly seated on the floor but sometimes joining in, and the vigour of this religious dancing, which carried on well into the night, was certainly superhuman. I put it down to the drum.

Often I tried to beat that hollow log with a python-skin stretched across it, but in the hands of the Temiar it became stirring and alive. I still carry in my memory the tiny, busy noises and the screech of a victim that unite in a great wall of jungle sound, but particularly I remember the throb of that drum.

Village life in the jungle had echoes of village life at home. Local flora and fauna supplied most of the hand-made furnishings, but in some houses there would be empty tins and refuse of the modern world. There existed also a fraternity, a moral obligation that one hoped no sophistication would destroy. Pat told me no instance of suicide had ever been brought to his notice, and there was a communal attitude in distributing agricultural produce to all members, including those mentally or physically handicapped, of which there were quite a few. Here in fact was the sort of commune that David had hoped to build with the Wild Geese, but failed.

We owed our friendly reception to Pat. Among the Malays, who are their rivals, the aborigines have an evil reputation, and the Chinese traders in their shop-houses on the edge of the jungle, who extort much for sarongs, knives, salt and cooking-pots, often find their shops burnt down in consequence. The Temiar looked on me as a woman of property, for their jewellery and currency were the small Czechoslovakian brightly coloured beads with which Pat and Kilton had come well stocked from a store in Singapore. In Arizona, Mrs Shadbolt had given me a belt at the trading post of the Hopi Indians, a solid leather belt with a handsome pattern of these beads imposed on it which I continually wore at the top of my slacks. The

Temiar girls, passing our camp to fetch water, could not resist fingering it as I sat typing.

*

Meanwhile, in the jungle we were cushioned from news of increasing hostility in Europe until about ten days before leaving, when a white man riding an elephant crashed in upon the village, as surprised to see us as we were to see him. Pat knew him; he had come from Ipoh, using a compass and the river as guide, and hoping his supplies would last until he reached upper Kalantan. He was therefore not averse to stopping a night with us, and when he learnt how long we had been here: 'Good Heavens!' he said. 'You people won't know Germany has marched in to Austria!'

It was strange to hear those tidings, stale by several days, in the heart of an aboriginal community; it made this community seem mature compared with later civilizations. Here too it was difficult to realize the implications; not till we reached Penang did it have direct bearing on our lives.

On the twenty-fourth of March we broke camp, which gave the same anxiety in anticipation as landing after a long sea voyage. All the trouble of the world awaited. As morning advanced, white linen suits appeared like blossoms flowering after rain, and after seeing them so long in trunks I had difficulty in recognizing my employers. Departure was timed for dawn and took place at midday, by which time we were mounted and there were elephants moving with that leisurely stride that covers the ground so quickly. Trailing creepers grabbed at our clothing and tweaked off my linen cap, and all my appeals to the moving elephant had no effect; but Puteh on the elephant following put up a hand and fetched it down.

I had been learning the elephant language, a vocabulary of about thirty words which produced different forms of action. The smallest child in our village had only to say *prap* to an elephant for it to stand close to a house while the occupant climbed on its back from the balcony. But when I said *prap* to an elephant nothing happened at all. Nor when I said *hoh* on losing my cap did the elephant cease from walking. It was ironical therefore that when we were elephant-ankle deep in the widest river crossing, and I was learning by repetition the word *gulin*, which means 'lie down' that the elephant should elect to obey me. I am unlikely to forget that word, for the elephant took it literally.

The animal stopped, and the horizontal matters on which we sat began to incline. I had no words for correction and felt like a motorist in a runaway car with no brake. How nearly were our linen suits saturated, but a lot of language from the little mahout averted disaster.

Where the jungle thinned out was a Chinese shop-house and the beginnings of a road, also Pat's car, ordered for this date six weeks ago. It had

131

been waiting about five hours. We drove to his house in Taiping, from which point he was shortly to set out on another expedition, and Kilton and I had to start for Calcutta.

The luggage Kilton had retrieved from the river was horrendous, several cases containing carved jade among mental tests, daggers among shirts, and quite a respectable dinner-jacket but no trousers. However, Noone subscribed an unwanted pair of trousers to go with it, for my two employers were much the same shape. All this I helped to sort and pack, for I was determined we should catch the steamer for Calcutta sailing in two days' time. We had no sooner got it all battened down than a large parcel arrived for Kilton from Singapore. Thinking it was a typescript, he was all for sending it on to this publishers. I was more sceptical and opened it. It was his laundry left behind in Singapore.

Kilton had none of that busy forethought generally noticeable in travellers, yet like the great Orient about us, by a series of accidents he seemed to arrive at results. Noone sent us in his car to the Penang ferry. Had the ship sailed at the scheduled hour we would have missed it, but having caught it there seemed no cause for all this haste.

On board was a letter for me from the Scotsman, written to catch us at Penang in case it should alter our plans. Since the capitulation of Austria there was a war panic and it was now impossible to obtain car papers for crossing central Europe. He and his wife were anxious to get their leave before war broke out, so they were going home by air. In fact the letter as good as said the car journey was out of the question.

We had been talking of this journey with an old sea pilot who was going to Calcutta as a passenger. When I revealed the contents of the letter, we sat utterly deflated. To soothe us the old man reminded us it was a terrible journey. There was a young lady killed only the other day, he had read in the paper. She was driving to London. A Swedish lady; he thought she was a Countess.

'Not a Baroness? Not the Baroness von Blixen Finecke?'

'It seems to me it was a name like that. It seems she was driving at night and went over the edge of the Bund into the Euphrates, then in flood. Her passenger was flung out, but she was pinned down under the car and drowned.' Kilton and I looked at each other across the table.

It had been arranged for Kilton to stay at Fort William until departure, which now appeared to be not so soon. It was possible with long waits and much discomfort to reach England by bus: I had gone into this on first reaching Calcutta. It was still possible to reach England by car via the North African coast, taking a ferry across to France and Spain, and Kilton with his profound faith saw no difficulty in buying a second-hand car and taking this route. If we could find reliable companions, well and good, but if not he believed we could do it on our own money.

I had had my quarterly Indian Military sent to Calcutta, and the money returned on my Calcutta to London steamer ticket had now arrived from Vancouver. I also had the handsome sum for my article on driving to Gopalpur. Kilton had, fast dwindling, the money he had made in Singapore. He also had a sublime faith that money owed to him was going to be waiting at Baghdad. Yet the second week in April found us still grasping at straws, and the telephone humming with the agonies of the secretary of the AA. He was urging us to amalgamate with a party going to England in a specially fitted station-wagon under an ADC from Government House. It proved, perhaps luckily for the ADC, that his numbers were already made up. I learnt later they followed about a fortnight behind us; no one was interested in their experiences but they kept hearing about the optimists in a 1925 car.

We were anxious to get cross the face of India – 1,500 miles – before it got hotter. We had to get visas in Delhi, as the necessary consults lived there and very soon they would be moving with the Government up to Simla in the hills, and we would have to chase up there after them. Added to this, the rapidly approaching Easter holiday was this year preceded by a Hindu holiday, so shops and offices would be closed for almost a week. And on Good Friday Avis and Deric were going on leave to the Nilgiris, hoping to shut down Number twenty-seven and send their servants on holiday.

*

On Tuesday morning before the holiday there was an advertisement in the paper offering a second-hand Studebaker with new tyres and battery for £30. It was a high, strongly built touring two-seater with a dicky seat at the back, out of range of the hood; a car of character as well as antiquity. Registered in India in 1929, it had belonged to a single owner who now, on leaving had sold it to the garage that had always tended it. No one knew its age, but the Studebaker agency in Delhi revealed to us eventually that it was a 1925 model.

We took a few turns up and down the street; the engine made a noise like a threshing-machine but ran sweetly. We got the inclusion of a second spare rim and tyre, and bought it. The garage proprietor, a burly Englishman deeply anxious we should succeed in our venture, had his hair in a bun at the nape of his neck, fastened with a hairpin. My journeys seemed often to depend on unorthodox characters, but I always found them pillars of strength, not least this Samson.

A mechanic from the AA office examined the car and was satisfied, and the AA secretary, seeing we now had all means for committing suicide, made out our *carnet de passage* and customs papers.

Tuesday was like a bottleneck through which a number of ingredients had to pour; we had to pay for the car, pay the deposit money on it – to be retrieved in England – and sign the deed of purchase. It was sensible to pay with my money, already in rupees, but the bank was shutting at four o'clock. Oriental arguments kept delaying me, but it was Occidental adherence to ruling that insisted I must have my brother-in-law's signature for the withdrawal of my money. This would not be possible before the bank closed, not to open again for three days, so I played the final card I had sometimes found useful. I burst into tears. On a hot afternoon in a crowded bank, the last thing a clerk wants on his hands is a weeping woman, and my cheque was cashed. I now had just ten minutes to reach the licence office, where Kilton and Samson had put many wheels in motion. They worked hard those British police officers, all other business set aside. Even tea was brought me while I signed my last signatures and while Kilton listened to stories of what frontier tribes do to their captives. Down near Calcutta, the Afghan route was viewed with suspicion, and it had been the last straw when I wrested from the AA the Afghan route rather than the one by Baluchistan.

The last rays of Tuesday saw us buying the maps of the Indian Survey department giving the route between The Khyber and Baghdad and finally getting a store of provisions before everything closed.

During the holiday many adjustments were made to the car, including guards along the running-boars for carrying extra cans of petrol. Samson volunteered some of the work and subscribed a St Christopher badge. His long hair, we learnt, had no religious significance; he just never seemed to cut it, and it was news to him that Mormons were a religious sect. 'Oh, I always thought Mormons didn't believe in God. I can't understand people like that.' Spanner in hand, he indicated the surrounding garage filled with disembowelled lorries. 'Why I just see Him everywhere.'

Throughout this time, hospitality at The Fort had been constant support: refreshment of an evening on the lawn of The Ramparts, cooling dives in the swimming-pools of expensive clubs to which the army had access and to which we were eligible as guests. A generous colonel had loaned us an idle car, without which we could never have got through our business on time.

The gift of a water tank, with a tap, fitted neatly on to a running-board, and held water for washing and the radiator. Drinking-water we carried in bottles that replenished, as we drank it, the water from the desert water-bags. I had bought the first of these bags at a filling-station in the California desert. The Shadbolts could not think why I wanted it, and at that point I hardly dared disclose the reason even to myself. Now came a time when nothing ever tasted sweeter, or cooler, than a pull from a desert water-bag. Kilton insisted on a spotlight, which seemed an extravagance, but a brilliant moveable light proved its worth in the end. What we really lacked were spare parts.

We had decided to get these at the Studebaker agency in Delhi, but the chaos in Delhi was such that the whole tour was in jeopardy and extra costs were mounting to a point where we could not spare the money for them. Against emergency we had only a length of rope, a puncture outfit and a couple of heavy-duty levers.

On the afternoon of Good Friday, Avis and Deric left by sea for the Nilgiris and we left after dinner the following evening. We came down amid much ribaldry to where the car stood ready-packed, but certainly not overloaded. We had despatched all our cumbersome luggage by sea, retaining each a camp roll and a modest case with the barest condescension to better clothing. Our provisions, with contributions from Twenty-Seven, were stored in a relatively cool deep recess behind the front seat. Kilton had retained a tent used on scientific expeditions, which could either be sold or in which, if we were bankrupt, he could set up a clinic. For much the same reason I retained my typewriter.

We turned on the car lights; the back light didn't function. Someone gave it a kick; it came on and never gave trouble again. At last the engine fired. Everyone said 'Ah!' and the doubts and hopes of the past week ended in exit, under our own power, through Plassey Gate, from The Ramparts, Fort William. It was the fifteenth of April 1938.

April–June 1938

TRAVELS IN BAKER

We came to call the Studebaker 'Baker', which was somehow expressive of its plodding advance that never exceeded forty miles an hour. With twenty-seven horsepower it could climb at any angle but could barely outstrip wild dogs that rushed barking at its wheels. The stark metal clutch and brake controls were not only hot to the feet but worn so smooth our feet tended to slide off them. Worst of all, Baker had detachable rims, lifting off with the tyre and taking all Kilton's muscular strength to get them back in position. I once saw Kilton kick Baker.

The hood shielded us from the sun, but an open car exposed us to the heat and we found the side on which the desert water-bag was hanging was so noticeably cooler that, sadly as it impeded lateral vision, we bought more and hung them along each side under the hood, bags which swayed with the motion of the car, causing Baker to resemble some prehistoric mammal. These bags gently dripped, but the slow evaporation through the wet canvas kept the water always cool.

On the other hand, Baker's generous front seat made it possible for whichever of us was not driving to lie over sideways and sleep in tolerable comfort, and this we did in turns all the way to Benares. Not only that, but Baker got us home. Or did we get Baker home? Certainly we all arrived together, by which time we were proud rather than apologetic about Baker's years, had grown to appreciate the finer points of this grand old veteran.

During those first days we hardly spoke; temperatures rose to 118 and 120 degrees Fahrenheit. It was difficult to keep awake; the mind would go wandering off, and I always knew when Kilton's mind was wandering as he started driving on the right side of the road. We were not in training; The Ramparts had softened us, and we wasted money stopping at railway stations to buy ice, which we stored in a Thermos and mixed with drinks of lime juice. In about five days, however, we were independent of lime juice; the cool water from the bags with its faintly canvas taste was all we needed, our desires growing fewer, our vocabulary in Hindi increasing. We belonged to the road, and there were still 9,487 miles ahead.

That road reaching across India from Calcutta to the Khyber was a good one, chiselled by a conqueror from Bengal marching against the Moguls.

136

Frequently planted with shade-giving trees, it consisted of a smooth strip of Tarmac bordered on each side by dust track, but all traffic, save the camel caravans, used the Tarmac. This traffic was mostly bullock waggons, camels and camel carts moving in slow convoy, and there was a similarity of pattern in the villages we passed through: beds out in the streets, pies of cow dung on the mud walls drying out for fuel, and a cluster of trees and splash of turquoise tiling marking where an Indian temple stood beside its artificial pond. The exception was the orderly little state of Chandarnagar with its huge Latin church and boundary wall inscribed *Vive la France*, an island of French colonization, also sanctuary for persons escaping British justice.

Early on Easter Day we reached Benares, where all the features of Indian towns enveloped us: fast-trotting pony carriages, Indians carrying tin trunks on their heads, the brown-legged water-carrier with his water-skin on his back, holy men on pilgrimage and inevitably the sacred Brahminee bull that wanders at will, often lying down in the street and a source of trouble to anyone who injured it. All along this route, in towns and villages, there would be women with bundles or pitchers of water on their heads, so graceful their carriage, their skirts swaying in tune to their measured walk. In all my journey I saw few to compare with the young Indian women for grace and dignity of movement.

Benares was made memorable for us by Mr Das, a clerk at the General Post Office, to which we went, hopeful for letters, to find it was shutting down for Easter Day. We asked where we could find a guide and Mr Das volunteered to come himself. Hastily we made it clear we had no money for a human guide, we were hoping for a map or leaflet, but Mr Das, who had been scrutinizing Baker, said he would come not as a guide but as one who loved adventure and would like to help other adventurers.

Thus we had a more penetrating view of Benares than a crowded city rising steeply from the Ganges, crowned by the palaces of the ruling Princes, while at river-level pilgrims washed themselves free of sin, and the still smouldering ashes of the dead were raked into the river after the mechanical ritual of Burning Ghat: bodies bound in white, laid on wooden stretchers on the pyres, a priest saying a benediction and the wife laying the first brand to the pyre.

After Mr Das had shown us the finest temples and taken us to the excavations at Sarnath, where Gauama Buddha had preached, he found us a cool and modest place for lunch, but would not eat with us though it was not Ramadan. Then he bartered with a boatman to take us down the river. Kilton had elicited from him that he was a Brahmin, a member, in fact, of the highest Hindu caste, and in an effort to repay his kindness we finally invited him to tea, but even this gesture of gratitude miscarried. Our guide took us to the tea house of a friend, who made a present of the tea, and Mr

Das ate and drank nothing in our presence all day. When afterwards he asked if we would go to his house, we were rather curious to do so.

We now penetrated a far more native quarter of the city, where no traffic plied, so Baker was left under the surveillance of our tea host. We followed a series of galleries under whose straw canopies sat musicians playing stringed instruments. Then we turned up a narrow alley past cupboard shops with a diversity of wares and smells, and an open door revealed a gyrating bullock in the process of milling. We met policemen walking three abreast since recent disturbances in Benares.

Thus we reached the house of Mr Das, and after a day in the company of an educated man, not poor by Indian standards, we were quite unprepared for the scarcity, the emptiness, the complete lack of household ambition within his home. It was not poverty so much as austerity.

By the light of a candle we were shown into a room where his young wife received us shyly, served us with water in small brass bowls and with sweet cakes that her husband slipped out to buy after opening up the house. His wife spoke no English, indeed we never heard her speak at all. Her sari and her bracelet were the only vanities in what seemed to be a two-roomed house empty of furniture. She sat discreetly on the floor a little distance from us while her husband apologized that they had no more to offer, but he did not like his wife to go marketing alone. We were only regretting that he had gone to the expense of the cakes.

He had now lit a lamp and spread a carpet on the balcony, where the air was cooler than within, but perhaps less spent. Here we talked and indeed the mind is keener when it is the sole resource of interest. Where were the books from which he gleaned his knowledge? Were they solely the tomes one saw students studying in the courtyards of the temples? Where would he keep a book save on the floor? We could not satisfy our curiosity without implying criticism. Even Kilton refrained from questioning. Nor indeed did we feel critical, rather more we felt penitent. This invitation had been a final courtesy. I can only hope that after we left they went out, bought food, and settled down to a solid meal.

*

At Cawnpore, some two hundred miles beyond Benares, we turned off the Grand Trunk Road to visit Lucknow. My desire to see the old Residency here was inspired by a diary belonging to my family in which Mrs George Huxham, my great-aunt and wife of a then Lieutenant in the Indian Army, recorded her experiences when confined in the Residency during the Siege of Lucknow. In such phrases as *How proud we felt of our dear countrymen ... they were so brave, so forgetful of themselves in their fatigue*, she gives a record of scarcity, endurance and death-bed scenes in which so many are commended for their bravery and patience that her own courage is completely obscured. *Oh, what an anxious group we were gazing at the flames and volumes of smoke which were causing destruction in our pretty station. ... Sweet baby is bright and healthy, and as long as my children are well I seem not to realize the dangers besetting us.*

So I now visited the scene where my great-aunt had lived with her family on half a pound of meat a day, about what Kilton and I were sharing, but at least our diet was voluntary. The Residency with its shattered walls was now a museum standing in a garden on the slight eminence that had given advantage to the besieged. The museum contained history of the siege that lasted four and a half hot-weather months until relief came under Sir Colin Campbell. The garrison had dwindled from 700 to 900 men; Lieutenant Huxham himself was wounded. A flag now flew from the Residency tower, the only Union Jack never to descend at sunset. I doubt it is flying now, or even if the museum exists.

With infinite trust in God and authority, those women must have been admirable subjects to command; their needs at best were few, no yearning for cigarettes or drinks. I am not suggesting our own generation would not have shown equal endurance, but would they have submitted to being blown up by their own kind while the men fought to an honourable finish? News from Cawnpore had made this a consideration.

I recognized the cellar where Miss Campbell died after the amputation of her leg. *The limb was so nearly severed by the ball there was not much work for the knife to do.* Here was the two hundred yards of open ground across which my great-aunt volunteered to go back under enemy fire, because many necessities had been left behind, when the mothers and children were ordered from the overcrowded cellar to the Brigade Square.

I found in the corner of the grounds a rose garden where there were a number of graves, including one tiny white stone cross sacred to the memory of Ellen Frances, beloved child of Lieut. and Mrs G. C. Huxham. This was 'sweet baby'. She died on the ninth of August 1857 during the Siege of Lucknow.

Dawn found us looking at another tomb, also white, also the expression of great devotion; its lily whiteness changed to palest pink as we walked up the gardens towards it and moonlight gave place to dawn – a wonderful introduction to the Taj Mahal.

When we had left Calcutta, moonlight was flooding The Ramparts and I was to see the Taj in moonlight too. This we had achieved, reaching Agra in the small hours, and we made out the dim pile rising before us was the great entrance gate to its garden. A night-watchman who was awake opened a tiny door in the big door, through which we entered, and in that pale light an ethereal, lace-like beauty enveloped the Taj, and utter stillness reigned. It was like walking through a dream.

139

We saw it in all its phases: the lily of the dawn, the brilliant creature of day, and finally the dreaming Taj of moonlight. It is a great piece of stagic scenery dominating the water garden leading up to it, while behind it flows the Jumna river but at a much lower level so the Taj stands like a sentinel on a cliff commanding river and plain. In the crypt lie the bodies of Shah Jehan and his beloved wife.

We were now among the chief cities of the Mogul conquerors, those dramatic kings who loved their wives and imprisoned their fathers, burying them afterwards in splendour. They drew from the areas they ruled greater revenue than comes from the land today and their architecture happily has survived, of which the Taj Mahal is not the finest example. There is the Pearl Mosque in Agra fort. The silken quality of its stone and the phasing of its arches need to be seen; they do not pose for photography. And marble inlaid with semi-precious stone reaches a superlative in Shah Jehan's palace in Delhi. Columns and ceiling in the Private Audience Hall were like an illuminated manuscript, with inlaid flower patterns on marble the colour of parchment. The confidence of the era is inlaid in Urdu: 'If there be a Paradise on earth, it is this, it is this, it is this.' I may also add that, as it is not in the Oriental nature to repair, it was thanks to Lord Curzon and succeeding Viceroys that these treasures were saved, cleaned, repaired and at that moment before the Second Word War were in their prime.

It was our habit in India to drive in turn through the night and spend the hottest part of the day in any large railway station, since the Grand Trunk Road was never far distant from an accompanying railway line. Junctions had sahib-reserved rest rooms with a bathroom, electric fans and cane sofas on which one could comfortably sleep. There would be for me an attendant ayah, who would wash clothing for a small bequest, and I scarcely recognized Kilton emerging form his quarters, his beard trimmed to an imperial; it suited him well. There was little competition at the hour that we called at these junctions but I doubt if authority knew we were not train passengers. If we stopped in towns we stayed at the Dak bungalows – formerly rest houses for the mail carriers. They supplied all needs, save bedding and food, but were apt to be crowded.

In contrast to our modest living expenses, the petty cash took eccentric leaps, which was the result of travelling with a philanthropist. The only hope for us, and he admitted it, was for me to hold the money. Kilton was unconcerned about spending, not merely income but entire capital, which was at that moment a rapidly dwindling sum with hope of a further sum awaiting him in Baghdad. Instead of pondering the hiatus between Delhi and Baghdad, he was concerned only with how to support the beggar population of the countries through which we passed, and how to give every pedestrian a lift.

140

Invariably when I went to sleep while Kilton drove, on waking I would find another pedestrian stuffed into, or beside, our dicky seat; and, on one occasion, that with our front bumper rail we were pushing a lorry which had run out of petrol. We were a sort of goodwill bus service, and I contended, not without cause, that all this philanthropy increased the likelihood of breakdown. Baker actively supported the view. Yet, for the conditions under which we were travelling, I came to see merit in Kilton's attitude, for we may have suffered a few punctures – even a broken spring – in giving aid, but as much as we gave we certainly were given in return. Not perhaps always from those who benefited, but it all equalled up in the end; otherwise we should have felt we were owing a big debt. The wilder the road became the greater the chivalry shown. Either in enthusiasm for our venture, pity for our dire economy, or just out of courtesy, we would be given free meals or presents that we came to find invaluable. Kilton's philosophy was not unreasonable.

*

Delhi and all the area around it is like a museum of tombs, monuments and cities, either buried or standing, built by succeeding conquerors and dynasties, and the Grand Trunk Road brought us dramatically to the Kutb Minar, the tower of victory built by the invading Mohammedans. The British were still constructing New Delhi, largely the work of Lutyens and Herbert Baker, but at the moment looking like a world exhibition in the making. The more tree-full civilian quarters were north-west of the Red Fort, the city of the Moguls.

It was the morning of the twenty-third of April when we arrived in Delhi and the migratory season of going up to the hills had already begun, but not with that orderliness that characterizes bird migration. Many officials were already in Simla, some on their way, while the Government of India would not be leaving for a fortnight. We hoped our Consuls were still remaining, but that was too much to expect. We had to secure visas for Palestine, Iraq, Iran and Afghanistan, in that order, as no visa could be obtained until we had one for the next country ahead.

We secured visas for Palestine and Iraq, issued in one, at the office of the Chief Commissioner in Delhi, and learnt the Afghan visa would be issued at its frontier, but only if we had the visa for Persia – as Iran was then universally called. But we found the Persian Consulate shut, and were told by a clerk that the consul had gone up to Simla.

There was no point in reaching Simla before Monday so we improved our minds around Delhi until Sunday evening and then resumed our road northward to Amballa. Here we turned off for Simla in the foothills of the

Himalayas, to find next day the Consul was not in Simla; he appeared to be lost, a matter of apparent indifference to all but ourselves.

Air-conditioning was later to render these migrations unnecessary, but we were victims of a disorganization occurring biannually when administration had one foot in Delhi and the other on pine-clad hills, where there was little room for office expansion and no wheeled traffic, only an expensive type of rickshaw. Four men were needed for a carrying chair on those heights, and cars had to be parked on a shelf below the level of the town. Here a horde of guides hovered like vultures. We asked a policeman for the Persian Consulate; he handed us to a guide, who charged a tall sum for taking us to a not-far-distant travel bureau, where neither clerk nor telephone was helpful. Thus started our tribulation in Simla, but at least the air was cooler and we had shelter for three nights with relatives of the cousin in Burma.

Now for the first time in India I had reached ground where I had been before, but not remembered, for Simla was my birthplace. It had then been an agreeable hill station but in the intervening years had become a complex where everyone seemed to be standing on his own toe. I felt apologetic about it to Kilton and, exhausted by the general struggle, we paused a while to requite our souls in the church where I was christened. Army Headquarters appeared to be the fount of all knowledge, but authority was always protected by a barrage of Indian clerks uninterested in what you wanted, only anxious to know what *department* you wanted, and we had no idea, nor had they. It took us till 11 o'clock of our second morning to find the Persian Consulate, which was empty. The gardener, who spoke no English, unlocked the door on shrouded furniture and enough dust and confusion to assure us the place would not be open for some time. It looked like the funeral of our journey.

The moment called for desperate action. At twelve all offices would again be closing. I left Kilton to have another go at Army HQ while I walked at high speed a good mile to the Afghan Consulate. I hoped to put the case to the Afghan Consul and invoke his aid, but again he was shielded by a clerk who began quoting the rules, so I played the same card that had been so successful in the bank at Calcutta. I put my head in my hands and howled. It was not altogether strategy but rather the despairing cry of a patience exhausted by office constipation.

My tears moved the clerk to fetch the Consul, and for the first time on those heights a cordial hand was held out. This charming old philosopher was our friend to the end; we owed our journey to his readiness to depart from office routine under special circumstances. At this point Kilton joined us from the Office of External Affairs to say he had been advised to wait a week in Simla or go back to Delhi, where they felt sure the Persian Consul must be. Neither of these could we afford to do, and travellers we met later confirmed that the Persian Consul was not in Delhi.

The Afghan Consul now revealed what no one else had told us, that he had to get sanction from Kabul before issuing a visa for Afghanistan. He said he would telegraph Kabul, but as it might take a couple of days, he suggested our driving the 550 miles to the frontier, and as soon as he got sanction he would phone Peshawar and the visas would be granted. He knew there was a Persian Consul in Kabul.

My own authorities considered us foolish to rely on this arrangement, which they felt sure would break down, and I was piqued to discover that this Afghan sanction applied only to the British passport. No doubt I was paying for past conflicts with Afghanistan, and a military permit which I knew I had to get in Peshawar may have been a protection, but Kilton had none of these irritations. He simply had to pay a sum of money for a visa for any country: he did not even have to have an endorsement, whereas each country of Central Asia had to be specifically named in a British passport before visas for such countries could be secured, and in the wide area of India there were few hands empowered to write these names. Small wonder, on studying my passport and finding the names Afghanistan and Persia were missing, that with a hotel pen guaranteed to disguise any handwriting I took matters into my own hand.

Our next stop was Lahore. I would have liked to stay longer in this fine city, the scene of my father's one-time ministrations, but we only gave it a day. On the road leading out of it was an AA sign which pointed in the direction of Quetta and read 'London 6,753 miles'. I don't believe London ever returned the compliment. This was the route through Baluchistan, avoiding Afghanistan but joining our route at Meshed in Persia. It was longer in distance and the going was just as bad.

The wall of the Himalayas had distantly accompanied the Great Trunk Road for many miles, creeping closer at Delhi, and we felt we were on the edge of exciting country as we crossed the five great rivers of the Punjab: Sutlej, Ravi, Chenab, Jelum and Indus. We crossed them either on iron-girt bridges high over the river, or on a pontoon bridge at water-level, the yellow waters now fairly obedient but with a look of brooding strength. The Indus was here joined by the Kabul river and the two flowed together through a deep ravine, the bridge over it heavily guarded and shut at sundown. Snow-clad mountains were looming ahead.

*

Inevitably we reached Peshawar on a Friday and had to wait till next day for the office issuing the visas to open. This was at the top of a long flight of steps, and on each step an Oriental sat patiently waiting. My heart sank. However, a clerk on the balcony above saw us arrive, came down and asked to see our passports and, on reading the names, hurried off upstairs

143

with them. Was this a good sign? It was. A moment later we were ushered before the visa officer and we, who in Simla had been less than dust, were now people of importance.

The Afghan Consul in Simla had not only instructed the granting of our visas, but had written a letter to the Minister of Foreign Affairs in Kabul for us to use in case of any trouble in obtaining the Persian visa. Written in Pushtu, but with a seal, it became a form of *laissez-passer* at various points of our journey.

Now without opposition we secured my military permit, whereon the portals of Afghanistan were open to us; and now, surprisingly, came other attentions. The Office of External Foreign Affairs, which in Simla had been unhelpful, sent an intelligence officer from the same office in Peshawar, calling at our Dak bungalow to ask if we needed any help. Could it be that by turning to the Afghans, we had touched Britain on the raw?

We had yet to get Afghan rupees and the authentic banks were closed till Monday, but each had a shadow bank in the old town observing only the Mohammedan calendar. Here we got a very good exchange, and Afghanistan proved also to be the cheapest country of our journey. This was lucky, as I had now come to the end of my money and must rely on Kilton until Cairo, where I hoped my next quarter's pension would await me. I had also come to the end of my films, but though in Peshawar one could buy a Bokhara rug or a rough-hewn wooden leg, there was not a film less than five years old.

This market where I waited in Baker while Kilton was at the bank, was rich in alluring scenery. Surrounded by narrow, tall buildings of irregular height, it had a slatted covering through which sunlight percolated, throwing a zebra pattern on saddle-bags, on hennaed feet, and on every type of turban, from those loosely piled like a rug on the head to the finest of all, the turban of the Punjabi Mohammedan – nine yards of material swathed around a central peak, the *kullah*. These made a man of any Punjabi, and gave to those of fine physique an almost insolent splendour. There was also a fair sprinkling of frontier tribesmen: Baluchis of strongly Semitic type, Afridis and Waziris – well-knit hill men that I had long heard made excellent soldier under British commanders, living peacefully side by side in barracks but raiding each other as soon as they got back to their hills on leave.

Sitting there in the car, I pondered the likelihood of either Germany or Russia taking over India, had we not already done so; indeed either was still a menace if we should withdraw, as surely we must do soon. In spite of many shameful deeds, we had let India retain her soul, expressed in that humped-backed cow lying down in the road right in front of Baker, and that shrivelled arm thrust into the car in leverage for charity. No imposition here of a standard uniform or official salute; so was India then lucky in her status quo? I could imagine the holocaust if either of those menacing

144

Beatrice Parsons, Claudia's grandmother, at Southbourne with four of her nine sons *c*. 1906

Clement George Parsons, Claudia's father, married Grace Boddam in 1885. All three children were born in India – Grace Junior (Betty) in 1885, Claudia in 1900 and Avis in 1905. He died in September 1912

Claudia's mother, Grace Parsons, before being presented at court, London 1908

Claudia's aunt, Muriel Boddam, known as 'Unnie'. She lived with Claudia's family and helped take care of Claudia and her sisters. Seen here in WAAC's uniform during the First World War, Unnie also served in the Second World War in the WAAC's successor, the ATS

Claudia, aged three, dressed as a clòwn for Lady Curzon's annual children's party, 1903, Simla

Claudia at Southbourne, her grandmother's house. Her hair is just starting to grow back following a bout of ringworm caught from their kitten

Uncle Dick Crawshay

Aunt Tinie

Their home, Scole Lodge, in Norfolk, where Claudia and family spent their summers and where she first developed her passion for cars by learning to drive

Claudia's sister, Avis, in the garden in India, 1909

Claudia's sister, Betty, in her twenties

Claudia in 1927 during the time she was living in Southwold as chauffeur-companion-'daughter' to the seventy-year old Mrs. Robinson. On one occassion they travelled to Morocco together and were nearly shipwrecked en route to Tangier

Claudia in foreground at a Women's Engineering Society dinner in London *c.* 1926, three years after she graduated from Loughborough with a diploma in engineering

Claudia in 1926 posing for a friend who was studying photography

The three sisters. From left: Betty, Avis and Claudia outside the old house, *c.* 1936

Claudia's mother, Grace, right, and 'Unnie', Muriel Boddam, in Wonersh

The dolls' house Claudia made (including everything inside it) for her niece, Heather. She is a skilled craftswoman and last made something in her workshop at the Old House when she was in her late eighties

Claudia in the 1940s at her desk in the Old House around the time of the publication of *Vagabondage*

Claudia at her desk in 1961

The Old House, Wonersh, in the 1940s

Mrs Seddon, in 1937, to whom Claudia acted as chauffeur on many trips in Europe, often in pursuit of religious relics

Baker on one of the many occasions on the journey from India to England when a river had to be crossed

Claudia and Baker in Afghanistan

Kilton afloat in the Dead Sea on Claudia's and his journey from India to England in 1938

Claudia joined Kilton Stewart, an American psychoanalyst (left) and the anthropologist, Pat Noone (right) on a study in the Malayan jungle

Grand Trunk Road across India, 1938

The well at Rutbah, which was also the Iraqi-Syrian border post

Baker had to cross five rivers in the Punjab before reaching Afghanistan

Baker in the Egyptian desert

Baker with a puncture on the road from Alexandria

Claudia beside Baker at a rare roadsign in the desert

Claudia, Kilton and Baker sometimes stayed in caravanserais in Persia and Afghanistan. Baker was always placed with the camels and livestock in the courtyard while Claudia and Kilton hired an alcove for the night

Claudia continued her independent travelling well into her sixties. Here she is heading towards the Arctic Circle in the 'waggon' on a trip made with a fellow member of the Society of Women Engineers

Baker and Kilton outside the Old House at the end of their journey. Kilton Stewart was invited to stay at the Old House at the end of their long journey, where he had to cope with Claudia's family, particularly Unnie, Claudia's aunt

Baker at the end of the trip in 1938 before being sold for £5, finally ending up as a tractor on a farm during the war

powers came up against civil disobedience, which was making India impossible for us to rule. I did not apprehend the blanket of war so soon to envelop us and create universal change. I was thinking more of the Afghan Consul in Simla, and his parting words on hearing that I hoped to write the story of our journey. He begged that I would say nothing that would cause ill feeling between our two countries. 'We are anxious for our people to be friendly towards Britain. We like her as a neighbour. She has enough land of her own. She will not steal ours.'

Peshawar, last city of India, lay on a plain encircled by mountains across which we drove to the gate of the Pass – a mud fort flying the British flag. Ever since entering the north-west frontier at Attock, the country had lived up to all that is implied in the word 'frontier': no isolated houses, only mud villages so tucked into the slope of the hills they looked like part of the soil. Even the birds were all scavengers. The Khyber has since become a tourist attraction so the barracks, watch towers, and regimental crests carved in the rocks by soldiers once billeted here, will be known to many. Its importance to the British was evidenced by the double route along the top of the mountains, one for fast motor and military traffic, the lower one for lorries and caravans.

In addition there existed a railway line and a line of telegraph poles, and it only dawned on me later how consistently we depended on telegraph poles in finding our way. There were few readable signposts, if any, and roads were often more tracks, but I noticed that telegraph poles were conscientiously marked on our Indian survey maps, and not without reason.

It was the first day of May when we reached the Khyber, and from the top of the Pass looked down on Afghanistan and its coloured hills lying below. At the bottom of the Pass we dropped off the end of the good road and were not to see another like that till reaching Lebanon.

It was late afternoon, and a Major in the Guides, who was taking his wife and daughter on a visit to the legation in Kabul, advised us to break the eighty-odd miles to Kabul at Nimla. We saw the sense in this on tackling a road like a dried water-course, and shared with the Major and family the lonely white house set within a garden with high walls, once part of a palace of the Emperor Baber. Roses in the garden and cypresses of great age were a contrast to the hot open country stretching beyond. So were the bed linen, the service and the evening meal a contrast to our normal Dak bungalow experience.

This part of the country was full of suspicion: flat-roofed mud houses with projecting beams were replicas of the adobe houses seen in New Mexico. These, however, had few windows and the front door was upstairs, reached by a ladder that the owner pulled up after him. Scarcely a man among these Bible figures had not a rifle slung across his back, and there was a distressing prevalence of clustered graves.

145

That was near the frontier; Kabul had no city wall and was heralded by a cinema with out-of-date film stars gazing from its walls – part of that emancipation that had been frowned upon and created strong reaction. Yet Kabul reminded us of the increasing difficulty of getting beyond reach of normal life. In a most native quarter of the city, towards midnight, we were in an Afghan tea-house, steam rising from a big samovar and teapots nestling in the charcoal embers. Room had been made for us on the carpets, and a hookah was being passed from mouth to mouth and offered in turn to Kilton. Here I had a feeling I was out of reach of Empire, that anyone searching for me this night would have a job to find me, but for our benefit, and proudly, they turned on the 'wireless' to the Empire programme, and we heard that unctuous voice from the BBC.

*

There was no difficulty in securing the Persian visa in Kabul, but in neither passport was there a page to put it on. For Kilton this was no problem – extra pages were added – but that was far too simple for the British passport. I had to go to the legation and get a new one. Empty, save for the additional visa, it was clamped to the other one, and I have retained this double-decker as a memento, one half issued in London and the other in Kabul. The time taken, however, was not wasted as while waiting I was given a heartening lunch, and Kilton meanwhile had come on a party of American geologists who had also extended hospitality, brought our itinerary up to date and paid a handsome price for Kilton's tent, which had become a burden to us. The money tempted us to visit Bamian, but Baker, since reaching bad road surfaces seemed to be suffering a secret sorrow which deflected us from the idea.

Kabul is crowned by the Bala Hisar, a fort on the hill above it to which a wall climbs steeply; a fort that has seen Tartar, Mongol, Mogul and Persian invasion, and the burning of their handsome covered market as a lesson to the Afghans by the British a century ago. This may have been better than slaughter but was a terrible desecration, and a piece of propaganda useful to the Germans who were in evidence everywhere, building bridges and engineering plants, in payment for which the Afghan government was exporting lapis lazuli from the mines of the Oxus valley.

Only small pieces of this beautiful stone were now being sold, furtively, and I was determined to snatch a piece from the Germans. It was Kilton, turning over sheepskin hides in a market, who came on a silver ring in which a good quality oval stone was precariously mounted. He bought it for a song and gave it to me. In a firmer setting I wear it still; the sincere royal blue is nourishing to look at, and reminds me I was once in a land filled with such colouring and richness.

146

It took us ten days to travel the 900 miles of Afghanistan from the Khyber to Herat on the further border. The map showed a road going due westward through the mountains, but evidently not a motoring road. The itinerary bade us go south to Kandahar, where the mountains give way to the Regestan, a great southern desert. Between mountain and desert the route then took a westerly direction to Girishk, and the crossing of the Helmand river still firmly in spate.

Here the Germans were building a mighty bridge, but it was not yet finished; building material, lorries, humans and animals were scattered along the embankment but the ferry crossing appeared to be private enterprise, under the control of an elderly ferry master enjoying his despotism. He had the eye of a fanatic and with a knotted stick and flow of language was laying about him, consigning animals to ford or swim, according to size, and giving priority to army lorries, which were mounted on the ferry as far as an island only, and made to ford the river the rest of the way. They invariable got stuck so it was not a comforting sight, and the growing conclave at the water's edge guaranteed a long wait. We waited twenty-nine hours.

Luckily there was a tea-house on the bank whose colourful owner took great interest in us, gave us benches to lie on, and for supper, which no doubt paid him well, a gorgeous pilau which to us was worth more than gold. Recently it had been chilly at nights but here it was sultry and clouds obscured the stars, and I lay in jeans and shirt on top of my sleeping-bag, longing for a refreshing thunderstorm to soak us all. Yet in spite of heat, dogs barking, animals coughing, humans spitting and a distant donkey braying, in spite of the bad reputation of lorry drivers all around us, I slept, and it was only my perhaps overzealous guardian angel who woke me on the faint sound of metal on metal. I saw a vague form standing near Baker's intake of petrol, and sprang up growling as in Japan. This woke Kilton, who shone a torch on a retreating figure, and never did man back away in greater alarm, aware that his white robe offered a gleaming target and that aroused sleepers were possibly taking careful aim. He kept making soothing gestures in retreat, but in fact there was no evidence next morning of siphoning, or even of the petrol cap being removed. Indeed nothing was ever stolen from Baker on our journey.

Next day transport of army lorries continued, followed by the governor of the district, whose private car, we were relieved to see, went on the ferry the whole width of the river. However, when other vehicles got taken in preference to the patient Baker, Kilton went and bearded the ferry master, taking the letter from the Afghan Consul. It is doubtful if the ferry master could read it, but crested paper and a seal got us across free of bribery, and only a modest sum was absorbed into the old man's thick wallet at his belt.

147

The landing-board on the far bank had so many broken slats, one might say Baker fell on to the further shore.

Now well, now haltingly, we staggered on from the Helmand river. There were times when the wind would rage, light funnels of dust, miniature typhoons, would go spinning across the land and Baker would run so badly on a route that was merely a track that I began to wonder if we would make it. Close to the mountains of the north there had been belts of verdant country, rich in vegetation, with orchards, with fields of green corn and clover, and banks of wild irises and other flowers beside the road. There were rosy-cheeked women working in the fields; in fact it seemed a paradise after India, making us both feel homesick. It was seven years, Kilton said, since he had smelt a good field of alfalfa.

Here in the south agriculture depended on the tunnel system of irrigation, a trench below surface bringing water from the mountains at an angle of gentle incline to the plains. *Kanats* these were called in Persia, sometimes marked by a series of wells dug down to them like giant molehills across the land. Villages were the soul of simplicity, a row of booths down each side of the street with a communal mud roof over the lot, often with a stork or two on it, and a communal wall extending along the back. The street side would be animated, the back side discouraging and windowless. All Afghans seemed to us to have rosy cheeks.

Our route lay between snow-clad mountains and 'painted deserts' far more extravagant in colour than those of the USA. Both here and in Persia the very rocks were colourful; they appeared to mend the roads with turquoise, not efficacious but beautiful. Often we were the only moving thing on a wide horizon, or there would be flocks battening on sparse vegetation, or distant black tents of the nomad tribes whose savage dogs came challenging us. Finest of all were the graceful camel-caravans winding across the plains; these camels had thick hair on their necks like beards under the chin, hair which conveniently provided halter, tassels and the rope securing the load on their backs.

In spite of these great isolations, our presence in the country was known. We lost a towel we had put out to dry and then forgot; it was returned to us that evening by a lorry-driver. Later, our itinerary, which had blown out of the car, was brought to us by a medieval character with skull cap, bobbed hair and fringe, certain he would find us at that night's halt. Such was the benefit of being unique.

*

We now had a different programme of advance, heat no longer compelled us to drive through the night, nor was there now a railway to provide rest rooms. In Afghanistan rest houses were few and far between and beyond our means. The one in Nimla and the hotel in Kabul had overtaxed the purse, and there was nothing akin to the Dak bungalows, the rest houses of India.

So now we had resorted to the caravanserais constructed for the caravans of livestock passing through the country. India had only squalid examples, for their importance waned where there was a railway service. In Afghanistan and Persia the serais were still a fine ornament of the road with their high brick walls and stout wooden doors, the animals – and Baker – driven into the courtyard, the herdsmen – and ourselves – hiring one of the alcoves in the walls from which one looked down on one's possessions and in which one slept. There would be a communal wash-place with a cold tap, also stone lavatories of great simplicity but generally kept clean. There would be no privacy, but I soon grew adept at dealing with that; after all, I had had my apprenticeship for all this in the Balkans. Sometimes an opportunist would bring a portable charcoal cooker to the gate of the serais and serve kebabs, individually cooked and garnished to taste.

Caravanserais lodged generally near towns; in the country we camped just off the roadside, and at such time our passengers, of whom we had relays, either left us or lay rolled up on the ground. Other foreigners that we met, including the geologists, said they also camped without undue anxiety. There is a certain protection travelling among people who expect you to be armed, but we had of course no firearms at all.

I had my Lilo, and thankfully Kilton had the lungs for blowing it up; I would spread it on the ground, my bedding roll on the top of it, and lie inside or outside according to the temperature. Kilton owned a sheepskin mattress that I felt to be less protective from snakes; however, it was an old friend used over long years. Many people passed by in the night; one heard the rhythmic footfall of camel feet, the sharper gabbling sound of donkey hooves, and there would be the measured swing of the camel bell repeating its melodious stanza, never missing a beat until the notes were lost in distance. May it never die from my memory, the song of that camel bell.

Our tinned food we left in the well of the car in case we got stranded in some desolate place, but soon learnt about *mast*, the sour milk of the camel, said to be medicinal even if one had to remove a layer of dust from its surface, and there was an excellent cheese made from it. *Non*, the Afghan bread, was a wonderful standby, like a giant biscuit, baked in an underground oven, flattened against the walls, and when ready flipped out on the end of a stick and left to cool in the dust. I remember our eating together off one tin plate in a fly-blown kitchen, sausage meat grilled over charcoal and fried with onions – the meal of a lifetime. The only thing to do about flies was to get used to them. We bought dates and dried almonds in the markets, and ate them while driving, and an Afghan doctor sharing a tea-house with us gave us a list of words and phrases and their pronunciation, useful right through to Iraq.

Tea-houses – *Chai Khanas* – now persisted all along our route: mud huts with a thatched verandah and carpets spread under their shade or in the shade of an adjacent poplar grove. There would be a big samovar filled with boiling water and teapots nestling in charcoal embers; the tea was served neat but with lots of sugar. We sometimes camped at these houses.

In all this journey we were both in excellent health, leaving it to our inoculations in Calcutta to keep us fit. We took no pills; most of them were not yet invented. I admit that people looking through my films said I grew progressively thinner, and my flesh was evidently no longer succulent as I was only once bitten, and encountered only one bug, in a cheap Russian hotel in Jerusalem. I marvel at the arsenal of protective pharmacy pre-scribed by present-day travel tours.

On course for Herat, we covered a cruel piece of country: thirty miles without sign of habitation, where small boulders were scattered over the ground with a regularity suggesting evil purpose. Our journey was in fact a study of different types of wasteland that come under the all-embracing term of 'desert'. Yet into this barren region a pedestrian was walking, and it took a hard heart to pass him without offering a lift, though we already had two passengers. He was not improvident; from the corner of his turban he untied his rations, a fistful of dried peas which he offered us to share, and he accompanied us for 170 miles.

He appeared to be a man of importance, inviting us to stop at couple of walled towns beyond the desert. Their gates were too narrow to allow Baker's entry, but he would go in and presently return with the whole population, who would spread carpets on the ground and give us tea. After they had smoked and exchanged a bit of gossip, we would resume our way, and soon we had to be grateful to this passenger. We reached a plain where the telegraph poles deserted us, leaving us to a number of divergent tracks, with a dust-storm brewing. We were guided across the plain and through the storm, meeting the telegraph poles again in the mountains, and finally leaving our passenger in a town seventeen miles short of Herat.

We had paid our respects to what monuments existed along our course but Herat, last city before entering Persia, had been glorious in the Timuirid or Tamarlaine period when Shah Rukh made it his capital. It was then the cradle of craft and miniature painting that spread to India and Persia. Of mosque and college, outside the city, only the minarets remained, leaning precariously and covered in seraphic tiling, and ruined in the defence of Herat against Russian invasion last century. To look down on Herat from its mud walls was to look on a city whose eyes were closed: flat roofs and few windows gave away no secrets, but its arcaded bazaars, like the aisles of a cathedral, radiated from a central point. They had high stone roofing pierced at intervals to let in a beam of light, yet excluding heat. They rang with the sound of the beating of silver, copper and tin, also the *prang, prang, prong* of the bow that beat the eiderdown quilts. Cold as a larder for food, these aisles also contained every other commodity, and such must have been that ruined market in Kabul, its remains now covered reverently in matting.

Here we bought *ghiva*, shoes common to Persia but obtainable on its frontier, with soles of beaten cotton and the oriental upturned toes. In Persia they were beautifully embroidered, but we bought the serviceable type, cool, comfortable and they didn't slip off the driving pedals. Another benefit bestowed by Herat was twelve gallon drums of Russian petrol at the cheapest price of the whole tour. We put a drum on either running-board, secured by goat-hair rope. Bulging out on Baker's sides, they brought us into line with the panniered transport of the country, and one of them remained as a useful tank to the end.

*

Persia was the very factory of red tape.

We had been warned to take plenty of passport photos, and details had to be taken of every travel document we had, and this saw us penned in the frontier office from nine in the morning till nearly eleven. There had to be an investigation of money also, and it did not look too well, that M. Stewart had $200 and Mlle. Parsons had nothing at all, but it simplified the filling out of the form. The frontier officer was quite sympathetic, and when he learnt we had not yet had breakfast he ordered tea and sent his servant out to buy us food. I naturally thought that we were paying, and the bread we hadn't finished I put in my bag. So it was awkward to find we had break-fasted as guests of the official, and equally awkward to hand back the bread, so I could but apologise – and we were sent with his benedictions into Persia.

From Afghanistan the route led down to the level of the great Khurasan, a desert that occupies a large area of Persia and was then a refuge for sub-versive tribes and malefactors. Completely ignorant of this, we had hoped to find better roads; yet Persia, that historic seat of sun worship, persisted in torturing us with a series of harrowing adventures which culminated in breakdown. We found the route more shattering than in Afghanistan, and thirty miles into barren country we had our first puncture, followed swiftly at sundown by another.

The second puncture revealed the outer cover had split, and was of no further use. This left us with only the retreaded tyre bought in Calcutta as a spare, and its retreading was already beginning to part company from its foundation. Also we found that we had left the keys somewhere between this place and the site of our first puncture. A great advantage to Baker, so it seemed at the time of buying, was that the spare wheel locked on the back with a foolproof locking device. We had both seen the keys lying on the back step of the car. They were not there now, nor apparently in pocket or bag. Our spare tyre was irrevocably locked and the blown tyre irrevocably damaged.

There was more to it even than this. Kilton had a habit of leaving spanners trustfully on mudguards and other places whence they fell off and were lost, bringing bitter words from me and the assertion from Kilton that it was human nature so to lose tools. I said it was a matter of training and that I never lost them. That word 'never' had committed me to a standard now shattered, for I had charge of the keys.

It was a night of strain and as foot-wearing as Simla had been. Stewart with a torch walked back the whole distance to the point of the former puncture, where a single castor-oil tree marked the spot, the only tree we had seen for miles. I stayed with the car, and couple of bewildered passengers, raking through my bag, my pockets, feeling I *could* not have left those keys on the step. At eleven o'clock a weary figure returned announcing he had not found them. Dejectedly we ate supper and slept, and I dreamt that I went back and found them, and Kilton dreamt that I knew where they were and would not tell him. What a powerful support for his exposition on dreams! With the first streak of light I rose to go and look for them.

Kilton was all for trying his strength on the spare-wheel grip, but also first getting more sleep, so I left him, only asking how far it was.

'About five miles going, over twenty coming back.'

I followed our wheel tracks, on the side the keys would have fallen, for over two miles. Then the sun came over the top of the mountains and chill dawn turned to grilling day, and I took off Stewart's cardigan. Ever since the dachshunds had eaten my coat I lacked covering for after-sunset and borrowed Stewart's cardigan since he never used it. I now hung this over my arm and strode on, my hands in my pockets, confident I would find those keys. I did. They were in my hand. I had put on the cardigan after we had packed up from that former puncture; they were all the time in the pocket of my linen jacket beneath.

I got back before the car was pulled to pieces. No one had stirred. We mended our puncture, built a fire and had breakfast in such jubilant spirit that when a third passenger applied for a lift and Stewart agreed, my voice carried little weight. I warned that there would be another breakdown shortly, and it was no compensation that in another thirty miles the engine petered out, a fat spark leaping out of a crack in the coil. And we had no spare.

Thanks to Baker's considerate nature this occurred twenty minutes before a bus passed by, the only bus, and not another for three days since we were again on the brink of a bunch of Sundays: Mohammedan, Jewish and Christian. We were trying elaborate repairs to the coil when the bus came on us, and Kilton thrust the coil in my hand insisting I must go to Meshed and try to get a new one. He would stay with the car.

Presuming the bus was making for Meshed sixty miles distant, I leapt on it. I had no Persian currency as here one could only cash travellers cheques at a bank, and Meshed was the first bank. I had no money at all but I knew there was a British Consul in Meshed and on this I pinned my hopes. I was, all the same, in a state of profound anxiety; before me was the unknown and behind me Stewart and Baker, for whom I naturally felt anxious. They were in a vulnerable position, defenceless against either bri gands or police. In the haste of departure I had carried away Kilton's pass-port, and Persia was a country where a passport was far more important than the owner of it.

I must have boarded the bus about nine in the morning but it was six before we reached Meshed. Not only did the bus itself break down but besides a full complement within, the outside was hung with extra passengers who had to be let down before we entered a town, while the bus drove to an office to prove everyone was a legitimate passenger. Yet such was the spirit of helpfulness on the road, the defective coil was produced and I was never asked for a fare. Which was lucky. On the far side of the town we picked up the hangers-on.

Towards midday I had discovered in my bag a piece of that bread we had stolen on the frontier; it not only became my food for the day but gave me the feeling God's eye was on me yet, and at one of our halts someone gave me a glass of tea, while the bus-driver studying the coil nodded his head and said, 'Meshed'. I could see nothing of the country because of the hangers-on, while the passengers inside were not attractive to look at since the law compelled them to wear European clothing, in which they did not look happy but rather drab. This was on the order of Shah Reza Pahlevi, father of the late Shah and then in command. The light-hearted repairs to the bus, on occasion of breakdown, showed me an optimism even greater than our own was able to triumph.

Meshed is a very dramatic city and a place of pilgrimage. Here are the tombs of Harun-al-Rashid and Imam Reza the prophet, and though the infidel may not enter these shrines their glow extends to the circular main street hard by. Into this street we crashed, where was every sort of trade and business, illustrated in oil-paintings above the doors for the benefit of the uneducated; horse traffic and buses were absorbed into a central yard. From here I took a one-horse cab to the Consulate General.

The Consulate was surrounded by a high wall and a stout wooden gate, and on driving through that gateway the change was overwhelming. One was at once in England. There were wide spreading trees, green lawns and

153

flower-beds, a comfortable-looking white house with people having refreshments on its verandah, and others dressed in white were playing tennis. I must have presented a strong contrast in the car-repairing condition in which I had left that morning. I had to drive right up to the Consul in my cab as I could not pay for it until I had found him.

Situated where the two India—England routes join together, the Consulate was not unused to visitations such as mine. The cab-driver was paid and a new coil secured immediately – but it was some time before it reached Kilton. No buses would ply till Monday, the Consulate car was already on call and anyhow not at my disposal, so on Friday morning they sent a servant on a bicycle, hoping a lorry might give him a lift. No lorry passed. Kilton had tinned food in the well of the car, including tepid tinned beer, and he had what water remained in the canvas bags, but there could have been no lonelier spot at which to be stranded.

Meanwhile there was I enjoying delicious food, hot baths, a comfortable bed and thinking guiltily of Kilton. Mrs Squire, the Consul's wife, had a cupboard of supplies for the stranded, so I had a loaned nightgown and the gift of toothbrush and toothpaste. In that interval of rest I recovered from a sort of hay fever one can get from road dust, which in Herat had robbed me for a time of my voice. From the roof of the Consulate one had a grand view of sunset caressing the golden dome of the Imam's tomb and the azure dome of the mosque of Gohar Shad. The wife and widow of Shah Rukh, Gohar Shad had been a patron of the arts and had designed the mosque, also her own mausoleum, of which we had seen remains near Herat. Clearly a woman of forceful character, she was assassinated at over eighty years of age.

On Saturday Kilton drove in through the gates of the Consulate with his rescuer and the bicycle. He adopted a strong indifference to his late ordeal, but after a bath and food he slept for fifteen hours.

*

No wonder Persia inspired famous poetry, it was so beautiful. Years previously I had tried to join an expedition going there but could not raise the money, and more recently had been reading in *The Times* of the impressive excavations at Persepolis.

Now I was here, and had the opportunity to see its diverse scenery, to discover how the work of man had derived inspiration from the work of God. In carpets and embroideries one saw the reflection of the siennas or smoke-blue of the mountains; and the bedizened page of a manuscript or even the more stylized tiles on a mosque were inspired by the vine or the wild flowers – lupins, chicory, poppies and stretches of bright blue irises like powder spilt on the grass. Turquoise was even more vivid in these rocks than in Afghanistan, and mud houses would have their lintels and their sills painted a cerulean blue.

Always there were roses; everyone wore them, in the hair or behind the ear, even a commercial traveller had one in a pocket otherwise given over to fountain pens. And always there were poplar trees marking where there was water; they would stand like tall paintbrushes, grouped in clusters, generally joined by cypress trees and a *chai khana*, and these tea-houses now became the chief scene of our camps. Then suddenly we would reach red soil where villages and headlands took on a rufous tinge at sunset, and all gentler cultivation would be given over to warrior country with mountains like battlements. The village of Izad Khast (God willed it) was piled on a high promontory, the only access by a doubtful drawbridge spanning a deep chasm. One took the hint and stayed away.

Persia, which had been at first rather brutal to us, now made up for it by a series of pleasures and gifts. It gave us a legitimate passenger for the 580 miles to Tehran. Boris, a Yugoslav resident of the city, had grown weary of waiting in Meshed for a bus and had gone to the policepost in hope of finding lorry or car, and found Baker. He paid us the bus fare and became guide, interpreter and friend, helping with punctures. At Shahrud we even left him to collect our passports while we drove six miles to see the multi-sided stupa at Bostam.

In Tehran, hotels of our price had a dormitory system; one engaged not a room but a bed, and for two nights I lay on a bed in shirt and jeans, Kilton on the next bed and, of the four remaining, two were occupied by unknown recumbent forms. There were, however, male and female wash-rooms. It was quite chilly here as the Elburz mountains, the backdrop to Tehran, were still snow-covered.

Persia gave us 'Balkan' roads, but these were less frustrating than having to submit to a passport examination at entry and exit of every town, a delay that could amount to half an hour. We had always intended to make a divergence of nearly a thousand miles to visit Isfahan, Persepolis and Shiraz, and had to get sanction to do this in Tehran at a post office the size of a parliament building. Here admittance to the required offices was hampered by a gang of porters expecting a tip before allowing entry. I doubted the Afghan letter could have influence here but, though we waited no longer than other clients, we never had to resort to a bribe. Arrived eventually at our objectives, we had to have police escort, but this had the advantage of free guidance and the escorts were fairly human, though the one at Qum allowed us only a brief look at the golden shrine of Fatemah, sister of the Prophet. Infidels here were not encouraged.

Persia was in fact becoming a dictator country, but the Shah was not yet in full control, and though he had robbed the people of their natural cloth-ing, there was no restraint on the handsome bridles, elaborate stirrups and fringes and tassels that then ornamented the horses. We came here just in time, with Isfahan in its natural state; and since there was only one road down from it to reach Shiraz, we saw everything twice, going south and on return, plus two long sessions with the archaeologists at Persepolis.

At the end of a conscientious morning in Shiraz we asked our policeman where to go for lunch. He took us to a walled garden where there were roses, and figs ripe for picking, and the white mulberry trees that had persisted since Afghanistan, when to shake a bough was to fill Baker with dessert. An officer sitting near us spoke fluent French and confirmed our belief in the natural goodwill of the ordinary Persian. He helped us with the menu, anxious we should have the best, but we explained the need for frugality and how we had got here. He regretted having to leave before hearing more, but might he look at our car on his way out? We could have stayed in this garden all afternoon; no wonder the poet Hafez would never leave his homeland. When at last we roused ourselves to go, we found our bill had been paid.

*

We had long since discovered the reason why Baker advanced at intervals in jerks. It was a worn seating in which the distributor shaft was mounted, causing vibrations on bad road surfaces and hence irregular sparking. In Tehran we had the seating rebushed with hard metal but in Kermanshah, the last city within the Persian border, we came limping in with a sorely tried, and now broken, mainspring, also the rebushing needed to be done again. Here this operation was performed very much better, and it was also remarkable that though the supply of spare parts was culled solely from vehicles abandoned by the roadside, a spring of the right size was nevertheless found.

The business of the tour had automatically fallen to Brawn and Brain. The scheming fell to me: the accounts, the food and the business of finding the way. The driving we shared and Brawn, besides blowing up my Lilo, changed tyres, spliced springs and heaved petrol from the containers into the tank, sighing over the labour involved. Once when I unwisely compared Baker to the Magic Carpet, 'Magic Carpet, Hell!' said my companion. 'I bet Ali Baba didn't spend half his time under the carpet.' Yet Brawn could start a fire with the minimum of kindling, and that soaking with dew. And, charitable to the oppressed, Brawn dealt severely with those seeking to exploit, and thus was a godsend at frontiers.

We drove all through that night, having little Persian money left after the repair garage. A great barrier of mountains lay between us and Iraq, and a chill wind blew as I breasted the first two passes, then handed over to Kilton and slept till dawn. I woke suffocating with heat; the sun was up,

156

and we were nearly down to desert level and had passed through the last high mountain range between us and home. We used up our last Persian money on petrol, knowing we could not take Persian currency over the border. We arrived at the frontier with a few negligible coins and Kilton's last traveller's cheque.

We had to flourish the Afghan letter to get through this frontier. They had enhanced the stamp duty to catch out those who, like ourselves, had only reserved a few coins for it after buying petrol. We were short of the stamp tax by a minimal sum, but the crest and the seals on a scroll they could not read persuaded them we were people of importance and they graciously overlooked the deficiency.

At the Iraq office we had intended to cash the remaining cheque, but found here such a crippling exchange that Kilton offered a Malay dollar he had found in a pocket towards the stamp on the carnet. The face of King George had some appeal but not enough for the clerk, who had recently worked under the British mandate. With a shrug he handed back the dollar and let us go.

Baghdad on the horizon looked immense and the same colour as the land approaching it, but for us it was a rare oasis, thanks to a most fortunate introduction. Our host and hostess had known Baghdad both during and ever since the 1914–1918 war. 'You won't find anywhere to stay under a pound a day,' they told us. 'That was the wartime price and no one has thought of reducing it. You'd much better stay with us.' Nothing loath, we stayed.

There was little the Wilkinses did not know about Iraq, where for the past twenty years Major Wilkins had been helping to form a police service on which the Iraqi government might lean after the termination of the mandate, and he had been asked to stay on another five years as head of the CID. It was not encouraging to sit and watch things one had built up being differently handled, but both felt Iraq would never decline to pre-mandate conditions.

Those were indeed Arabian nights when we sat out on the verandah, hearing of the hospital of which Mrs Wilkins had been matron, where no one was ever turned away, even a hundred lunatics when their asylum was flooded, and a few conspicuous cures were then effected. Mrs Wilkins' eyes gleamed as she detailed revelations coming to light under that exodus. 'The ones we couldn't release at least we could wash,' she said. It was hard to think of that hospital now.

In Major Wilkins, Kilton had found a host after his heart, one to whom hours of sleep were superfluous. They never went to bed. Unfortunately, normal meals made me so sleepy I had to retire, so I failed to hear at first hand of bandits being turned into useful agents of the law, of criminals who would escape into the desert and take refuge among their tribes. Then would come a nice problem. An armed force would only alienate the whole tribe, but a man well known to them, and respected, might get them to deliver up the criminal, but the moment of arrival was ticklish, whether the tribe would receive the emissary or shoot him. 'Poor old so and so. They shot him. One of the best.'

In telling these stories 'Wilkie' was going over ground that he cherished – he himself at times had been an emissary – but he was quite unconscious of being an advertisement for the British Empire. I had noticed Stewart's growing enthusiasm. He was repeating a story I had missed by going to bed, of how Wilkie and his man had trapped a whole bunch of bandits in an old fortress, arresting them without firing a single shot. 'Heck! I'd like some of our folks at home to hear this. You know you British just love being inferior. When it comes to the real salt, you keep it hidden so it's only by accident that outsiders get to know. We'd have taken a *tank* to attack that fortress.'

Baghdad had for some time been a focal point for celebrated characters, but the heroes it most revered were scarcely known in the West. Leachman, of the Sussex Regiment, had got to know most of Arabia by 1914. Carrying never more than a light switch in his hand, he had worked all though the war amongst hostile tribes. He never approached the Arabs with bribes, but his extreme mobility on camel or horse, and his personality, had won him such fame that Arab children were still being called after him. He was murdered in 1920.

There were other such heroes, beside whom Lawrence faded into insignificance, and one got a different slant on those whom the West revered. On asking after Gertrude Bell, whose treasures from Ur were on view in Baghdad: 'Know her? Lor' yes. Good old Gertie. What a nuisance *she* was.'

For us the Australian brothers Nairn were particularly important celebrities. Coming to Mesopotamia in the war, they had afterwards built up from a couple of Ford cars to a three-tier service of motor transport between Damascus and Baghdad. In winter, the rainy season, the desert turned to mud, when no wheeled traffic could ply, also then the tracks of the Nairn coaches were apt to be obliterated. Yet never for long was the Nairn held up, and the express service had to average thirty-eight miles an hour to do the distance in the time scheduled. In fact the driver had to know the route by heart, as though there were miles of billiard-table surface, but the tracks were apt to end abruptly with small outcrops of rock, unseen but very damaging if not anticipated.

One could pay the Nairn Company to get a car across; one could go in convoy, but the convoy did not wait for a breakdown. Most motor vehicles went on their own, which was what we were intending to do, following the tracks of the Nairn.

*

We had fairly raked Baghdad by the time we left, but the flooded
Tigris had balked our seeing its surroundings, or the Arch of Ctesiphon.
Flood-water was the first bunker of a journey that differed from former
desert driving where we had driven always alongside the desert. Now we
had close on 500 miles right across, with only the oasis of Rutbah for
water. Food and petrol imported to Rutbah were above our price.
Wilkie had got permission for us to follow the oil pipeline direct to Jerusalem, cutting out 200 miles, but not desert miles. It had the advantage of telecommunication but it went through Jordan, for which Kilton
would need a visa, and was extremely lonely. He himself finally decided
we had better stick to the Nairn route. Wilkie, who had experienced all
the hazards of the desert and looked back on it lovingly, was extremely
nervous on our behalf. People often remarked on my courage, but I
don't think I was courageous; I simply knew it was going to be all
right.

From Baghdad the road led bravely out into the desert and continued
past the airport, where we were accompanied later by a little bus which
stopped at intervals to put down white-robed passengers, rather like a
laundry van delivering washing. There was nothing in the whole landscape
save tents on a distant horizon, so one wondered how the passenger judged
the point at which to descend, what he asked for when booking a ticket.
The road had now become a track, but forty-five miles from Baghdad it
recovered itself to enter Falluja on the Euphrates, which, for us, was the last
petrol station. Normally Ramadi in another forty miles offered petrol, but
Ramadi was cut off by floods.

We left Falluja with sixty gallons of petrol on board, distributed between
our various containers; a liberal allowance, but we had to cover bad
running if the distributor again started playing up. It wasn't comforting on
the road outside the town to see the burnt-out body of a car with exploded
petrol tins all around it. We were in an unnatural state of solvency as,
besides living free in Baghdad, true to expectation, Kilton had been paid
the money owing to him.

We left Falluja at the same time as a police patrol going towards Ramadi
which offered us escort round the floods. It was possible Wilkie bade them
look out for us, this smart lorry, mounted with gun and spade and a
company of deeply considerate policemen, with cartridges in their belts and
the silver star in their caps.

On our way we called to leave supplies at a police outpost: a fair-sized
tent, where instantly tea was made and a couch with a cloth on it offered us
on which to rest. There followed what sounded like the inevitable quarrel,
but interpretation would probably reveal it was the local news, and then we

159

were escorted on round the floods cutting off Ramadi to where we picked up the Nairn tracks.

The tracks around the flooding now led out into the desert, and the remaining 450-odd miles we did alone. It was then just before sundown and we reached Damascus about noon of the second day. It was mid-June and heat induced us to drive during the night till the small hours. A moveable spotlight enabled us to do this. With only the fixed headlamps night driving was not recommended; Wilkie had warned against it, but if we did, and lost the track, we should sit still till dawn. He also cautioned us not to remain on the track when we pulled up to sleep but to get a little way off it.

However, I was travelling with someone born and bred in desert country, and it was he who now started driving into the setting sun, while I slept until my guardian angle woke me – to find the spotlight in action and no sign of the tracks. I remarked on this. 'You *would* wake at this moment,' said my companion. 'They're on our left.' We kept bearing left but failing to find them on awkward ground full of bluffs and hollows. Then suddenly there they were. 'Trust a desert man,' said Kilton. I didn't, but know few occasions when two people should drive a car. So I resumed sleep, soon aware that we had come to a halt, but the watchdog within me was fully alert. In the small hours I woke to hear a droning sound.

With a searchlight sweeping the ground before it, the Nairn Express was advancing towards us, the path of its light already scattering brilliance and shadow on the ground about us. We seemed to be fully in the line of approach, with wheel tracks to right and left of us. I put out a hand to turn on our lights, to find Kilton had turned off the battery switch; and in trying to get at it I encountered his recumbent form. The air was rent with the curses of a man roused from sleep, and by the time the lights were on, the Nairn Express was disappearing over the other horizon. We were parked on a bluff where no car was likely to climb. This sad want of faith in a desert man was held against me for some time.

Crossing the desert in a couple of days, one got the impression that it was intensely populated with human and animal life. Camels we saw in plenty and graceful gazelle would go leaping across the ground at a speed that put Baker to shame. There were sand-grouse, salamanders, hares and jerboas, which Kilton called kangaroo rats. He assured me their bone construction strongly resembled the human frame; we were as closely related to them as to the ape. This made their massacre at night all the more terrible as, leaping higher and higher before the approaching headlamps, they were ignorant of the art of sidestepping. All this livestock was feeding on vegetation so sparse it was barely visible. Cars passed or met us on an average of one every four daylight hours; there were often black tents on a distant horizon, while early on we had met a little knot of a tinker tribe, the Solubba, believed to be descended form the Crusaders, whose security

160

depended on their being thought too contemptible to be included in the blood feud.

Our dependence on telegraph poles had ceased with Iraq. They were no longer marked on the maps of Central Asia we bought in Baghdad. They were substituted in the desert crossing by metal kilometre posts with Arabic numbering, each one within vision of the next, if it hadn't been knocked over. They were generally within sight of the Nairn's tracks.

The smoothest piece of our journey was crossing a big salt basin where we were deceived by a mirage, despite our long training. It seemed that a salt lake had formed here, and there were wheel tracks where cars had pulled away to avoid it. The only reason I did not do so was that distances in the desert are hard to measure, and it did not seem to me yet necessary to do so. We never reached that water.

The well at Rutbah is a constant miracle of salvation; it is a solitary and copious supply of water where there is no other water-hole within a radius of 200 miles. It is enclosed in a fortified wall, for until there was air service across the desert, whoever held Rutbah held the desert. It was also the Iraq customs office before reaching Syria.

Here the rich could sleep and dine in quarters provided by the Nairn company. We merely refilled our water tank and water-bags. An empty glass of beer in the lounge was nearly our undoing, but we resisted temptation. Mrs Wilkie had supplied us with plenty of food which included home-grown tomatoes and grapes. We allowed ourselves a basin of water a day for ablutions, and the desert at sunrise or sunset makes a very satisfactory bathroom. We were driving across a surface like a shimmering golden ice-rink towards evening when on our flank two stone pillars appeared on the horizon, and the tracks were heading towards them.

These marked the Syrian border, and they seemed to round off a stage, so we decided to eat here, and I began scratching some food together while Kilton walked over to one of the pillars, lay down in its shadow and went to sleep. Presently a lorry drove up and a man jumped down from a seat by the driver, and in bad French offered me his services as a driver. He would only charge a modest fee. When I thanked him but said I had no need of a driver, he insisted I needed someone to show me the way, and finally that it was more dangerous in Syria for a woman driving alone.

For answer I nodded towards the recumbent form of Kilton, which this man had evidently not seen. He advanced towards him cautiously, then paused.

'Is he ill?'

'He sleeps.'

The man looked at me nervously, crossed himself and got back in the waiting lorry, which drove on.

'Maybe he thought you'd laid me out,' said Kilton, opening his eyes.

161

We moved further into Syria before camping that night under the glittering tiara of Heaven, and a pre-dawn start brought us to where the road from Damascus comes forty miles into the desert. Smooth road like this had not been under our wheels since India, and soon we were among cypress, olive and eucalyptus trees, with canals beside the road, and fat oxen. Never had land looked more abundant as we came into Palestine just north of the Sea of Galilee, verily a land flowing with milk and honey. Out in the desert we had also crossed a line between Near and Middle East, aware suddenly of our appearance: dust in clothing, eyebrows and hair, mountains of it on every horizontal surface of Baker and almost obliterating the BI (British India) plate and Baker's number, 16061, with no lettering.

Damascus for us was a wonderful French lunch and a slow approach through the street called Straight, now a market. We went on to find a modest hotel in Tiberias by the Sea of Galilee and bathed in the sea next morning; Kilton, with always a slightly Biblical appearance, seemed to have found his natural surroundings.

Palestine then was in an explosive state, full of war *matériel* and young British soldiers, their youthful faces out of keeping with their tin hats, rifles and ammunition. In fact the whole of Europe was like a volcano about to erupt. I had left it in company with ejected Jews, and now approaching it again I was meeting Jews at their point of landing. The German-speaking people who had poured in here had brought their country with them. Jaffa Road was becoming a Kartnerstrasse with a selection of most excellent cafés.

True, one was free to see everything, though having to declare one was not Jewish before visiting that greatest and most beautiful treasure, the Dome of the Rock, and the scarcity of tourists resulted in no pestering guides. Baker and occupants rather resembled the Solluba, those tinker tribes too contemptible to be included in the feud, whereas the High Commissioner, who passed us with outriders, armoured cars and expensive tourers full of important people, was a target as tempting as driven grouse. We had only a week here as Kilton, an alien, was confined to a transit visa of only seven days, but we used them well.

We had learnt with relief that there was a Studebaker agent in Jerusalem for, having got us safely across the desert, Baker had again indulged in its old habit. The agent replaced our distributor with a new one of quite different coupling which never gave trouble again. But he was horror-struck at the state of our tyres, and since we could not afford a new outer cover as well as the distributor, he *gave* us one he had of the right size, admitting there was no general demand for it.

The start of that journey, Beersheba to Suez, was just gruesome desert, not a particle of vegetation, no bird or animal life. It was undiluted sand moulded by wind, but it had a road. At intervals, to prevent sand drifting across it, were tar barrels side by side along its edge. All the same, we sometimes had to dig the sand away. During the first hundred miles there were police posts with wireless transmitters, petrol and water. At the AA office in Jerusalem we were given a chatty pamphlet biding us call at these as they kept a tally of the passing traffic. We found it strange to be so tenderly nursed but, willing to comply, found them tightly shut down for the night. Ah, that was more the sort of thing we were accustomed to. The sun sank on us, the moon grew brilliant as we studied the excavations at Sbeita, the colour of the sand clearly visible in its light. In the former desert there had been starlight; here we saw the cold impersonal beauty of moonlight over the desert, a beauty at which one tries to grasp but which is complete, outside one's being, belonging to nobody.

Yet on my gypsy pilgrimage I had grown near to sun and moon, the only constants in a life of change; I felt the sun was my guide, the moon my courier shedding a gracious light on the rarest vistas of my journey, and often no roofing between myself and them. We found it extraordinary in this open landscape how the headlamps formed a meaningless circle of light, absorbed by unimpeded distance; only the ground protracted its range. Night driving in the desert was always a hallucination of being enclosed in a lane whose tree trunks were just outside the limit of radiance, but to switch off the light was to reveal an empty horizon.

The last hundred miles were mountainous, the desert forming rocky tablelands near the Mitla Pass; telephone poles loomed up and the road took on a coating of bitumen, but nothing could be more unostentatious than this canal that revolutionized world communications: we saw a tramp steamer apparently plying through the desert, and then at Kupri near the Suez entry, a notice 'To the Ferry'. The ferry we shared with a camel.

A road like a ribbon of rubber carried us ninety miles to Cairo; it was so smooth and the early morning sun so hot that a terrible drowsiness overcame us. Our greatest danger yet. Finding myself charging towards a tar barrel at the roadside, I decided I had better hand over to Kilton, who was all too soon charging a tar barrel on the other side of the road. It was extraordinary how we gravitated towards those barrels that only occurred at intervals and were the only features of the landscape.

It was now July, and on entering Cairo, flame of the forest trees stretched out along the avenue to greet us, trees now in full and glorious bloom. In every sense a warm welcome.

*

In spite of the heat there were many advantages in out-of-season Cairo, where prices dropped to their normal level and one could enjoy its assets at reasonable cost. Museums were almost a tenth of their winter price, which we found a godsend. Another advantage was the absence of visitors, apart from a few concentrating mostly on Tutankhamun. Except for a guide, we saw the great pyramid of Giza, the Cheops pyramid, entirely alone. We ascended its hall, sloping up through the body of the pyramid, and not unlike an escalator on the underground in design, but on far greater scale. It led into the silence, the terrible isolation of the King Chamber, where there was an empty sarcophagus. Here the coffin and all the funerary treasure had been sealed in by a stone door, to be plundered at a later date. Yet the personal belongings of Queen Hetepheres, hidden underground, had been found and now formed one of the most beautiful and interesting exhibitions in the city.

At sunset we climbed to the top of the Cheops pyramid and from the peak of these thirteen acres of masonry looked westward at the trail leading across the desert, a three months' camel journey to Algiers. The scale of the architecture in the Nile valley overawed me, the extreme accuracy achieved by such primitive methods and simplistic measuring contrivances.

Cairo was then still an Oriental city, its suburbs had not yet lapped to the feet of the pyramids at Giza, but the absence of visitors had not reduced the pestering of would-be-guides. 'Can I help you, lady? Are you going to the Blue Mosque, monsieur? Yes? I will go with you, lady. I show you. . . .' It went on like a gramophone, the scourge of the Nile valley.

Cairo was important to me as here I was again to become solvent, no longer a kept woman, though inevitably we had to wait till Monday for banks and poste restantes to open. Until then our meals consisted of beer, as Cairo had the habit of issuing with alcohol a small hors-d'oeuvre, a snack about equal to our usual meal, so we lived on beer till Monday. Then the bank not only produced my quarterly pension, but the post office brought a cheque from my godmother, who was very interested in my journey. To Kilton came news that money awaited him from Utah at a bank in Alexandria.

These bonuses had a demoralizing effect. The Coin de France restaurant henceforth became a habit.

We took the road bordering the Nile as far up as Memphis, and in this short distance I became imbued with the idea of one day following the river itself as far as one could go. Would a Nile steamer go to Luxor, even to Aswan? Kilton said he would go with me. Little we knew what lay between inspiration and fulfilment years later when I went alone.

We now had to make for Alexandria and the coast road to Libya, quite unaware of the red-carpet send-off that awaited us. We were staying at a hotel recommended by the customs officer at Suez as being reasonable in price and central, and we had found it fully adequate. I doubt many Westerners came here, thus verbal communication was sometimes strained, but a jeweller next door, who spoke French and English, seemed always ready

164

to come and help. Meanwhile Baker had increasingly become an object of interest; as soon as Far East gave way to nearer East, it gathered such a crowd that an attendant was now needed until we could find a garage. In the early stages Baker was nothing unusual, and in Persia whenever a gathering formed anywhere it was dispersed by police; but now the number of tanks embracing it, the pendulous water-bags and the roll of iron wire netting on the bumper rail gave Baker a very singular appearance. It was thought to be at least the winner of the Grand Prix; we had a job to get into it at the hotel door, so it was rather humiliating, after this glorious departure, that nightfall found us returning humbly to the hotel on foot.

For outside Cairo the winner of the Grand Prix had suffered the collapse of another mainspring and was now in a repair garage whose owner was searching for a substitute spring of correct size. There was nothing for it but to collect bare essentials for the night and return to the only cheap hostelry we knew. When we, who had left with such a flourish in the morning, returned without a car or luggage and on foot, the jeweller could not arrive quickly enough to discover the cause. It seemed whenever we were nicely in funds Baker instantly claimed a share.

After leaving Alexandria, we drove swiftly along the Mediterranean coast, through scrub-covered country that appeared desolate until one pulled up and got out of the car. Then the area seemed widely populated by deeply inquisitive humans. If we had a meal, the moment we opened a tin there was obvious curiosity to see what was inside; in fact, picnicking by the roadside in Egypt was rather like giving a demonstration at an Ideal Homes Exhibition.

On the Libyan border we filled up with petrol almost to our sixty gallons capacity, for we were entering territory where petrol was far dearer than anywhere else. In Baghdad and Damascus it had cost just over a shilling a gallon, but thanks to the Shell agent coming down in his pyjamas to help us fill up, we covered 970 miles of Mussolini's high road without using Mussolini's petrol.

We travelled this road across Libya at the right moment, 1,142 miles of smooth tarmac recently laid, the upkeep of which was likely to be a greater expense than its building. I can imagine its state after the war. It followed the coastline, with a cool breeze form the Mediterranean softening the heat of the day, but at the eastern end and at the centre it flanked extremely barren ground with miles of boulder-covered desert such as we had seen in Afghanistan. Yet after a long span of arid ground, on the first sign of nourishment in the soil there would be some form of human habitation, and one wondered which had induced the other.

There were wide areas of Libya where a little determined effort could revolutionize the landscape, and evidently Mussolini meant to make use of it, transplanting 20,000 Italian families, who were shortly to arrive. *Ente*

Colonizatione Libya was written on flat-roofed white houses that stood like lumps of sugar scattered now and again inland: tolerable dwellings, each with some acres of ground, a wind water-pump and a barn.

The best land, the natural oases, had rich groves of date palms being vigorously cultivated, the sand dunes pinned down a network of faggots and creeper plants grown on them to keep the sand from blowing. Tasty as a marron glacé, soft as a pat of butter is a date fresh from the tree, and for a small charge one could get more green figs, dates and tomatoes than one could conveniently carry.

One must be grateful to Mussolini for opening museums and galleries free of charge: a grand gift of education. Near most of the oases there were Roman remains. At Leptis Magna the tread of sandalled feet seemed scarcely to have died from the paving-stones of its wide arcades. At Sabratha was a theatre ready for use, with a semicircular auditorium facing seaward, the stage backing on to the shore, with a high backdrop of pillared galleries protecting its acoustics. Here mosaics like embroidery had been relaid in museums out of reach of sand and weather.

Of living cities I remember especially Sirte and Benghazi. Sirte, pressed close to the sea with desert behind it, had ancient fortifications, white walls and oleander bushes bordering cobbled streets. Benghazi, which we passed through in the silence of dawn, was also white and decorated with pink oleanders, and with no traffic was quiet and beautiful. They were both later destroyed by bombing. Tripoli gave us our second legitimate paying guest, an Italian despairing of a bus, the owner of a small fishing fleet at present off Tunis, which he was hoping to reach next day.

*

It was late afternoon when this offer was made to us at the Tripoli frontier, and we were glad of it as we had no idea of the cost of the ferry from Tunis to Marseilles. Thoughts of continuing along the coast to Gibraltar had long since melted. We decided therefore to make for Sfax on the Tunisian coast, but once into French territory we came on a large military camp where passports were examined, and though Kilton's and mine caused no hindrance, our passenger was taken to headquarters and closeted there for half an hour or more. Meanwhile American and Briton sat in Baker, conscious that they had only eaten figs and dates all day, that the sun was slanting towards the horizon and an enviable smell of soup was coming from an adjacent officers' mess. This had a canvas roof and wicker fencing round it and, in the aperture between, a row of heads was visible. A conversation in French ensued:

'You come from far, madame?'

'Yes. Very far.'

'From where do you come?'

'From India.' Much laugher.

'And what do you like best on that journey?'

'The smell of your soup.' A chorus of offers. Soup-plates appeared above the fencing.

'But it is not good at all. You will find better at Gabes.'

'Thank you, we won't take your soup. But if you could liberate our passenger we could get soup of our own.'

'But you present problems. Three persons of different nationality. Are you one family?'

'No.'

'You were friends only?'

'Not exactly.'

'Then why do three persons of different nationality, who are not friends and not related, travel in one car from India to Tunisia?'

'We are the League of Nations.'

'Ah, no. You lack a Frenchman.'

'It was the will of God.'

'Ah! The will of God.'

There were messages of *bon voyage* and *bon potage* when at last we resumed our way, and in fact stopped for dinner and the night at Gabes.

At dawn we rose to fulfil our programme, but at the huge amphitheatre at El Djem a guide made mysterious mention of a Roman glass he had found, and when we saw this slim tall glass, the core of earth still inside it and iridescent scales slaking off its surface, we knew it must be genuine; to make so good a fake would cost twice the humble sum the guide was asking. All through our journey Kilton's case, and hide-outs in Baker, were filling up with trophies and now, four miles out from El Djem, he felt it was folly for a few francs not to have bought this glass. Back we went, our passenger in a state of frenzy, but we got him to Tunis on time.

Now came high-pressure activity for Brain, and I just managed to get a booking on the ferry leaving next day. Kilton had yet to get a visa for France; the Consulate was firmly closed till next morning. So having done what we could we drove out to Carthage, stood on the heights and watched the sun go down in splendour. I think we were both a little resentful that roofing would soon shut us off from our friends in the sky, whose phases we had come to know as the fisherman knows the tides.

Deck-class had seemed more exclusive to me than stuffy cabins on a warm, calm night that enveloped the crossing to Marseilles, so we lay out on the deck in a line with other bodies, the masthead above us, like a pointing finger, tracing a wavering line across the sky. The cool breeze for which we had been grateful in North Africa became a trifle too chilly as we approached Paris, which also produced rain. We had forgotten about rain; it fell through Baker's hood straight on to our laps.

There was a lot of rude laugher when we landed in England. On the Channel auto-carrier of those days the humans had the deck and all amenities, while the cars were stored in a hold from which they were lifted on a small platform to the quay by crane. We knew that Baker was the next to arrive, by a pause in the operation, by the angle at which the ropes became taut, and so it was. Looking rather like something brought up by mistake, it joined company with a line of sophisticated sports cars and tourers, all in perfect trim. Yet as the BI plate came into view, the purport of all the odd accoutrements was realized, and the owners of that glittering array forsook their own cars to come and stand round Baker, to admire, exclaim, ask questions. And had not Baker done ten times the work of any other car upon that quay!

Now we had to stoop to the indignity of being insured, lately introduced as a compulsion. A mint of money in one cause or another was spent before, with full tank and empty pockets, we were released. The port officer, whom I knew well, asked all details of this imported vehicle, including the engine number, to which I replied we had never found it yet. It was refreshing to find an official who simply wrote 'never yet found'.

It was Sunday night; darkness and rain fell as we groped our way on the narrow Reigate–Dorking road against the glare of streams of oncoming headlamps, all reflected in the wet road surface. Presently my companion remarked, 'I guess this is the most dangerous country we've yet driven.'

Nevertheless we got home, to find it just as I had left it: the money for the laundry on the hall table, the tabby cat in the same armchair. Half the spice of the unknown would be gone if there was no one waiting to share its relish. But for this constancy, this solid ground, the journey would have lost much of its attraction.

Yet the mind, long accustomed to caravan life, does not easily stop travelling. In the small hours of next morning I woke to see dim light on beams and sloping ceiling and thought how wise to seek out this warm barn, this comfortable hay. Then doubt crept in. Was it a barn? Was it hay? Good Lord, where had I got to now?

1939–1950

WORKING IN THE WAR

I had anticipated it would take delicate handling, my return to a conservative environment, accompanied by a male with unorthodox ideas, after travelling with him for 9,500 miles. There were, however, mitigating circumstances, not least Kilton's forthright charm and Baker's stern mien – no love-nest here – and a helpful precedent had lately been established by Peter Fleming and Ella Maillart together bursting through established convention in an epic journey from China through Turkestan to India. Above all, we returned only shortly before the Munich crisis in September 1938, and most minds were occupied with what looked like inevitable war.

My mother greeted Kilton with a friendliness she had always extended to friends I brought to the house, whether or not of the accepted order. Betty received him with amusement, and I was spared castigation from Dora by her absence at a home to which she was now obliged to retire at intervals. My aunt received Kilton with reservation, shortly to break into open conflict.

To me it was soon evident that in my absence my aunt had got a firm grip on the house, and Kilton found me at breakfast one morning in a state of gloom, having been reminded that, after a year and a half of happy liberty, at home I must suffer persistent persecution. The writing-table chair I had been using for typing had, during the night, been removed by my aunt as belonging to her. A canvas garden chair had been substituted.

I went and found a suitable chair and went on typing, when the sound of my aunt's voice raised in furious indignation reached me from below stairs, and I realized she was receiving an interval of unsolicited psychoanalysis. My mother now came from her bedroom, suggesting I should go to my aunt's rescue, but I said I thought this was the best thing that could happen, and we smiled conspiratorially at each other and left well alone. Presently Kilton joined me, laughing delightedly; I cannot claim there was improvement from henceforth, but it cleared the air. No further aggravations occurred.

The typing was important as Customs & Excise had levied a tax of £30 on this foreign car brought into the country, whereas the highest offer we had obtained for it was 30s from a dump. By dint of further correspondence, the tax was reduced to £3 6s 8d, and the payment of this extra-ordinary sum released the £22 deposit paid in Calcutta. We were now able to calculate that the journey, Calcutta to Wonersh, had cost £184 shared between us. Then the Studebaker Company in the USA paid us quite handsomely for an article on the journey published in their magazine, so funds began looking up, and Betty had kindly extended the period of insur-ance, so we kept Baker for some time.

I was hoping before war broke out to get down to writing an account of my world journey, and Kilton was wanting to work for a Ph.D. at the London School of Economics, so the happy solution of the Munich crisis was a bonus to both of us, though with Baker at the door there was every inducement instead of getting to work to visit our friends. For in fact it was a time rather of unforeseen reunions, as it was generally assumed that 'peace in our time' was only temporary, and autumn brought sons of Britain home by the shoal to enjoy leave while they could. So we finally took Baker on tour and paid a round of visits.

Deric and Avis were home, then with Mrs French in Norfolk; Pat Noone was in Cambridge, and the Collingses, with whom we had stayed in Singa-pore, gave what one might call a houseparty at Eleanor Collings's family home near Southwold. We met Edmund Leach, with whom Kilton had shared one of his earliest expeditions among primitives, in London. The Morrisons were also in London; Esmond was curious to meet Kilton, who went down well with both Morrison brothers. Father Barker had taken a keen interest in my journey and now invited me to lunch in London; so it was much easier to drift on this tide of friendship than to get on with life's struggle. There were also exalted occasions.

There was Kilton's lecture to the Anthropological Society on Dream Psy-chology among Primitives, when the 'trousers found around Noone's place' blended miraculously with Kilton's own dinner-jacket. I could hardly recog-nize the lecturer. There was a weekend at Cambridge when Pat gave a lecture on his work in Malaya at his college and we dined in hall at the high table. There was an evening when, at Miss Haslett's suggestion, I gave a talk, supported by Kilton, on the journey from India, and the hall con-tained almost as many of our friends as women engineers.

Elspeth was now well established in her house in Sydney Street, and on postponement of war, she decided to go on a visit of some weeks abroad which she had earlier deferred. Often in her absence she lent her house to friends, and she now let Kilton use a room of the house for psychotherapy, and I happened to know someone in London in dire need of it and anxious to meet him. Between us we launched Kilton on a London practice; this was further advanced by Dr Jensen of the London School of Psychology, who was interested in Kilton's theories and subsequently lent him a small empty flat in Brook Street. Kilton both lived and practised there. The room for the patients was the only one furnished, and inevitably there were 'hangers-on' in the back rooms, but of a higher order than those carried by Baker.

In late September Kilton and I drove Baker to a final destination. A friend had offered us a small sum for it, if we would drive it to his house in Dorset, where he had arranged for it to be exhibited in the local garage. I painted a line in white enamel round the bodywork, giving the names of the different cities it had passed through on the way home. When war came, the tyres were removed and Baker was used as a tractor by a local farmer, helping to feed Britain.

By August 1939 most sons of Britain had been recalled; Deric was back in India, Avis at home awaiting transport for wives. Pat Noone had returned to Malaya and Kilton had gone over to Paris with him to see him off, and couldn't get back. An alien leaving England temporarily had to obtain a return visa before departure, and Kilton had known nothing about this. Most aliens were only too ready to leave, but Kilton intended to finish the course he had now started at the London School of Economics, and it was generally assumed that the USA would remain neutral. I learnt that Dr Jensen had sent him some money in Paris and told him his only hope was to get back to the States.

On hearing this I was shattered; certainly with the writing of my book and Kilton's London practice our occasions of meeting had been rare, but the Atlantic was a ruthless separation. Would I ever see him again? I had underestimated him on our first meeting, but since working with him and travelling with him – always a test – he had risen in my esteem, was always enlivening in discussion, and a sturdy and protective friend. In the jungle I had felt that both Pat and Kilton needed a 'nanny' – for Pat Putch largely filled this role, but to nanny Kilton would be a full-time job. Had I been a nobler woman I might have taken it on, but I had tasted the pleasure of independence and had other things I wanted to do.

There was one ridiculous argument recurring at intervals throughout our journey; Kilton was intrigued by the imaginary families I had made up for myself in childhood, particularly by a single daughter who would, I reckoned, now be seventeen. 'And I certainly wouldn't introduce her to you,' I had said. Kilton was incensed. She became the focal point of dispute at intervals all along our route until, somewhere in France, on the strength of a higher estimation, I revised my ideas and the matter happily closed.

Some days after Kilton's departure for America, I had a ring from one of the hangers-on at the Brook Street flat to say it was being sold and there was a cupboard still full of Kilton's belongings. I had a premonition it would happen: that luggage so frequently lost, shipwrecked, marooned, ended up in a boxroom in The Old House, to await further orders. It remained there throughout the war.

171

During the phoney war, when neither Germany nor the allies seemed anxious to start fighting, I continued writing *Vagabondage* and found it exacting, as always in writing personal experience. Fiction allows blissful freedom to follow any course, describe any scene, but truth imposes responsibilities; bold assertions need to be accurate. At that time some excellent bureaux of information existed; Selfridges had one, purely as advertisement, and made no charge for conscientious research.

It was generally assumed that at the first bomb I would leap into the driving seat of ambulance or lorry, but in fact my inclination was towards the factory. Of what avail those years at Loughborough if I couldn't use them now? But a rolling stone, such as I had been, discovers that each occupation has its own terminology, and concerning factory processes and tools I had forgotten the language.

Miss Haslett, who had moved from strength to strength, was now advisor to the Government on recruitment of women into munitions work, and Verena had devised a three-month course in workshop practice so that women would be put into useful jobs, and those recruited as personnel managers would have knowledge of the work being done.

These courses were being given at technical schools around the country, and there was one at the Beaufoy Institute in Lambeth, within easy reach by train to Waterloo and tram. I had missed the autumn session but took the one following, which still gave time for writing in the evenings and at weekends.

It was a fascinating course: lessons in machine drawing accompanied the making of simple metal devices using the general run of machine tools, also a micrometer to achieve results correct to decimal points. Though this was all ground I knew, I can't say I shone particularly. There were all types of professional women from architects to actresses, mingling with housewives and society women, all delighted to find that, given the tools, they could make things in metal as much as in cloth. We were visited one morning in the workshop by Queen Elizabeth (now the Queen Mother), who was fascinated watching the processes and longed to take the course herself. Miss Haslett, who had brought the Queen, came and dug me out to shake hands with her, but as my hands were covered in oil I was obliged to curtsey, which did not somehow accord with trouser overalls. The Queen was told of my former Loughborough training, and I described myself as a reconditioned engineer.

A day before the end of the course the workshop was invaded by a Mr Freeman, a good-looking man obviously accustomed to exerting influence, who soon had our works manager at his bidding and was demanding the three best pupils to go at once to his firm. Somewhat overawed, three of us were bounced into working at a rather squalid but massively equipped firm in Ealing, meekly accepting the deplorable wage then paid to women factory workers. We were thinking in terms of patriotism rather than personal benefit, and influenced by Freeman's compelling propaganda on the importance of the work. Thus I look back on a rather abortive war career, from which my two fellow workers escaped before the Essential Works Order held them prisoner. One of the fellow workers was an artist living in London, but she retired early on getting a war contract more in her line of business. The other, Dess Forshall, a star pupil at the Beaufoy, lived not far distant in Sussex and we became great friends, but after some time at Freeman's she escaped in marriage.

By the time we joined this firm, Germany had invaded and encroached up the face of France; the heroic drama of Dunkirk had been enacted, and day and night raids were aiming at the destruction of London. Wonersh was not strictly in the path of the bombers, but the blackout had caused the death of two valuable young neighbours, while planes chased out of London were apt to jettison their bombs inconveniently close. Refugee children from the East End were billeted all about the village, but not at The Old House, which was replete with what one might call a crèche of old ladies: my mother, my aunts and a posse of elderly PGs. With the war Dora had taken on a new lease of life and was back cleaning, my mother doing the cooking. Avis had early discovered one could still reach India by an Italian line and had crossed the continent to Venice before France was invaded.

In Ealing I had found a ground-floor bedroom in a private hotel – more accurately a boarding-house – within easy distance of the factory, and Dess found a similar room close by. There was great advantage in being no further away from home, and Dess and I took it in turn to go home for the weekends. Freeman made no comment when one or other of us clocked in an hour late on a Monday morning and dutifully made up the hour in the evening, for the factory closed at an indefinite time. I told myself I was perfectly safe on the ground floor at night, and indeed managed to sleep through outrageous noise, but when we first joined the factory the bombers were passing over us in favour of more spectacular damage in London.

Soon daylight raids got too expensive for the Germans; they hadn't expected such opposition, and before long their tactics changed again, concentrating on factories round the perimeter of London. These bombers took the roof off Freeman's factory and reduced to rubble a small house at its entrance where Mrs Olson, the cleaner, lived with her family. That night was the first occasion of their going to a shelter, so they saved their lives but lost their house.

That night I woke to hear an approaching plane, to know that a bomb was coming at us; there was no scream such as generally presaged the *wump* of a falling bomb. I heard and felt only a mighty explosion, with a loud

173

crack as my window turned into a series of daggers pointing inwards, but luckily not launched from their frame. The house staggered, leant over, and then with Victorian demeanour recovered itself. Two new houses across the road slid down like a pack of cards. That night the bombers kept returning, setting fire to an adjacent church which conveniently lit up the neighbouring targets for them, and bombs went on dropping all night. By that time I was in the cellar with the rest of the household.

Though I worked in Ealing and then in London throughout the war, that was the nearest encounter I had with the enemy. There were minor crises when one found the boarding-house cordoned off because of a land-mine or unexploded bomb, and suffered the ridiculous situations resulting in overcrowded, makeshift quarters. I remember a night sleeping beside a total stranger under a double bed of someone I didn't know but who offered shelter in portions of her house she considered safe. Everyone had his or her bomb story, and that was mine.

*

On the whole Freeman – and in fact all of us working for him – did pretty well out of that night of bombing. His machines, under a coating of rubble, were unharmed, and we were given a few days' holiday while Freeman used his powers to secure other premises. This resulted in our taking over the showrooms and repair shops vacated by a leading motor firm, even closer to my lodgings. The previous name was removed from above the showrooms, but not the Prince of Wales's feathers or the Royal Coat of Arms. There was now a much more comfortable spread of activities in a much larger machine shop, with even a tea-making offshoot to it; there was a yard for spray-painting and delivery of goods, and above all there was heating. The former premises had been the epitome of discomfort.

We witnessed the machine tools being levered from their bedding on to steel rods acting as rollers, and then on to low platform transporters. The oil trays at their bases resembled Victorian skirts shrouding the never-to-be-seen ankles, but in this case they revealed not ankles but a glut of broken tools and botched work, conveniently pushed out of sight – not, I fancy, peculiar to Freeman's firm, but at this point starkly revealed.

It was evident from the start that Freeman's was not an orthodox type of factory. He described it as an experimental firm, which gave him more liberty and made it more interesting for us as we were turning out individual work rather than batches of components. Dess and I were put in charge of a large turret lathe which was Freeman's pride and joy; its only drawback was that it constantly gave trouble. The automatic feeds did not always stop where they were set to stop, and once he was convinced it was the machine and not the women who were at fault, he would strip the

174

whole thing down and send for an authority from the firm which made it, a man who came in some state of alarm.

We would then return to the job to find things much as they were before but, forewarned, we no longer relied on the automatic stops. We managed well till an evening when concerted effort broke down. A ⅝-inch drill fitted up in the capstan was just not clear of the cross-feed coming in at right angles, and as they met there was a blinding flash of light and a loud *ping*, and a large chunk of metal hit the far wall of the machine shop, luckily encountering no human body on its course. We had broken a large and costly tool. Freeman was absent, but remembering what we had seen under the uprooted machine, we made a point next morning of accosting him with our confession and the broken fragments. He was so astonished he said nothing at all – that is, not to us.

There was no doubt Freeman treated us with a deference he certainly did not show to the general run of his employees, whom he described as 'scum'. They were a diverse lot: some quite skilled refugee Jews from Germany, local lads hoping to avoid call-up by going into munitions, a few local girls, while his foreman was an amiable Italian, always taking the way of least resistance, and formerly an ice-cream seller. They minded a lot when Freeman lashed out at them, and it was soon evident he had a violent temper which made itself audible in spasmodic outbursts above the noise of the machinery, sounding rather like Donald Duck. I found 'My' one morning, who made tea and managed the tool store, mascara mingled with tears on her cheeks, as she whimpered, 'He called me one of *them*.' And the foreman was so shocked he couldn't contain the information and had to tell us that over the breakage of the drill Freeman had called us 'two bloody cows'. I think he was also shocked at our reaction, describing it as justifiable if not wholly accurate. There was no doubt that Freeman also had a modicum of charm, and these employees that he both scorned and underpaid held him in highest esteem. Before the raid, while we were still barely twenty in number, he took the majority of us to the local pub for drinks before breaking up for the holiday.

Once into the new building, there was an increase in staff – one or two useful workers – also more machinery, and a night shift was started. Dess and I were saddled with a huge capstan lathe which should have been automatically turning out dozens of similar components, but which we were using in the place of the former lathe, turning, drilling and screw-cutting individual projects which Freeman brought us in the form of a blueprint and a lump of steel. He then left us to get on with it. This was so fascinating that when Dess left to get married I remained on, fully aware the firm was not of the importance we had been led to believe, that there were chronic misdeeds I felt I ought to report; but probably they were not unique to this firm, and where was the dividing line between loyalty to one's firm and to the nation?

A further reason for making no move at this time was a sad rebuff from Chatto & Windus, telling me *Vagabondage* was too long for the present shortage of paper; I must cut it down by at least a quarter. To do this, and since I was on individual work, I asked Freeman if I could come to the firm at six in the morning, to which he agreed so long as I did the eight hours. I believe at the time it was illegal for women to be employed during the night shift, but Freeman was a law unto himself and by this scheme I left the firm at four o'clock in the afternoon.

I spent the evening in the tedious and delicate task of pruning my manuscript, thankful only that raids were now sporadic and Ealing no longer a target. I sat in a bedroom rightly termed the 'garden room', where as winter advanced, the damp crept up to a high-water mark on the walls, unrestrained by a small gas fire. Then, before dawn, I repaired to the factory, often to find the machine shop reeking with the smell of spray-painting done in the warmth rather than out in the yard. The night shift, on leaving, opened everything up to dispel the fumes, which, however, were still hanging around when I came back from breakfast. A factory inspector who came at intervals was obliged to have evidence from her own eyes and nose, but they were never there at the right time.

During this period there was an increase in wages for factory workers of both sexes, but not a sign of it at Freeman's, nor any agitation from those employed until they met workers from other firms, when there was loud complaint. I was asked to tackle Freeman, for my independence resulting from not being beholden to the boss for present or future career had been noticed. I tackled the Technical Officer from the Ministry of Labour, who said he would report it to headquarters, and to my surprise the pay was granted. This led to my becoming a sort of unofficial personnel manager: would I tackle the milkman to come before rather than after the tea break? Could I tackle a landlady charging an exorbitant price for a refugee German? Certainly it taught me that Germany was not the only country that exploited Jews.

*

Vagabondage came out in 1941 and ran merrily through the two editions allowed under paper rationing. Freeman appeared to appreciate having an author in his firm; he ordered three copies, got me to sign them and gave me leave, when the book secured me a contract with the BBC to talk on *Woman's Hour* about Malaya. Here many husbands were now posted. I learnt afterwards the machines were switched off during the five-minute talk so that I could be heard, and later I was allowed to fulfil a couple of lec-

176

tures on the journey from India, for which I was booked by two clubs in the North.

Then there was a remarkable gesture, based I think on a false premise, when who should turn up at the firm, resplendent in Air Force uniform and now in charge of a coastal balloon barrage, but David of the *Wild Goose* venture. He had read *Vagabondage* and learnt my whereabouts from home, and the first knowledge I had of his presence was through Mrs Olson, wreathed in smiles: 'Oh, Miss Parsons, there's a lovely young airman asking for you in Freeman's office.' The machine shop was agog when Freeman brought him in to show off the firm, and I learnt David had secured my freedom for the morning, for it was a Saturday and David had one day's remnant of leave.

Now we talked, walking along the towing-path to Richmond, lunching on a balcony overlooking the river and then seeing the enthralling film *Target for Tonight*, when I was assured the control room of a balloon barrage was not as dramatic as the one shown, that managing balloons was very like managing a square-sailed schooner, to which no doubt David owed his present promotion. I learnt also of his own publishing triumphs, one of which brought him fan mail from the then Prince of Wales. Then he returned to the coast of Cardiff and I went belatedly home.

All this I must concede, and it was summertime, the spray-painting was done in the yard and my bicycle bell a different colour on every occasion, until the number of coats of paint rendered it mute.

I missed Dess a lot when she left the firm to get married, but was consoled by sharing in an important job: supplying to Admiralty, Air Force and Army Headquarters a small mono-radial hydraulic pump with exceptional driving and lifting power. It was a French invention, but with the fall of France many English firms were producing it, and castings supplied to Freeman's were duly machined and assembled.

My job was to turn the flange of its cover to an exact fit with an orifice, already machined, in the body of the pump, a fit which had to be exact to a fraction of an inch. I found that this machined part could vary in size, even if only by a fraction, and thus each pump had to have its individual cover, and I was careful to despatch each pump body with the cover in position.

On the days when a van called for a specific number of pumps, the foreman was scuttling round like a scared rabbit to have the quota ready, and I was sceptical of the last pumps assembled ever having been put to test. No complaints appeared to have been made, but the work at Freeman's often troubled me. I was to feel this acutely one morning arriving at 6 a.m. to find one of my covers fixed up in a fitter's clamp, and he was about to *file* the flange. He said, rightly, it did not fit the pump body. Nor did it. I went and found covers spread about indiscriminately, but amongst

177

them found the correct one. Thereafter I marked each cover and pump body.

I had closed my eyes to too many lapses. Complaint to Freeman merely brought vengeance, not correction. I must find another firm. Yet I was wary of appealing for help from Verena as I knew she wanted me to assist her at the Ministry of Labour, and not only was an office job anathema to me, but surely it was better to use my experience at a factory. At this point, however, all was taken out of my hands by the passing of the Essential Works Order, which clamped me down. I must now prove evidence of a superior job offered me if I was to obtain release from Freeman's.

Thus I was still working at the firm when a drama arose into which I was drawn to a point of no return. One cannot live with oneself for forty years without getting to know something of one's own character, yet any positive statement I could make about mine, equally the opposite seemed to be true. Mine was a nature that only the proverbial last straw roused to action in self-defence, yet there was a tiger inside me which would stir my fury and incite me to impetuous action in the face of rank injustice.

*

There stood in the machine shop a massive diamond grinder, said to have been part of a consignment being shipped to France from America at the outbreak of war. On news of the fall of France, the ship was diverted to Southampton, and Freeman had been at the ship's side to acquire bargains. Industrial diamonds were being increasingly used for cutting, shaping and surfacing, and this machine which offered improved methods had stood idle ever since I joined the firm, either because there was no call for it, or because no one knew fully how to use it; but firms all over the country were screaming for machine tools.

I was much relieved, therefore, one morning to see a young man stride into the machine shop, approach the grinder with every confidence, and study a blueprint spread out on the bench. This was an Irishman, one Barney by name, though I never spoke to him, I learnt later had been engaged by Freeman as a foreman, yet was put on to what he considered unskilled work and, much disappointed in the firm, was seeking his release. An employer, however, was now as much restricted as an employee and could not dismiss a worker save for insubordination or sabotage. This was no doubt the cause of an argument when Freeman later came to see Barney at work, and soon Donald Duck noises were resounding through the shop, suppressed smiles visible on the faces of all the older hands.

It was Friday, when there was no tea break as the firm closed early, so we went to the tea hatch to fetch our teas, and Freeman's face was showing every sign of resentment when Barney went to fetch his. It so happened that, while he was at the hatch, the electric motor of the grinder burnt out, black smoke pouring out of it as it so often did. Each machine had its own electric motor and one of them was always giving trouble in spite of constant repair, and since the big grinder was never used, a swap had been made, consigning the faulty motor to the grinder.

I did not actually see the smoke as I was still leaving at 4 p.m., but I did see and hear Freeman shout at Barney across the shop: 'You're fired!' whereon Barney, only too thankful for release, walked out of the shop as jauntily as he had walked in.

During the following week Freeman, the foreman and a couple of troubled-looking policemen pored over the grinder and the component. I had already witnessed this sort of scene when one of the Germans had come in for a course of intimidation, but everyone seemed to think it would all blow over, only it didn't. A week later it was reported in the local paper, very much from Freeman's point of view, that Barney was being taken to court in a fortnight's time, clearly on grounds of sabotage.

It struck me Barney would not even have known that the electric motor was faulty, and that a statement ought to be secured from the firm's electrician. As no one seemed prepared to make the move, I stuck my neck out so far as to write to the electrician myself, to receive in reply the address of Barney's solicitor, who evidently had forestalled me. I felt this let me out of any further interference, but I now got a letter from the solicitor asking me to see him and give my account of the incident, and he certainly seemed to think the case serious, if nobody else did. Barney, an Irishman, was in a vulnerable position, and after I had given my evidence he asked me to give it in court. I was harrowed by this idea; I knew nothing of court procedure and how could I get leave... ? The solicitor could get me subpoenaed, and my evidence in court would make all the difference, and that of any other worker if I could get it. Only one was prepared to support me; most advised me not to touch it, and looking back on it I seem to have been left with the whole thing on my shoulders.

*

Barney and a quite different solicitor were outside the door of the court when I arrived, Barney in highest spirits and quite convinced Freeman 'was bats'. Within, I encountered Freeman, who nodded to me brightly, and the foreman with him, who grinned. Witnesses for the accused were not allowed in court till called; nevertheless, Donald Duck noises soon penetrated the walls, which I felt was all in Barney's favour.

When I was called, the first thing I noticed was Barney's face, white as a sheet. I faced four magistrates, two of them barely awake, one a bright little woman, very alert, and a big man much in charge who established my

179

identity, the position of my machine in relation to the grinder, and passed me to Freeman's solicitor, who I noticed could not look me in the eye. His trump card was to ask was I a wartime worker, hoping to establish imbecility. I agreed I was, and should have mentioned the Loughborough diploma, which no one knew about, but it made no difference. The vital moment was when Barney's new solicitor, with little knowledge of the case, it seemed, asked me to tell the court what I had seen on the momentous date. My confession that I had not seen the electric motor burning out made him drop his hands to his sides like one dealing with an idiot, so I quickly added: '*But I've seen it happen many times before.*' The deadly silence throughout the court suggested this was the first hint of truth.

I was about to step down when the little bright-eyed magistrate asked if there was much trouble in the firm and, having been told that brevity added force in giving evidence, I put much eloquence into the one word, 'Yes.' I was followed by the union representative giving evidence in favour of Barney, but no one appeared deeply interested; the Court seemed anxious to adjourn, which they finally did, leaving me with the reporters. One came over to me. 'This is the most extraordinary case: an employee giving evidence against her boss! D'you know you've saved this man?'

I said that was what I had come to do, but I found it hard to believe, on such brief statements, that I could have done so. I was asked many questions about myself but also learnt that all cases of sabotage were taken up by the Government. It was the Director of Public Prosecutions who had brought the case on Freeman's evidence. Thus Barney had no comeback if he wished to make a countercharge.

At this point all came back into the room to hear that the case had been dismissed. As I passed Barney on the way out, he wrung my hand in a convulsive grip, but could not speak. He was on the verge of tears.

No retribution ever came; in fact there was little Freeman could take, as he was not even able to sack me. The following Friday when I went to work I found the night shift had spread on my bench the *Middlesex and County Times*, which told me I was an 'estimable woman'. It gave an outline of the case brought against Barney of wilfully overstraining his machine, but in the light of later evidence it was submitted that the charge should never have been brought, and the case was dismissed.

I now had no other motive than to get clear of this firm, and Verena was emphatic about coming to the tribunal to see that I did. During this time I had learnt that at the Ministry I would not be divorced from factory life, even if no longer a machinist. Also I would be earning a decent wage. I put in my claim for release, and Freeman blocked it, so I had to apply to the National Service officer, who found this incredible in view of recent events; but I knew that Freeman resented outside interference and had a useful worker at little cost. It was this which won me my freedom. I fully described the work I was doing, the limits to which I worked, and tossed in my diploma from three years' training at Loughborough. I got my release.

Let it be added, however, that having severed connections with a machine shop, and sitting alone in an office of the Ministry of Labour HQ, I longed for my bawdy companions, yearned for the noise of the machinery and to be using my hands instead of my yet untutored brain. I loathed the messenger who came at intervals to look accusingly at my empty OUT tray and left me with files that I did not know what to do with. Verena, when time spared her, came and briefed me on office routine and took me to meet officers of my section whom I must get to know. My general reaction was expressed in my catching measles at this point, and having a blissful span of sick leave.

*

When I was convalescent, Betty came for a weekend, bringing a friend, Mary Cornish, who had volunteered at the outbreak of war to escort children to Canada and America, at that time of course by sea. She had since become famous by surviving eight days in an open boat, a solitary woman with six small boys, two ship's officers and thirty-six Lascars, crew of the *City of Benares* torpedoed on its way to Canada. We listened to many things not related to the press or even to Elspeth Huxley, who was later to give an account of it in her book *Atlantic Ordeal,* and Mary kept up with the boys for the rest of her life, two of whom went to sea.

Mary Cornish lived close to Portman Square, where I would be working, and told me of a conveniently adjacent restaurant run by a remarkable Irishwoman, Miss Morone, who gave such good lunches at moderate cost that those who discovered the place – almost underground beneath George Street – formed a daily clique of which I soon became a member. Another friend of ours, Sybil Clement Brown, recommended her boarding-house in Hampstead, so I was well established on return to the Ministry of Labour.

I saw many more of my friends working in London, including Elspeth, now a cook in the WRNS; but later she was sent to Alexandria on intelligence work. Dr Jensen remained at his flat in Berkeley Square, where his collection of early armoury proved invaluable protection seeking raid casualties, for the West End still saw sporadic bombing.

I often visited Mrs Robinson's niece, Barbara Buckmaster, living in the much bombed and burnt Temple, where she had been allowed to retain her top-floor flat in Kings Bench Walk after her barrister husband died. The flat was now solitary and prominent at the top of an empty building, a burnt-out ruin on one side of it and a bomb-site on the other, and its survival was due to Barbara's courage in remaining there. From this elevation she could see where the incendiary bombs lodged and could instruct the firemen where to find them and, above all, where to turn off the gas main. She saved much more than her own flat. Barbara's daughter Celia had married Edmund Leach, then working in Burma, and I sat riveted listening to her adventures on the approach of the Japanese and getting a newborn daughter home to England. Edmund meanwhile was an officer in the Burma Rifles.

Sometime in the brooding calm of 1939 Esmond Morrison had called on me before departing for Malaya, asking me if I could give him any good tips about the country. I told him if he ever got a few days' leave to go to the Green Cow Tavern, even higher up the mountains than Cameron Highlands, the popular resort. A doctor's widow had turned a Chinese shop-house into a hotel, and she was an excellent cook. I had met her in Singapore and paid a brief visit to Green Cow to find, on the edge of the jungle and by the simplest and most ingenious means, she had made a delightfully cool and comfortable place to stay. I knew Esmond would appreciate it, and I got an enthusiastic letter before he was called on to fight a rearguard action all down the length of Malaya, finally to be taken prisoner and recruited for work on the Death Railway.

His sister, called Tommie, gave me his first prisoner of war address, to which I wrote a long letter, avoiding all sensitive subjects certainly, but otherwise giving a picture of life at home. I did the same for another prisoner of war, and strangely both letters arrived. They were the last to do so, but gave a tremendous boost not only to the recipient but to the rest of the camp, as I learnt later. Correspondence, when finally organized by the Red Cross, was a printed postcard with a couple of lines for free expression, over which one spent endless trouble trying to express maximum cheer in minimum space.

As the anniversary of Pearl Harbour approached, I was asked to do a quarter-hour talk on Japan. I found my knowledge of Japan barely filled the time. This was at the sacred hour of 6 p.m. – the news in those days was at nine o'clock. However, with Jean Rowntree at Broadcasting House coaching me, I seemed to edify those listening, though I always found it more harrowing talking to a machine than to an audience.

At Broadcasting House I met Christina Foyle, who put me on the Foyle lecture agency, and it was bliss now to have the spadework done for me: date, terms proffered, rail ticket and sleeper or hotel booked for a night, the cheque discreetly following. At the Ministry I could usurp days from my leave to meet random events, and how I loved the comfortable old sleepers then being employed, with all their accessories: coat-hangers, places to hang one's (turnip) watch by the bedside, and a cup of tea brought in the morning. So now I experienced a diversity of halls, from a huge cinema with radio transmission to cosy lecture rooms, and flattering introductions. These lectures were mostly on the journey from India.

In London I found my fellow lodgers quite inured to the old-fashioned air raids that were by then restricted to night-time and concentrated further south than Hampstead. I had not been long at the Ministry before the flying bombs started, a day and night hazard and at first no all-clear sounded at all. Moreover, some were aimed at specific targets, including a concentration of Air Force dwellings north of Regent's Park. I was afraid of the outer wall of the lodging-house collapsing, leaving my bedroom, and those below, exposed to the world like a doll's house with the door open, a common sight in London at that time. As my bed would have been teetering on the outside edge, for a while I slept below, but as none of these bombs reached further than Regent's Park itself, we all returned to our natural bedding, inured even to the horrendous noise of our defence. Very soon, during the daily round, one listened for the cut-out of the flying bomb, and when this and the explosion were fairly distant one remained utterly indifferent.

I feel I should mention that one of the first reports I read on return to the office from measles told me of a chronic shortage throughout the country of skilled grinders. So if I did nothing else for the war effort, at least I had helped to save one of them from going needlessly to prison.

*

Surprisingly, I remained seven years in the Ministry of Labour. My first office was in a block of flats commandeered in Portman Square, then we were moved to a house in St James's Square between the headquarters office and the London Library – very handy for taking books home at weekends. Finally we were installed in a private house (now demolished) in Berkeley Square, where my top-floor office was no doubt once a housemaid's bedroom, looking down directly on to where the Roosevelt statue was later installed. I had an uninterrupted view of the statue's installation, and later the unveiling by Mrs Roosevelt with a gathering of the whole Royal Family.

The loneliness in the first of these offices was soon dispelled by the intrusion of a second lot of furniture, followed by Magda Phillips, with whom I was to share the room and who showed a blatant contempt for her amateur room-mate. She recognized me as a fish out of water and belonging to a despised social class. Magda, with Communist sympathies, had been to Russia on a fact-finding expedition, had been one of a team of secretaries for Lloyd George, in fact had all the experience and self-confidence that I lacked, and while approving of my engineering training, she found my connection with Empire unforgivable. It was quite a time before the opposing forces in the life of this large-hearted, entertaining and religious woman were revealed to me, a tangled web unravelled by degrees; in fact, our con-

fidences considerably illuminated that dreary office, and Magda, despairing
of my ignorance of modern poetry, read 'Little Gidding' aloud to me
between the entries of the messenger.

Neither of us at that time had enough work to do; measles had upset my
programme, as the photographer booked to accompany me to remote factories had been transferred to other business and I had to await his return.

Verena had found it was the employer as much as the women who
needed training. Those early courses at the Beaufoy were largely wasted as
the women were put on such elementary jobs that they left. It became my
job to find cases of women on sensible work, have them photographed and
get a book compiled. Quite a number of employers, on conversion, became
rather proud of their skilled women, but others preferred to keep women on
low wages to do the donkey work. There was a strong tendency for the
machine tool to do the precision work, leaving the dead-end job to the
human.

I remember an arms factory very proud of a new automatic precision
gauge for checking the dimensions of bullets. These were fed mechanically
into it and emerged with a green or red light according to whether accurate
or faulty. It was the duty of generally a young girl to disperse the bullets
into 'Reject' or 'Retention' bin according to the light. Cheap labour
encouraged this sort of unfinished invention, and when I said I would
admire it more if it did its own selected ejection, I was of course told of the
additional cost. They did admit, however, that they often found the human
fallible, and I did not wonder. Sometimes there floated into my mind the
memory of the women breaking stones by the roadside in Greece, and I felt
they had the better bargain.

My reports to Verena were useful, so I was kept at visiting factories long
after the photo handbook was launched and distributed to the regional officers. Sometimes I visited two or three firms a day, a generally exhausting
but interesting ploy. Factories of over a hundred employees were still exceptional, and I found the workers preferred family firms; they liked to know
for whom they were working – it promoted a personal touch sometimes
lacking in the larger factory with every amenity. What I never quite
resolved was the source and the inspiration of enthusiasm that existed in
some factories and not in others. Why, in what seemed a deserving firm,
should there be a lethargy and indifference that one could sense from the
moment of arrival, when a dirty scruffy little firm, defying countless Home
Office regulations, could display a community working like bees, each
feeling a share in the final enterprise? Ultimately it must be a question of
management; some were rather more subtle than others.

Sometimes Verena accompanied me. We did a tour of factories in Scotland together and I realized how hard she was overworking. Her profession
had long been exposed to some of the meanest male prejudices; she was

184

only now winning the merits she had long since earned because they could no longer be withheld. We returned to Edinburgh late one evening after an exhausting day, to find most things gone from the menu at the Caledonian Hotel. In the main, Scotland was bountiful compared with England; one found soap supplied on washstands and a greater choice of good food, but it was not inexhaustible and we were late. Verena would have accepted baked beans and gone to her bedroom to write up her notes; however, I seized a waitress and asked, where could we get a good meal?

'Wait now while I tell you. . . .'

I think it was in Prince's Street. One sat at tables enclosed in loose boxes; there was soothing lighting, and it would have been sacrilege not to have had wine. Definitely not the place for the prescribed Government allowance, but we had eaten below level for the best part of the tour, so I had no conscience, and Verena succumbed under the influence of a most acceptable meal. The Irishness, the amusement, the warmth of her character again blossomed, and I hoped that that night she slept.

*

During the years of drifting from artist to adventurer I had neglected my early enthusiasms, rarely attending either meeting or conference of the Women's Engineering Society. Fellow members looked on me as a rolling stone and with every cause, but I had kept up my subscription and had spasmodically written articles for their magazine.

I certainly attended the lecture given by Amy Johnson – then a mere child in appearance – on returning from her solo flight to Australia. It was a memorable and rousing evening in the drawing-room of Lady Shelly Rolls. There was to be supper afterwards but the lecture got so out of hand with the combined enthusiasm of audience and lecturer that Lady Shelly Rolls had to keep withdrawing to get supper postponed.

Miss Haslett never looked on me as a lost member, and after I had returned from the Balkans, at my request, she arranged a member's visit to the Dagenham Ford works to see the Ford of the day through all processes from a pile of iron ore to the finished article. I had even asked her to join the Pacific Settlement Company, feeling her stable character would be such an asset. She considered it an honour to be asked, but thought it was not her *métier*.

I was now firmly back in the fold, and at a conference when Miss Haslett was President, she asked me to give a short talk on my general review of British factories. During this talk I thought I saw listeners getting hot under the collar and remembered that managerial staff often attended these conferences, and Miss Haslett was plainly enjoying secret amusement when she later thanked me. It appeared I had innocently said what needed saying

185

and what many had longed to say, though I never learnt what it was. Miss Haslett would have smoothed ruffled feathers; she was an expert chairman, never forgot anything or anyone, or ever had to grope for a name. She was soon to become Dame Caroline.

By 1943–44 the pattern of life had changed. Verena was busy on apprenticeship schemes and was soon to leave the Ministry for other interests. I no longer had my room-mate, for Magda's allowance of sick leave had ebbed away in two operations for a tubercular knee joint, though her vigour seemed in no way impaired by a resultant stiff leg. We were to meet again in civilian life, but in the meantime the bulk of her work was now handed to me, of which the only part I enjoyed was the editing of the Ministry magazine. Magda had secured a clerk to do the proofreading and often roped me in to write or edit an article for the technical staff. So I slid into the task of making this journal interesting, even sometimes amusing, to balance the more boring reports it had to contain; and a seasoning of lighter, less official entries seemed to be appreciated. I got fan mail.

I was recruited nevertheless for one further expedition to the regions; the Ministry of Labour, at Admiralty request, did a survey of Admiralty drawing-offices which were suffering both a shortage of staff and disaffection. A powerful team under C. P., later Lord, Snow was mustered, and my recruitment was due to the many women tracers employed.

I found it an awesome ordeal. Though in the dockyards women were doing ship's fitting, were welding and wiring, and WRNS had taken over a lot of men's work, yet in the bosom of headquarters – installed in Bath during the war – a woman was an inferior to whom no one of importance spoke. It was a shock to them to find one in the Ministry team, and as the dining-room in which we were to lunch was strictly reserved for men, I was asked – certainly with slight embarrassment – to have my meal with the tracers.

However, I learnt at this lunch of the women's loathing for the wiring diagrams they had to trace, and the consequent shortage of tracers. I fear my suggestion of using some form of copying machine would not at that time have been implemented, though I trust it is now. So really my only contribution to that survey was a page of portraits of our team, which I did for my own amusement but eventually showed them at our final meeting in London. I often did these pencil portraits, slightly caricatured, and noted now that each regarded his own thoughtfully but roared with laughter at the others. Someone suggested getting copies done on the Treasury photocopier, so it was sent there, but the Treasury was promptly bombed. Nevertheless, as if of vital importance, it was retrieved from a dust heap where it had been blown across a yard, and copies of it were eventually supplied.

That was typical of wartime London; people carried on exactly the same, nothing too small for consideration, nothing they would not do to reduce the set-backs, and it was this spirit that, in spite of the bombing, made me love London in the war. It was dirty; there was no one to clean the streets, and during a bitter winter the buses, on drawing up, piled up hummocks of snow over which they came leaping to a halt. To stand too near the kerb was to get splashed to the waist with what started as snow and soon turned to mud. Everyone accepted these trials with universal goodwill.

One weekend towards D Day – whose date was still unknown – I was late going home on a Saturday, so I bicycled to Waterloo and put my bicycle on the train. Thus I had my own transport to Wonersh. It was a clear night, the sky lit with stars, but I was aware of a droning sound, though there had been no air-raid warning. On reaching Wonersh I got off my bicycle and studied the sky. It looked as if the whole constellation of Heaven was moving across the sky, but these were not stars. I was looking at a tremendous fleet of planes moving in slow formation, but on what errand and to what destination I could not know. Never was there an exercise of greater precision and discipline. I hope they were not setting out to bomb Dresden.

*

The eighth of May 1945 we were at peace. Or were we? Korea, China, Vietnam, Japan were all to continue fighting, but anyhow Britain had a national holiday, for which I went home. When I returned I felt constrained to go to St Paul's, that great symbol of defiance, that assurance that God was in His Heaven; but He was not at home that evening. It was a shock to find the doors closed, with a conclave of people patiently waiting on the steps and finally drifting away – the first hint that a paucity of control could not contain the crowds now flowing into London.

A trickle had started returning to the city as early as 1943 but this was now a spate, resulting in such congestion that soon it was difficult to find a bed in London at any price, and the character of landladies stood revealed. Some remained loyal to the lodgers who had seen them through a long lean period, others got rid of them wholesale to raise the fees and make easier terms for themselves. In contrast to the latter, Miss Morone celebrated peace by giving all her clients a free lunch. Since I had continued to patronize her cellar, none of my offices being far out of reach, I was one to enjoy this handsome gesture, which must have been quite costly for one who only at rare intervals apologized for having to raise her price by a few pence.

At the Ministry, those who had encroached during wartime, as I had, were now facing dismissal or seeking to get established. I had no appetite for the latter, but saw no reason to divest myself of the best salary I had ever earned, so I decided to stay on till sacked. This did not happen for nearly three years because amongst other ploys they decided to get me to write an analysis of the engineering trade as a training course for vacancy officers. Engineering covers a wide field; it amounted to writing a book with accompanying diagrams, and looking at it now I don't know how I did it.

Staying on in London, I saw many warriors returning from overseas, amongst them, surprisingly, Kilton Stewart, from whom I had heard little since Pearl Harbour. He was now anxious to resume his studies at the LSE, and had brought with him a high-powered secretary, Clara, under whose influence all negotiations had been made. They had secured at minimum cost the top flat in a house shortly to be demolished, and this was soon adorned with *objects d'art* from the luggage retrieved from Wonersh. Here Kilton was to dictate his thesis, to hold evening sessions of group therapy, while Clara cooked meals, laundered clothes and saw to it that all would-be hangers-on were firmly turned out of the flat.

Kilton had indeed acquired the needed nanny, and certainly she was tidying up his life, but he believed he was going to regain his independence on their return to the States. I foresaw this was forever, as stubbornly as he saw I would get caged up forever if I went back and lived at home. Mine was the more accurate forecast and the only solution likely to survive. Seven years after returning to the States they got married, and they suffered two years of ebbing fortune in London before the thesis was accepted and the Ph.D. acquired. By then they were living on coffee, the flat bare of ornaments and the knackers at the door.

I therefore saw Kilton rarely, especially as, along with the other old-timers, I was soon to be shot out of our Hampstead lodging, and for want of other was now commuting between London and home. When we did meet, each hoped the other had heard news of Pat Noone, a warrior who had never returned.

Last official knowledge was in November 1942 when Noone was known to be alive, suffering from malnutrition and bouts of malaria, but it was not these that killed him. He had a beautiful mistress, Anjang, a half-caste Temiar Malay, but with the approach of war and no knowledge of where he would be sent or if he would return, before he came on leave to England, Pat gave her in Temiar rites of marriage to the headman of her group, who had always languished after her. When he was sent back to almost the same area but behind enemy lines, reporting to army headquarters, he was rejoined by Anjang, of her own volition, and Pat was eventually killed by poisoned darts that Anjang's husband, like all his tribe, was so skilled in using. All this came to light eventually but the act so shamed the aborigines that none would speak of it. Dennis Holman in 1958 published an account of Noone's life and death in his book *Noone of the Ulu*.

Esmond Morrison survived the Death Railway. He and Tommie visited us at The Old House one weekend, and I found myself apprehensive as a much shrunken figure got out of the car. I feared that what he had endured must have embittered his normally level judgement. There was in fact no bitterness; he dwelt more on the clemency of his own men when the situation was reversed and the prisoners became the guards, able to take any vengeance. The atomic bomb was deplored except as a harbinger of peace.

Esmond had been one of those making contracts outside the camp, thus obtaining necessities without which many more prisoners would have died. He chanced betrayal and detection and admitted his terror of discovery at the investigations that took place at intervals, when those proclaimed guilty were tortured and killed. We were told also of a diminutive 'wireless' smuggled into the camp, listened to in concealment at minimum pitch but a lifeline of increasing hope. When the whole camp was moved to new quarters, it was concealed amongst the luggage of the Camp Commandant, placed there and extracted without detection, a feat that lifted everyone's spirits.

When I next saw Esmond he was regaining his natural size.

*

I have to be grateful for those remaining years in the Ministry; they supplied me with glorious holidays, mainly in Scotland until the continent was unlocked. I went with Sybil Clement Brown one cloudless summer to the Outer Hebrides, sharing with gannets, tern, oyster-catchers and the like, also with a thriving weaving industry, every cottage having its loom. Out on the rocks the wool dyed with local lichens would be drying in the sun. Impossible then to get a modest skirt length; the Americans were ordering it by the bale. I fear it is a waning industry now.

I went to Sweden to say with Barbro, husband Stig and teenage young, all now at Alkvettern, a lovely old timber mansion standing in farmland. Sigrid, now widowed, had a flat in Stockholm with a wide balcony looking out on treetops, where we breakfasted in the morning sun. She gave me a lavish sum for buying clothes, which were still rationed in England, and I cannot describe the joy of coupon-free shopping as I used up the money for self, family and friends.

On the first chance offered I went to Rome, where I had always wanted to prowl on my own without being a chauffeur-courier. What added to the relish was a ticket from my Catholic friends for the canonization in St Peter's of Maria Guiseppa Rosella, of whom I had never heard. Far too conspicuously dressed, I sat in a privileged seat at the end of the north transept, where we were all neatly stowed in separate pens – the diplomatic corps, the aristocracy, the common herd, of which I was one, among a party of nuns and mothers superior, almost embarrassingly close to the Papal chair. We waited a long time in the dawn and dim lighting till the sound of distant chanting proclaimed the Pope's approach in his litter,

189

when every bell in Rome started pealing, music broke like thunder from the great organ, the choir from the Sistine Chapel burst into song and every candle, sconce, chandelier from eye-level to vaulted ceiling burst into light, and the congregation began clapping.

Never had I expected to see St Peter's in such a state of pageantry, and never was there such a posse of cardinals, each with a cardinal's gentleman. As the cortège filed down the transept the tall dignified figure of Pius XII was conspicuous in mitre and gold and silver tunic, the jewelled ring flashing on his finger as he made the sign of the cross to right and left.

When seated in his chair, a deacon on either side of him, we all resumed our seats, including those who had stood on theirs for a better view. In ceremonies following, of which only the sacrament at the high altar was beyond vision, there seemed little reference to the lady being sanctified, but perhaps knowledge of Latin or Greek would have revealed more.

Also the Ministry gave me theatre, and never was there more brilliant theatre than in those postwar years, never more talent. We had Cochran, Ivor Novello, Noel Coward and though the Old Vic was still in shambles from bombing, its directors, Laurence Olivier and Ralph Richardson, leased the New Theatre in St Martin's Lane and put on a repertory of Shakespeare, Chekov, Shaw ... *Arms and the Man* was presented with Ralph Richardson, Laurence Olivier, Sybil Thorndike, Margaret Leighton and Joyce Redman. What more could one want? I kept all my theatre programmes until they fell out of the bookcase and, looking at them later, I could hear the lovely voice of Edith Evans playing the lead in James Bridle's *Daphne Laureoli*, her diction so pure that even in soliloquy she could be heard in the furthest gallery.

Up till the time of working for the Ministry my visits to the theatre had mainly depended on invitation; now it was bliss going when and to what plays I wanted, and even after retirement I would go up in the evenings, bicycling to and from Guildford station as late-night buses were not for some time restored. The Old Vic seemed almost on my doorstep, so near to Waterloo Station, and added to this the Yvonne Arnaud Theatre was soon to be built in Guildford.

I spasmodically attended meetings organized by WES, to keep abreast of the many engineering and scientific developments of the day. Turbojet propulsion and nuclear power were now almost part of life, but I gave up the pursuit about the time of the laser beam and microwave. Membership of the WES had enormously increased and I noticed the difference between the later members and those of the twenties. None of these were afraid of their own voices or waited to be asked their opinions; they gave it freely with confidence and clarity, fully assured of a career ahead.

Influenced originally by David and later through my own factory experience, I had always voted Labour as lending strength to the worker, but I grew disillusioned with the long crippling strikes, so eventually entered the Conservative fold.

I was still a black sheep in Wonersh, however, when commuting to London, driven to and from Guildford station with three hard-baked Conservatives. They would have read the headlines of their morning papers and I was clearly responsible for the fall of Churchill and the handing over of Empire. I made no attempt to refute the snorted accusations tossed in the air ostensibly against Labour but clearly aimed at the socialist member present.

It so happened at this time my mother, a highly esteemed occupant of The Old House, had retired from being voluntary diocesan secretary for the Mothers' Union. It had been difficult to find a replacement or she would never have kept on to such an age, but now that someone had been found, a grand dinner was given for my mother in Guildford and she was presented with a cheque for £100 raised through modest voluntary contributions. I remarked on this to my fellow travellers, going to the station next morning; it was received with deadly silence. Then one of them said, '*A hundred pounds!* Gift. Doesn't even have to pay income tax!' Then again silence. It would seem my political views had contaminated the whole family.

*

It was in the spring of 1949 that I left the Ministry; my analysis of engineering had been read and discussed in, of all places, the ballroom of Spencer House, which was empty and at the disposal of Government requirements. Looking out from its windows at Green Park, it seemed to me sacrilege to submit this beautiful room to such mundane usage, to this gathering of vacancy officers – as those officers placing people in industry were called – along with a sprinkling of higher grades.

All the same it was a great climax.

Almost straight out of the office I was booked for a chauffeur-courier job in Paris, which was heartening, but a one-off job not likely to happen again. At home the elderly PGs had long since departed, to the relief of all, for they could never pull their bedroom curtains so that a shaft of light did not penetrate the street, and Dora was convinced that persistent offenders were going to be shot. Our air-raid warden was nightly on our doorstep.

During the war my mother and aunt spent holidays at Cliff Hall, a charming country hotel near Devizes that Betty had found when working at Westonbirt School. She gave them these holidays, for in the forties hotels were not yet so expensive or pretentious as they later became, and Aunt Tinie was now living in Wiltshire not far distant. Hotels were finding it difficult in wartime to provide linen; guests were asked to bring their own sheets, and the old ladies were soon sitting out in the garden helping to mend tablecloths and napkins, bosom friends of the presiding family. I would join them from London at periodic weekends, and Avis and her small daughter were eventually to join the party, but Aunt Tinie died suddenly in the year of the peace. I had seen her shortly before, but with no idea that the warm heart of this beautiful old lady was presently to fail.

That the roof of The Old House was still over our heads was due to that special protection my mother enjoyed. A friend who lived in London had, during an early air raid, the front door and windows blown out of her house. She phoned my mother asking if she could come for a fortnight while this was sorted out. She settled her own terms, which my mother considered far too generous, and stayed for the rest of her life. It was unnecessary to have any other guest.

Mrs Billy Martindale, generally known as 'Mrs Billy', was in her seventies, quite happy to sit by the fire with her library book and to take mild walks. She enjoyed bridge, good conversation and the company of the young generation, but had lent a kindly ear to the elderly PGs while they remained. She got on well with Muriel and had three grandchildren for whom she was responsible. They stayed in the neighbourhood during school holidays and she took them away in the summer while the old ladies went to Cliff Hall.

Mrs Billy took life as calmly as my mother did; it troubled her not at all that she had the unfortunate habit of falling down; however, she was apt to do greater damage to what she fell on than to herself. I don't known if she was aware of what was soon to dawn on my mother, that these falls were a form of fit, but she looked on them with amusement, and if left for a while could get up of her own accord. When out walking with her granddaughter one day, she fell in a field near the hedgerow, and told me gleefully that next morning she could not think what the pretty trimming in her hat was and found it was barbed wire.

Just such a fit had occurred one Sunday when our forces were converging on England in preparation for D Day, among them a Major who had been billeted on Avis and Deric in India. The Major lived not far from Wonersh, thus he had been asked to call and see the old ladies, and had elected to do this just as Sunday lunch had been laid on the table, and Mrs Billy had fallen flat on the floor, the drawing-room end of the long room.

My mother's inclination to ask people in was modified by this time, but the Major was already in, had seen the meal on the table, and was saying he wouldn't stop now, he would come in later but couldn't pass the door without just. . . . My aunt had by now joined my mother in bright conversation, neither of them skilled in deception and both confident that Mrs Billy was hidden from view. In fact the Major had clearly seen, and wrote to

Avis saying he thought her mother and aunt perfectly sweet, but could not account for what appeared to be a dead body lying at the far end of the room. Luckily an account of the scene had already reached Avis.

1950–1960

PUTTING THE PIECES TOGETHER

Over the years changes had taken place in Wonersh and were still doing so. The parkland of the former Grantley Manor – now pulled down and become an exclusive building estate, but cushioned from the street by a church green and the grounds of a large recently built house adopting the name of Wonersh Park. Two unoffending smaller building groups had grown up, and two stately homes were now occupied by more than one family. In population terms Wonersh was no longer strictly a village but a wide spreading residential area, yet still enclosing common and farm land.

Our shoemaker tenant at The Old House had been forced into retirement, not so much by age as the difficulty of securing shoe leather in the war. Reluctantly he had abandoned his trade and the shop that he had retained at the west end of The Old House. He now became warden of Wonersh church and grounds.

For us this opened up possibilities. It was growing increasingly evident that cooking and shopping were getting beyond my mother's capabilities, and there were three empty rooms besides the shoemaker's shop. The fact that they had been left as box-rooms was not merely for lack of funds to do otherwise; an outdoor lavatory was clamped to the wall of one of them and the status quo seemed justified in consideration of the shoemaker. Peace, however, had revealed a grave housing shortage, and I was still in my palmier days at the Ministry. What if we made these rooms into kitchen, bedsitter and bathroom and offered a small ground-floor flat in exchange for cooking? Betty came in on this too.

My mother agreed, and moreover was eligible for a grant towards it. I made out a plan but, on showing it to our plumber, learnt the grant would never be issued for an indoor lavatory when one already existed outside. We went out and looked at this uninspiring equipment masked by a lean-to shed, and I saw a light come into the plumber's eye and knew we were both thinking the same thing.

When the council viewed the site and gave its blessing there was only a pipe above ground level with a tap on it, obviously for a garden hose, even if this might seem excessive for a small patch of ground separated from the main garden by a massive spiraea hedge.

I can't say the grant went far to cover the fittings I installed, but a tolerable flat resulted. What I hadn't foreseen was the toil of finding a tenant pleasant, useful, and not merely seeking a roof. Only in the last years of this arrangement did we get near to the ideal, a woman I chose, apart from her record, because she had kind eyes.

Now, however, I had the shoemaker's shop as my workshop, feeling proud to move my bench and tools into a room that had supported a craft for over a century. And now I had time to get on with a project very near to my heart, for when I learnt Avis was expecting a baby I wrote urging her to have a daughter, as I had always wanted to make a doll's house. She had co-operated.

I hadn't got far with it because my all-too-brief weekends had been massively filled with lawn-mowing, apple-picking, copious repairs and, in cold winters, climbing into the attic to release a frozen stopcock to let water into the cold tank before the hot-water tank exploded. There was reward for this, however; in shining my torch along the full length of the attic, I saw a serried line of lean-to-beams meeting at a common apex like ranks of faithful soldiers forever on duty. It was an inspiring sight.

Another hindrance to the doll's house was that in wartime one had to apply to the Government for supplies of wood, and I doubted it would be granted for so frivolous a scheme. I had made an architectural plan of the house, scaled an inch to a foot, and had sufficient wood of my own to cover most of it, but needed a plank of certain width and thickness for four dividing walls, and this I lacked.

It may be remembered that most of the furniture in The Old House belonged to my aunt, who had in her bedroom a stout cupboard used exclusively for hanging clothes, but there were shelves that could be installed if desired, and these to my horror she had put in the shed where I stored the apples, whose structure though stout and waterproof was riddled with woodworm. There they were going to remain forgotten, so I went and prospected, to find them under a mountain of dust neither warped nor attacked. Without the smallest conscience I appropriated them.

Thus, now that I was at home, I assuaged my early yearnings towards architecture in building a house vaguely classical in design, with hipped roof and balcony, with staircase and bathroom, and had now reached the stage of making furniture and decorating. A black and white parquet floor was a severe test of patience and of a steady hand. I was under no delusion that the child would ever get the pleasure out of it that I was enjoying, or was providing for neighbours who looked in.

Yet I was not at peace. I must find a job, subscribe to the household. Courier jobs were now cramped, not so much by currency restrictions as by a belief that the continent, not yet restored, was engrossed in rebuilding. So it was, but my visits to Rome and Paris had shown me that foreigners were

195

very welcome. On the Paris tour I was driving Mrs Robinson's sister-in-law, whom I had met at Roos; her Gellibrand husband had died and she was now Mrs Nicholas, her later husband a delegate at the UNESCO conference being held in Paris. While he was pent up at work, Grace and I enjoyed a Paris never more light-hearted, and when we all three drove to the theatre of an evening we found it never more talented. It was a rare gift but short-lived.

I had lost my writing contacts; the *Bystander*, now clamped to the *Tatler* and under a new editor, was quite different in character. There was no hope of a reprint of *Vagabondage*, a travel book far out of date. I must seek something more stable than writing.

I visualized a steady part-time job, preferably away from home but giving me enough time on my return for myself and the household. The Labour Exchange seemed to have no part-time work available and was pressing me to be a full-time personnel manager at a small factory near Guildford, within easy bicycling reach and well paid. In fact the job had everything in its favour except it would usurp all my precious time.

The Labour Exchange, deeply impressed that I had worked at headquarters, was determined to place me in it and urged me to go anyway for an interview, and conscience at least compelled me to comply. I had an interview with a secretary who seemed equally enthusiastic and felt I had all the right experience, and I found myself being sucked in. Little can be achieved in official life, however, without the filling in of a form, and it was this which pulled me from the brink. It asked the date of my birth. The secretary was bowled over on finding I was just fifty; she thought she was good at assessing age, would have said late thirties or early forties. Never did I bicycle home with a lighter heart.

Did my youthfulness spring from following my inclinations? If so, it was now given an extra boost by my throwing aside my pious intentions and accepting an invitation to go with Elspeth to Cyprus.

*

Elspeth, when posted to Alexandria, had sold her Sydney Street maisonette and on demobilization had bought one of the coachman's cottages in Markham Street, Chelsea. It had a room on each of four floors, starting with a basement kitchen up to a second bedroom, and the walls were as elastic as had been those of the house in Sydney Street, the same wide sofa accommodating when bedrooms were filled. This had been my resting-place on Friday nights when commuting to the Ministry, to save the journey up for four hours of work on Saturday mornings. The latchkey of the flat was on a string in the letter-box, known to privileged friends, and a duplicate key journeyed to and from Australia in the pocket of a fellow ex-WRNS who had now returned to her former job on a liner which harboured six days at each end of its run. It was easier to find harbourage for a liner than a human.

This house was a great meeting-place. I even found Dolly here, of whom I had not heard a word since she stayed at The Old House soon after the Balkan war. I had learnt, however, that she had gone back to Romania and settled down with a Romanian husband and during the war, fluent then in three languages, she had worked for the allies. Later she divorced the first Romanian husband and married another, after which – never a letter-writer – she totally disappeared. Lib Parker, my fellow parasite, would write asking me, had I an address? – had I heard? – but nobody knew anything. 23 Rue des Belles Feuilles was sad and empty when I was in its proximity, at the time of the UNESCO conference in the Avenue Kleber.

When searching for a roof, Elspeth had stayed at The Old House and described to me places in Lebanon, Syria and Jordan that she had visited in bouts of leave from Alexandria. They had stirred my resolve. Cyprus had been much extolled and she was all set to go there, but the war ended too soon. Now, settled in Markham Street, the moment seemed opportune and I put up no opposition to being her guest. We sailed from Marseilles in a small Greek vessel and had evidence of Cypriot hospitality from the family at our table who invited us to dinner in Nicosia, followed by a dance! What no one had anticipated was finding Cyprus under snow – quite exceptional – and the dance hall so freezing that the women wore their coats. The snow soon melted, revealing the patiently waiting spring flowers.

Elspeth had an introduction to a family owning a fair-size olive plantation, a family who, to a man on our arrival, abandoned work to put on a meal so liberal that it was hard to do justice to it. We came away slightly dizzy and each clasping a bottle marked BRANDY but containing the rarest olive oil. At this time the island was still under British rule, Greek and Turkish Cypriots were living apparently in harmony together, and Archbishop Makarios was unknown to the outside world.

What made this visit outstanding in memory was the hire of a seasoned Chevrolet from Odysseus in Nicosia. At the main ports of the island smart American cars, legacy of the war, were available with drivers, at a price, but the choice was less opulent and more confined in hiring a self-drive vehicle, and only Odysseus appeared to oblige. What we acquired had no safety glass in the windscreen and stuffing protruded form the upholstery, but one could not afford to be too particular when engine and brakes were in good order. The Chevrolet appeared perfect for our needs.

In it we explored small white Levantine ports and sandy bays, rode alongside carob, olive and orange groves on well-kept roads, but to stray on to side-roads after rain was to encounter the all-too-familiar patches of bog. Some of the newer mountain roads were also good. The monasteries of

Cyprus were a great feature, with fine churches containing valuable icons, and generally at a height that give magnificent views, but the roads that reached them varied considerably.

For one of the monasteries we had to take a road built at a time when, other than on foot, there was only equestrian transport. To add to the spice, this narrow road clung to the side of a ravine and was severely cornered, with little or no protection at the edge. We were told we would find a telephone at the entrance to it, and could ring up and learn if the road was clear, but by the time we found out there was no telephone we had reached a point of no return, so drove the whole distance in a cold sweat. On arrival we learnt that a new road had been opened to the monastery by the building of a bridge, so the old road was no longer used. This information, in place of the telephone, would have been helpful, but there was a happy *laissez-faire* attitude prevalent in Cyprus, a sort of Irish leave-it-to-God outlook that I was to find later also in Turkey.

One might have expected this to cure our passion for the mountain roads, not to mention the frequent sight of abandoned war lorries lying upside down in the valleys beneath them, but a High Court judge staying in the same hotel with us at Pathos extolled the magnificent position of Khrysorriatissa, the monastery of the Miraculous Virgin, as the finest in Cyprus. This was backed by the proprietor of the hotel, equally enthusiastic. There was a good road shown on my map in Panayia, with the monastery a short distance beyond, but a rainstorm in the night before we attempted it made me anxious about that remaining thread of road beyond Panayia; Cyprus indulged in pernicious seams of clay. In fact, I had a sort of premonition about this venture.

Next morning was bright and sunny, the proprietor certain the monastery track would have dried up by the time we reached it. A picnic hamper had been prepared and Neophytus, one of the waiters, was pressed into service to give us help. We climbed to Panayia without incident, by which time we were at an immense height. The monastery capped an adjacent hill, but the track branching off to it was undulating and not far along dipped into a rutted hollow in a state of slime.

I approached slowly, keeping as far as I dared to the outer edge, which was dry, but the slope of the hollow sucked us in and we had not advanced far before the wheels were churning. Noble efforts at pushing, by Elspeth and the waiter, were unavailing, so they decided to walk up to the monastery and get help. Meanwhile I studied the track ahead, which beyond this quagmire was steep, narrow but sound, until round a bend on the hill there was a second quagmire waiting. It was now afternoon.

With whoops of joy a wild band of vineyard workers arrived, evidently accustomed to this exercise. They began pushing almost before I got into the car, and with four men bent to the task we were swaying along with all

198

promise of reaching sound soil when, with no alteration in steering, the car suddenly slewed sideways so we were now athwart the road. Firm command from Neophytus in Greek might have arrested the pushers, but none was given. The vineyard workers, blind to what they were doing, pushed me over the edge.

*

This must have been as harrowing for Elspeth as it was for me, as she believed there to be a sheer drop into the valley far below. I had also believed this until left to reconnoitre, when I saw that the road we were using had been carved out of the side of the cliff in place of an older road lying like a piece of looped string beneath it, but easily accessible to the higher road at the far end. In the moment of crisis – in a car over which I had no control – I was struggling hard to pull it away from the edge and at the last moment the car responded, but too late. Yet it resulted in my rolling sideways over the edge instead of head-on, which was a mercy. I just had the wit to turn off the ignition before the car turned clean over and crashed through bushes to land on its head on the old road below. I found myself kneeling on the inside of its roof, the driving door still functioning upside down, so I was able to emerge, but a car with its wheels in the air is a distressing sight.

Not so for the hearty pushers, to whom the whole thing was a mighty joke, and who established contact with Panayia by shouting, the mountains echoing and the message taken up by a shepherd who relayed it to the village. By the reverse process we learnt the village lorry would be with us presently, and so it was, a double-wheel lorry with a bunch of highly experienced lads. They came down, righted the Chevrolet without pushing it over the further edge and got a tow-rope on to it, and the lorry drew the Chevrolet to the higher level. I was asked to sit at the steering-wheel; I knew what lay around the corner, and dreaded, when even the double wheels started churning, that the lorry would descend on me. However, it got a grip and we eventually landed in the courtyard of a noble monastery, a place of pilgrimage. Here our adventure had raised us to the level of VIPs. Clearly the Miraculous Virgin had saved my life. We were received by the Abbot himself, the Archimandrite, his hair in a neat bun, and he seemed very satisfied that an English lady had gone over the edge of the precipice, for now he might get the long-sought after grant for making a proper road.

We were bidden to his parlour and seated amongst much holy bric-à-brac. A small acolyte came and removed our shoes, coated in clay, replacing them with monkish slippers while he took ours to be cleaned. The radio was bringing news in Greek of the election results in England, of

199

which we could only follow periodic reference to 'Ut-lee'. There followed an excellent dinner served with heartening wine, and a consequent drowsiness descended, whereon the Abbott asked, had we night attire with us? We hadn't, so he took us to a cupboard and, with a coy glance, produced monastic pyjamas of ample girth but spotlessly clean. We were to be thankful for their warm texture as the air was keen in the pilgrims' dormitory, of which we were sole occupants. It commanded a tremendous view of country dreaming in moonlight. There was a lavatory of simple construction: the floor at one end of the room was extended beyond the outside wall and had a hole in it. Jutting out over a sheer drop of fathomless feet, it was walled round, with a door into the bedroom.

We lay in bed wondering what was a fair sum to place in the church box on departure. Pilgrims gave only the most modest offerings, but they might not have dined with the Abbott nor slept in his pyjamas, and we had to express gratitude to the Miraculous Virgin. We went to sleep over the knotty problem and woke next day to the sound of a great bell and distant chanting. The village lads were back again as promised, with supply of acid, oil and petrol to replenish what had been lost, yet damage to the Chevrolet was surprisingly modest. There was a deep depression in the roof on the passenger side but it did not leak, in fact kept us supplied with fresh water, and could easily be hammered out; there was a crack across the windscreen, and acid had eaten into the upholstery, but that seemed to have happened before. I knew insurance demanded immediate reporting after an accident, and by rights we should go straight back to Nicosia, but we were rendering up the car there in two days' time, and were doing no harm to it if we finished our programme. When we did report the accident to him, Odysseus was at first very put out, but finding all in order and that insurance would make good the car's two existing weaknesses, he wrung my hand on departure, begging me to hire again from him if I should ever return to Cyprus.

Before we left Khrysorriatissa we sat a while in the quiet of its cathedral-like church, our thoughts concentrated on the immediate past, and I am glad to think neither of us had an inkling of the future. I had put in the church box all I had in my purse, which wasn't a great deal but would be slightly more than the average offering. I was shattered to hear later what Elspeth had given, and accused her of spoiling the market. Elspeth agreed it was rather ostentatious. 'You see, I felt I ought to put in the value of your life.'

She had put in five pounds.

That summer, while the old ladies were at Cliff Hall, I asked Elspeth down for a holiday at The Old House – garden, books, walks, drives and a diet of Cornish pasties made by the Women's Institute, relieved with lunches at the adjacent restaurant. After that, nailed down by my new ploy, I saw very little of her and the following winter she and her sister, Susan

Backhouse, were invited to join their father and stepmother on a cruise to the African ports. Susan described Elspeth as a very poor sailor, always having to go and lie down. I found this a little surprising and Elspeth said nothing of it on the phone to me but sounded lukewarm about the cruise.

Elspeth, however, was a private person. In all the years I had known her she had never once mentioned her mother, who had suffered what must have been polio after Elspeth was born, resulting in an awkward upbringing for Elspeth and a correspondingly awkward child. She had lived down the disapproval of Crofton, had made many friends, but the first real mothering she ever received was from the head of her finishing-school in Paris, who had at once engaged a dressmaker and hairdresser to show what good grooming can do for a girl. I was to meet this wise woman often in Markham Street, for Elspeth, though shrewd in assessing character, was always touchingly loyal to those who had been kind to her.

In private Elspeth had lived down an unhappy love affair, and one might say almost in private she died. Hindsight compelled me to believe she was in pain on the African tour but preferred her family to think it was seasickness. I happened to call at Markham Street with a gadget I had made for her, and found her washing her hair. She told me she was disturbed at getting so fat and had ordered a surgical belt to give her support. I am sure neither of us imagined when she came to the door, her head in a bath towel, that we would never meet again. Some weeks later one of her Chelsea friends rang me to say Elspeth was in hospital, severely ill, and Susan Backhouse was arriving from Ireland. That same evening Susan rang to say she had died.

I couldn't believe it. *Elspeth*. Her zest, her vitality! I thought of that attic bedroom in which she had found me in Paris. Didn't the trams keep me awake? How did I survive all those stairs? I had said all I longed for was grass. Paris didn't know the meaning of it. And grass she had given me, all down the length of France, and afterwards chunks of education, chunks of glorious life. She was not young when she abandoned a cushioned life to be a cook in the WRNS; she knew cooks were needed. Alexandria had been her reward. And now, one thought aimlessly of the things one would have liked to have said, and which would have heartily embarrassed her.

Elspeth was barely fifty.

*

On return from Cyprus there was a duty I had to perform. I had to take the doll's house to its expectant owner, my niece Heather. In Cyprus I had completed a final furnishing – its sitting-room carpet executed in petit point, done generally in the evenings in a hotel bar, a ploy not really in keeping with the general atmosphere.

I had foreseen the need for the doll's house to be mobile, so had made it to dismantle, yet even when base, walls and roof were lying flat they were not easy, plus the furniture, to push along into a sleeping-bag, which seemed the best container, and it did look rather as if I were travelling with a corpse. The porter at Euston asked me what it as, and when I told him he said I might have to pay on it as luggage was restricted to personal property. 'Leave it to me,' he said, which sounded comforting, and sure enough when I went to my sleeper it was lying in the unoccupied sleeper above, and at no extra price save an enhanced tip.

Heather had received the doll's house in Wonersh but was now in the Highlands. Foiled of further service in India, Deric had retired from the army to fulfil a long-felt desire to farm in Scotland. His mother had been a Miss Rose, which made him acceptable, for without a Scottish connection one could be made to feel very alien, a foreigner owning Scottish land. Indeed, I was impressed, some years later, on driving his sister Doreen (Aunt Dor) to stay at the hotel at Kilravock, to see the reception she received as a member of the Rose family. This hotel had formerly been the Rose stronghold.

In Inverness I was met by a Jeep and carried to the village of Drumnadrochit, from which a one-time test hill rose steeply into the mountains but at its top emerged on to more level ground, the property of Balchraggan. Tucked into this land was a house and stables, backed on the north by continued mountains, looking south over Loch Ness and on the west over Glen Urquart. It was a perfect setting, and for some years paid Heather's education while the raspberries they grew were carried fresh to the Inverness market. The deep-freeze was to debase the price, but by then they had a large flock of local pickers coming annually, and the land supported side-shows such as bees and geese, and only the later restrictions on milk distribution compelled Avis to give up her beloved cow. After that they received milk by the simple method of a farmer, further along the hill, putting bottles every morning in the cold waters of the burn which divided their properties.

All that was in the future. When I came to Balchraggan, more work had been done to the farm than to the house, and Avis had just learnt that the local market-garden fête was about to be held in a neighbouring garden in Drumnadrochit. All they had of live-stock were hens; however, these were laying so she sent a box of eggs, which won first prize, and followed this up with display of the doll's house. At so much a showing – electric lighting in rooms and curtains pulled – it brought a handsome profit to the cause.

I stayed on, as a load of timber in the stables enabled me to make two built-in cupboards and a bookshelf in the house, while Avis painted walls and window frames and made curtains with a child's sewing machine given to Heather.

202

Balchraggan was to usurp custom from Cliff Hall; the old ladies began spending their holidays in Scotland, and what a perfect journey it was, the night train up the east coast to Inverness. One could dine comfortably in the Euston Hotel, then sit out on a seat on the platform opposite the sleeping-car until the time to board it. The sleeping-car attendant looked after one like a mother, brought tea in the morning, and double-berth sleepers were not only very comfortable but not then an outrageous price. In the morning one moved to the breakfast carriage, looking out on the Vale of Nairn, one of the loveliest views of Scotland. My aunt did not stay at Balchraggan so much as in Edinburgh, with friends she had made in the WAACs. It was to be some years yet before I drove to Scotland in my own car.

At home there still seemed to be a dearth of part-time work, but I was increasingly thinking, was there not some money-earning ploy I could pursue in my own workshop? People had already brought me small items of furniture to mend, but I never felt this would be a steady flow. It was the woman from the Labour Exchange, nevertheless, who gave me the all-providing clue.

I thought I knew the face of the woman sitting next to me in the bus but it was not until she asked me had I found a job yet, that I knew who she was, and said I hadn't. 'I know what I'd do,' she added. 'I'd take up china-mending. We're always being asked for china-menders. I see now they're charging half a crown a rivet! *Well...*'

In my ignorance I looked upon china repair as the end, but someone whose furniture I had repaired asked me if I mended broken china, of which she seemed to have a ready supply. Wood for repairing was not easily obtained and furniture was bulky. No overheads were needed for riveting and the unattractive wartime china was all you could get in the shops. No satisfactory glue had ever been found, far less any hint of synthetic resins. Good riveting was not obtrusive to the eye, but I had not the faintest idea how it was done.

In Wonersh was a wonderful character who knew everyone and everything, which resulted in my setting forth, with little appetite, to be a paying guest and pupil at the house of Air Commodore and Mrs Athol Milne, to learn riveting. This was at Northiam, a village on the eastern flank of Sussex where the Rother river makes a boundary with Kent. The beauty of the countryside softened my feelings, not to mention the kindness of host and hostess. Certainly I was well versed in what a PG should and should not do.

Having spent seven years at the Ministry of Labour I was entitled to a bonus on leaving, a gratuity which now neatly covered the outlay on living and learning. The Milnes, I soon found, were suffering the same chilling experience that I was, that of reduced means on retirement, after a more lucrative life. As a result every inch of a fine old barn belonging to them was devoted to making up the deficit. The growing of mushrooms occupied one end of it, intensive chicken farming the central portion, and a bench under the north-facing window at the far end was given over to the riveting of china, as well as teaching the art.

Holes had to be bored with a diamond to a certain depth in, but not through, the china. The rivet, made of half-round brass wire, had to be shaped with legs just short of the depth of the hole, and spaced apart so that the rivet had to be pulled into position, thereafter forever exerting pressure. The rivet, in fact, is a clamp; the Gypsies know the secret of it, as did the Romans.

After a long battle, and surrounded by discarded rivets, I would hand the finished job to Athol, who, with a seasoned thumb-nail would pull out rivet after rivet that I had spent hours getting in place. In fact, I wore out my own thumbnail, and made myself a metal thumbnail to fit over it. Eventually, just before the gratuity ran out, I got the knack. By that time I felt even five pounds a rivet would barely pay.

*

For a considerable period I sat working for love, or that was what it amounted to. I could not possibly charge for the time it was taking me, especially on the eggshell-thin china I was frequently brought, when it was a nightmare not to bore right through. There was no lack of custom. Athol in the country was sighing for work; here beside the village street I was overloaded, and when someone brought me eighteen pieces of dinner service needing riveting, I rang Athol and said I could give him plenty of work if he would come and fetch it, which he did. It ran up a huge bill, I got commission and no one ever knew I hadn't done it. The riveting end of the Milnes' barn was certainly the most lucrative.

What brought me to terms with riveting was one of those clownish events, like sleeping in abbots' pyjamas, that seemed to intrude on my life at intervals, and now brought a humble little soul to my door. She was maid to a formidable invalid we knew, and had dropped the lining to a commode, which now had a crack from base to lip growing ever wide till at the top it was an aching void.

I said I did not think it could be mended, that it would not be sanitary to mend it, that I doubted rivets could do it, but the real question was could *I* do it? She looked so distressed, and it was a challenge. I rather wanted to try, so in the evenings when no one was likely to find me at it, I tussled with it. I had to mount a larger diamond, to bore a deeper hole, to use a thicker wire, and each time I pulled the track closer with the rivets, those at the base loosened. I had to go over them all at least four times before the crack closed. It was like buttoning up a coat. I left it overnight full of water and standing in a bucket, expecting next morning to find the water in the bucket. The pot was still full. I had sought to keep hidden this article that debased the standard of my workshop, but now I felt like putting it in the window. My reward was not monetary, but the mastery and speeding-up of riveting. I was later to train two pupils in the art, and I soon found I was making a little money!

Then came the introduction of synthetic resins. Two ingredients when mixed together gradually solidified into a permanent bind. It was quick and, if applied skilfully, as reliable a repair as riveting. Moreover, it brought me a greater variety of work.

For there had been an afternoon at Northiam when Athol and I, sitting in the barn, had been visited by a light van, and a boy sitting beside the driver had called out, 'My father is the china-mender', a statement I felt Athol did not altogether relish. Frederick Curl had come to bring plates needing riveting to Athol, as he himself was not interested in riveting but always getting it sent to him. He was wondering if he and Athol could not supply each other with work suited to their respective skills. It appeared he was a restorer of ornamental china, but we had no idea that he received applications from collectors, antique dealers and private owners in England and America asking him to restore porcelain of museum quality.

This sort of repair interested me far more than riveting; had I not done a fair amount of modelling in the Paris studio? And though I might not have an ear for singing a tune, I certainly had a good eye for matching colour. So I asked, might I move on to a course with Frederick Curl in this kind of mending? He said he would readily show me the processes, but I could only find out by practice on my own whether I could reach a satisfactory standard.

Thus at a later date I felt I was privileged to be instructed by such a brilliant craftsman, and in an environment that one might say was out of this world. Slithering and bouncing across marshes, the light van carried me to New Barn Farm, which stood on the Kent bank of the Rother river. I wondered how valuable china survived this journey but was to learn that Frederick surmounted all problems, and with practised skill he opened and shut several gates, keeping herds separate from each other meanwhile. These constituted an almost natural barrier between New Barn and the outside world, which personal friends and the daily postman alone penetrated.

A timber-framed house, built around 1425, it had had improvements and comforts added over the years, but remained definitely beyond the tentacles of town mains. There were sufficient trees to supply firewood but an Aga lately installed provided the main heating. A hand pump brought water from the river, a windmill supplied electric light, and there was a chancy telephone line whose breakdown it was generally Frederick's job to repair.

Every winter the surrounding fields were submerged for a time by the flooded river Rother, but the builders of the house had sited it carefully, for only once had the water encroached indoors.

I was to return many times to this sanctuary, which Frederick, his wife and two sons shared every summer with owls, larks, nightingales, copious butterflies, and lambs cavorting in the fields. Across the river were acres of golden corn. The fertile soil rewarded Judy's gardening; no difficulty in cultivation, only in protecting it from the beasts of the field, but Judy was not so enthusiastic about the winter evenings when the boys were absent and she longed for the friends who came so eagerly in summer. Yet an interesting feature of this remoteness was that when violent storms, extreme cold or periods of drought brought blackouts, frozen pipes and water-rationing to citizens, New Barn carried on serenely – all basic needs to hand.

Meanwhile, the long evenings were no hindrance to Frederick doing miracles of restoration by a number of inventive ways. Nothing seemed beyond the scope of his handwork with no other machinery than a pedal lathe. He had made cameras, a telescope – there was nothing he was not expert at making except money. His fees covered their needs, and the best craftsmen get enormous satisfaction from their work; the more demanding, the less it is seen in terms of money than as a test of skill.

He could have asked three time the sum he charged a collector who brought him broken pieces, with some missing, of a Nymphenburg group designed by Bustelli of which only two examples existed. The museum which held the complete one allowed Frederick to take photographs of it and measurements, but would not allow him to take a plasticine impression of the face of a little midinette, the head totally missing among the broken pieces. To copy the face, preserving the pert expression given by Bustelli, Frederick needed to mould it on a larger scale, so he modelled it in a dental plaster which shrinks on drying out. When it was slightly reduced he made a mould from it, and cast it again in the same plaster, repeating this process until he had a mould of the required size. From this he cast the final head in plaster of Paris, joined it to the broken neck, modelled an exact copy of the little hat she was wearing, and after he had painted it one could not tell the one in the museum from the one restored.

This was the kind of work emanating from New Barn. From such a master I learnt the methods and ingredients used, the pitfalls of which to be wary, but not a penny would he take. He was one craftsman helping another, he said, and certainly there was no fear of rivalry. Thus I was launched on an absorbing, but often harrowing craft – my fifth vocation.

*

I spent fourteen years crouched over this sedentary, exacting but absorbing job of mending and restoring china, which synthetic resins did so much to advance. Mixed with specific powders they formed a dough-like paste which could be cast, or modelled as it hardened, then smoothed to a refinement much like unglazed china, and more durable than plaster of Paris, which it replaced. The harrowing part was painting and glazing, getting an exact match with powder pigments and solvent, and bleeding this off where it met the china surface. Acrylic paint and polyurethane only came in towards the end of my career.

Always work flowed in faster than I could deal with it. In the first years I was guilty of the same fault as Frederick in not charging enough. Brought up to modest expenditure, I felt guilty imposing a price that really covered the time and toil, but as I came to be recognized as a worthy restorer, was visited by quite a few authorities on china and was restoring some beautiful pieces from great houses, the sheer weight on my time compelled me to exact a higher income from the job.

In those fourteen years I made many friends and had only two awkward customers. I trained an assistant, Joan Fordham, who became a very efficient partner, enabling me to be selective in the work I chose to do and protecting me in moments of crisis from the caller at the door. I had often envied Frederick his isolation, for if one was disturbed in the act of painting or over-glazing, a caller could wreck hours of patient toil. New Barn took a flattering interest in my progress. Judy and Frederick came over when I was working on a charming Chamberlain-Worcester inkstand, and one of the two little ink-pots attached to the stand had lost its lid. I was using the existing lid to make a casting for the other, and Frederick reminded me to add some shot in the paste to make it heavier, otherwise it would be half the weight of the china lid.

Restoration, with its ruses for disguising the false from the real, was sometimes condemned as encouraging the antique dealer to pass it off as genuine. There is, however, immediate disclosure under ultraviolet ray: the china loses all colour and lustre, and a line of luminous silver, like a thin wire, betrays where synthetic resin is seaming two parts together. A built-up part looks like a luminous beacon. And this is as it should be. The Germans claimed to have developed resin that defied the ray, but while I worked on china they had not succeeded, and shops selling the china of leading firms were often equipped with the ray to prove the perfection of their stock.

I no longer earned money as a chauffeur-courier. I had no time for it and anyhow times had changed. People now drove themselves abroad, and though I performed just the same duties for those who did ask me to drive them, they now paid my expenses only and had to synchronize with Betty's holidays, my only chance of escape. As Kilton had foretold, I was becoming tied up with my obligations to the household being taken for granted, and needed someone to replace me if I went away. No mercy for the daughter at home.

Mrs Billy had died shortly after I left the Ministry. I was away at the time, and it was from one of those fits that she never recovered. It was like losing a member of the family, but at least she was well and her usual self up to the moment of death, and her grandchildren were now independent. Nevertheless we very much missed an endearing personality and she had gallantly seen us through a very lean time.

I escaped on an Easter tour the year after Cyprus, taking Magda and her teenage daughter to the châteaux of the Loire, and one summer down to Rome. As we were a hen-party and funds were scanty, we stayed when possible at convents, as I had often done with Mrs Seddon and later on my own. They gave us simple fare, but adequate, the cost was modest and you did not have to tip the nuns, though Mrs Seddon perhaps gave liberally to the order. Some convents would even accept husbands, and we discovered one that gave a 'late-night pass'.

Another occasion of absenteeism was the Queen's coronation, for which the WES had bought an expensive ticket to raffle among its members, and I had won it. Thus in the Mall near Admiralty Arch I was in a seat at just the right height for seeing into the carriage windows of the procession both going to and coming form the Abbey. This, my second coronation, reached a far wider public than my first; the old ladies at home, watching at a friend's television, would see far more than I would, but at least my vision was live.

I went to London a day in advance of the great event, a London full of goodwill and carnival spirit, of tanned skins, dark skins and white skins, of people in wide-brimmed hats, turbans, toques. I had lunched at the Stewarts restaurant, then at the foot of Bond Street, sitting next to an Australian family with whom I was soon locked in firmest friendship, but to whom I gave quite erroneous directions as the buses had mostly strayed from their usual circuits.

Now I was in a stand with elegant fellow kinsmen and a sprinkling of foreign visitors, dressed mostly for the occasion rather than the chill of this second day of June. The British, however, had discreet carrier bags of sustenance and mackintoshes, and nearly all had newspaper, which can be useful protection against rain.

At the hour that we reached it, the Mall was in a state of confusion with Heads of State getting into line for their advance to the Abbey – the Queen of Tonga clearly visible in her open coach, and Nehru peering out from the brougham, wondering why he was receiving such an ovation. All this got tidied up when the radio took over, leading to a crescendo as the Princesses of the Blood Royal passed by in their glass-panelled coaches, and then the Irish Coach bearing the Queen Mother and Princess Margaret at her side.

The Princess looked like a Dresden ornament, and even more so on return wearing a little crown. Could this be the same crown I had seen fall from Princess Mary's golden hair forty-two years before? Then the salute of arms ripping down the line of guardsmen told that the Royal Coach was on its way, preceded by so many servants of the Queen in royal splendour that it was some time before the golden coach came into view. Then we were reminded of something transcending the pomp and splendour and even the music of the mounted band, and that was the extreme youth and freshness of our Sovereign. She looked so young, her smile so genuine, she seemed delighted to see us all and was enjoying the day.

In loyal silence we followed the broadcast service, when the only chattering was from the birds in the trees, but the ceremony was still in session when birds as well as broadcast were drowned in a steady downpour of rain. Garden-party hats and eye veils began embracing the cheeks of the wearers, and the Queen's loyal commoners began looking commoner and commoner, finally disappearing under protective covering. Nothing, however, dampened the spirit of the day.

When the rain ceased, giving over to a wan sunlight, I took exercise to try and get warm, and in doing so met Mercy Summerhayes. She had worked for the Ministry of Labour in the war, and I had got to know her well. It was her brother-in-law, then Governor of Nepal, who had sent the message to the Queen on this auspicious day, a message on every hoarding as I made my way that morning to the Mall: 'EVEREST CONQUERED'.

*

For some time after Elspeth's death, property arrived at The Old House that I doubted had ever belonged to her, for Markham Street had been a repository for belongings as well as humans. Elspeth had made no will or provision for her death, and when Susan rang me asking was there anything I would like in memory, I could think of nothing except I would be most grateful for her London telephone directories. These were sent. Presently her father and stepmother came to London to disperse her belongings, and I fancy I was the friend of Elspeth's they knew best. So, amongst other things, I received a typewriter, though Elspeth had never typed in her life. Eventually these were followed up by a beautiful brooch, a lovely opal with a diamond surround which I assumed must have belonged to Elspeth, though I had never seen her wear it. I wore it gratefully and with effect for many years.

All that was in the early days of riveting and penury, but in the years following the coronation, as I advanced as a china restorer, I found I was not merely subscribing fitfully to household expenses but was making a small but steady income. More than that, in the house of a friend I had met a most valuable Miss Ranby, who bolstered her retirement pension doing bouts as a companion-housekeeper. Miss Ranby, who had led an interesting life, paid us a visit, approved of us, and for a modest fee would supplant me at intervals when convenient to both of us. This meant I need no longer usurp Betty's holiday time, and could now go on holidays of my own choice and time, and Miss Ranby had enough experience to ruffle neither my aunt nor the cook at the time.

This broke up the habit of leaning on daughters, and gave me a freedom I immediately used, taking my bicycle and bicycling up the Hook of Holland to visit its famous art galleries. With my own transport, and relying on guest bedrooms, of which the tourist bureaux had lists of addresses, my ten-day holiday was not expensive. I was also lucky in having a following wind going northward which conveniently changed as I came south again.

As bicycles were the main traffic in cities, there was less noise from motor vehicles, and one entered the towns bicycling to the tune of large hurdy-gurdies that enlivened the main streets, and it was wonderfully restful riding to music. Yet the Dutch seemed to bicycle mainly as a duty. I bought a Michelin map and reached my objectives by the towing-paths following the canals. Thus I saw on a wide canal what I took to be a large pleasure steamer approaching, towed by two pinnacles keeping it in midstream. But they were not tourists reclining on deck under the awnings; the white-clad figures moving around were doctors and nurses and the people in bed or on deck-chairs were patients – a touring hospital. I learnt later it was a gift from a millionaire. With the geographical layout of the country now so changed, I doubt if even the canal exists. The practical common sense of the Dutch shone through all amenities such as eating-houses and places for buying picnic food, and Dutch architecture was as inspiring as the art galleries.

It was a year of unexpected surprises. Later on Barbro and Stig Hegardt suddenly turned up in a seraphic blue de luxe Studebaker, and with them was another married couple in a Jaguar. The idea was to do a round of British golf-courses, the men playing the women accompanying them, but the women had, not surprisingly, grown bored and decided to go to London. This would leave them with a surfeit of luxury cars, and when they came to Wonersh to take me out to lunch, they said if I would show them the way into London to the Piccadilly Hotel, I might have the Hegardts' Studebaker to use as desired for at least a week.

I felt rather nervous taking it over under the eye of its doting owner, but the car more or less drove itself and I purred back along the Portsmouth–Guildford road. Feeling I might never again have such a box of tricks under my control, I decided to try everything, and turned on the radio to hear the most glorious music. I was tuned in to Stockholm. At that time no car was left unsheltered overnight and I had some trouble finding a garage long enough for it. Also, I had too much work on hand to make maximum use of it but, to their delight, took the old ladies to see friends and relatives beyond normal reach – to the amusement of our neighbours, for with both of them sitting beside me on the front seat there was still room for more. There could not have been a wider contrast between this car and old Baker, but I think had the older Studebaker seen the present one its comment would have been, 'Sissy!'

Then came the climax of the year. I got a letter from a solicitor which told me that Elspeth's family shares in Lea & Perrins Worcestershire Sauce, now amalgamated with HP Sauce, had been made over to me. It took me a little time to digest the full impact of this news and not till I heard from Lloyds Bank was it clear that I had received capital far greater than anything I had ever earned, waiting to be parcelled up in gilt-edged-securities. In fact I was rich beyond my wildest dreams. It would not replace Elspeth but, denied Elspeth, it was a wonderful compensation. The difficulty was to find expressions of gratitude that had not already been used.

Evidence of this opulence did not appear for some time; I was balked by postwar impositions: a tax, said to be temporary, on car purchase, and oppositions from the council for a garage so near to a dangerous street. Not till the late sixties did I obtain either garage or car, but in the meantime that basic urge to write, which lay deeper than any other vocation, had impelled me to write a light-hearted novel on village life in the war. Unfortunately it got held up by the riveting and I missed the market. People had grown tired of the war, they wanted to forget it, and even a very enthusiastic American agency had eventually to return it to me.

I was hampered by too many interests. I now had the money to travel; but travel needed freedom, which I had not got. China repair needed infinite patience over a long period, and impulsive writing also needed time. Each of these occupations cramped the other, but I enjoyed all three and brought to them a powerful enthusiasm which is in itself a form of strength.

Thus no sooner had I abandoned the novel than an idea began forming in my mind that the simpler china repairs might well be done by the housewife herself if she had the instruction. I eventually discussed this with Frederick, who felt, however, that foreknowledge would be needed to recognize the simple repair. What he wanted was a book on the whole craft of mending and restoring china to save it from the terrible botched repairs and restorations he was continually having to undo on valuable china. He would give me the support and supply the photographs. So I began on a book far more ambitious and costly than I had visualized, but once started there was no looking back.

*

My day, with a sprinkling of household jobs, was given over to china; late evening and night to writing, and in bed after midnight I read *The Times* of the day before. I now rarely asked anyone to stay; I had no time for being a hostess but I rejoiced always in Betty's holidays and her friends joining us. In fact it was in an effort to give me a greater diet of my own generation that, the day before returning to her school, Betty brought in Kay Lines to meet me. This was a Sunday afternoon, which I always gave to writing, and my lack of enthusiasm for Betty's gesture was plainly obvious, giving quiet amusement to Kay, as I learnt when I knew her better and was more grateful for the introduction.

Kay was a Canadian who had trained in Toronto as a children's librarian and had published a book, *Six to Sixteen*, which had become a Bible among mothers and people involved in selecting books for the young. She had recently taken rooms in the neighbourhood while she was compiling a further book, and a mutual friend had asked Betty to call. Her life was not so cluttered as mine and she became a delightful and most helpful friend.

My holidays were of necessity brief, two of them spent at Annagh Begh, a lovely old domain in County Tipperary. Here lived Susan Backhouse, Elspeth's sister, now widowed and looking after a brother. Here of an evening the Shannon nearby became a social centre, neighbours turning out in small boats for an evening's fishing and exchange of gossip. In Ireland history could stand still for countless years; when we drove round the coast of Kerry we looked down from a height on a small bay where a coracle rocked on the water, a seal surfaced and dived out at sea, and on a rough-hewn quay a Benedictine monk was walking up and down reading his breviary.

Soon Susan was yearning for the continent, but it cost a fortune to bring a car over from Ireland, and as so far I had no vehicle I hired a Ford Escort from a London firm. This resulted in extended holidays, in five or six weeks of truancy from china and book. The monetary restrictions still in force brought the standard of our lodgings to the sordid by the time we reached the coast. The irony was I now had a garage worthy of The Old House, set well back in a small yard at the west end, where it took no light from the workshop and allowed a wheelbarrow-wide passage to garden and flat. But I had nothing to put in it for want of a car of my ambition.

It was not until the Volkswagen buses were exported from Germany, the seating removed to allow purchasers to convert them into caravans, that I acquired what Bulgaria had impressed on us as the ideal for travelling remote countries. It was not a heavy vehicle and had good clearance for fording rivers. I had the space between driving seat and rear baggage store adapted to be kitchen, dining-room or sleeping-quarters, but I never intended sleeping in it where a hostelry of the country was available. All the same it would have been useful under the monetary restrictions. It was a 1958 model.

It was at this point also I signed a contract with Faber and Faber for the china-mending book, which was developing into a far more comprehensive work than I have envisaged. No fixed delivery date was at that time established, and I had made it clear to Faber the number of jobs with which I was involved. I was also beginning to appreciate how often I had to refer to Frederick to be briefed on the wider issues of restoration.

Towards this the Volkswagen was most helpful. Eighty-odd miles separated Wonersh from New Barn, and at sparse intervals we would meet halfway along the route on Chailey Common, the Curls producing from their car a delectable meal, and the Volkswagen acting both as dining-room and office. Here I would batten on Frederick's superior knowledge, and we would arrange the compilation of this book.

In due course one of these sessions coincided with Betty's half-term. She was now teaching at Stroud High School for girls (and growing alarmingly enamoured with Gloucestershire as a place for retirement), her association with Westonbirt having wound up when that school was commandeered in the war. The Curls suggested, instead of Chailey, that we should both spend the weekend at New Barn. I went in advance to get the business with the book done and Frederick later met Betty off the train at Northiam.

I knew Betty would relish this bird-watcher's paradise, but as those multiple gates closed behind her and she saw ahead unrestricted countryside, she began getting nervous; she had to catch a train early on Monday morning for London. Could she ever get there in time? I told her Frederick always found a solution to problems, as indeed he did now.

I did not witness the solution as I had to leave on Sunday, but some years back an old rowing-boat had washed up on the Curls' bank of the river and, no one claiming it, this became their property. The woodwork was starting to rot, but still sound enough to make a pattern, and Frederick made a mould from it, both interior and exterior, which, fitted together and primed with fibreglass, produced a most desirable fibreglass rowing-boat. The Rother is a tidal river as far as Newenden, a mile or so upstream. I hope it was in his favour when Frederick rowed Betty to Newenden bridge, where the coach from Rye picks up London passengers in the early morning.

*

During the time I was in Cyprus I was not the only member of our family to suffer a fall; my mother had fallen down the two steps leading to the bathroom and, unable to get up again, had lain there cold, and severely bruised, until my aunt found her. Learning this on my return, I had speedily installed a handrail, but the fall had left her nervous of stairs, so I had taken to breaking off from the china every morning to go and help her downstairs. It also revealed to me how isolated she was over at the east end, and I moved my bedroom to the spare room we had formerly given Mrs Billy, next to the bathroom.

Apart from the staircase, my mother retained her independence, resuming her normal ploys, which included the making of a trifle annually, a birthday present for a neighbour. I now found she topped it up from the Cyprus bottle marked BRANDY which in fact contained olive oil. She resented my interference on discovery. The neighbour had 'always found it delicious'.

February 1958 saw her ninetieth birthday, with a lunch given her by her friends and with visitors arriving all day; but the late fifties and early sixties were to bring great changes. That same February Deric died of lung cancer which an operation the previous year failed to stem. This meant the eventual sale of Balchraggan, but Avis hoped to keep the raspberries going till that time. Neither old lady went to Scotland that year, but opinion seemed to be unanimous that I must take the Volkswagen and help Avis with the raspberry harvest in July. The 'waggon' had not yet even been delivered, but I was not averse to the idea, which would have to be my holiday of the year, and I was delighted when Kay volunteered to come too.

We streaked up the 300 miles to Bigland Hall in the Lake District, where Chilly, the Croftonian I had driven to Budapest, now rented the older half of this fine manor farm – and Kay survived the haunted bedroom. The popular areas of Lakeland and Scotland had seen great changes in recent years: either they were invaded by campers, or fields and woodlands were wired off against intrusion; but we had another roof extended to us on our way. It was bitterly cold and had set back the raspberry harvest by a fortnight or more, and to my disgust the Volkswagen would not take the test hill leading up to Balchraggan. We had to leave our vehicle, as did other visitors, in the car park of the hotel and were driven up in Deric's Land Rover by a neighbour, who told us Avis was only just back from hospital for a 'tired heart'.

In India Avis had had a bout of diphtheria, which may have weakened her heart, and I suspect she had been spraying the raspberries herself, a heavy job with tank and spray,. She had a couple living in the flat above the stables – the wife was her housekeeper – and since her return from hospital she had been almost overwhelmed with offers of help with the picking. I could not wait for the belated harvest, so it seemed sensible to stay for a limited time only, and hand over our bedrooms to friends who were old-timers at organizing this job. So I took Kay to some favoured haunts further into the Highlands before we came leisurely home.

I had left Miss Ranby with the old ladies, but now found my mother had given up the struggle of getting downstairs. No staircase in The Old House was convenient for the elderly, so, fully dressed, she had meals and received friends in her bedroom, and was busy destroying her diaries, all save the one from which I have quoted. She said they were not worth keeping. In the meantime I had contracted shingles round neck and throat, and was dreading an approaching weekend when there would be no one to help me: Betty and Miss Ranby were unavailable, Dora was doing a spell in a home and our now reliable cook was on holiday.

That Saturday the little nurse who came to wash my mother called at the workshop to say she had put my mother back to bed as she was feeling rather giddy. Not to worry, but she thought I ought to know. I went up and sat with my mother and we had a long peaceful talk together which seemed to dissipate the giddiness and soothed the shingles, hidden by a scarf. My aunt was in Guildford, so not till her return did I start doing lunch.

The old ladies slept in the afternoon, and we had tea together, my mother sitting in her chair and apparently now well. Yet with no justification for the thought, I had a feeling she was not going to be with us long, and when I tucked her up that night I felt she too knew this was a long farewell.

All night I kept coming in to see her; she lay in the same position, breathing steadily, but in the small hours I fell into a deep sleep to awake with a start in the broad daylight of Sunday. She lay in the same position, but there was no breathing. Her flesh was still warm, her expression one of perfect peace.

*

Some years back my mother had made over The Old House to her three daughters, and had once asked me what we were going to do with it. I wish I could have said over my dead body would we leave it, but in fact I did not know. I would have been quite content with my workshop and the flat I had made, but Betty had a mind for the Cotswolds and Avis sought somewhere more rural than Surrey, and had been offered a share of a house in Suffolk when bereft of Balchraggan.

Yet it was obvious if we could bring ourselves to divide up the long room, the house could be made into three independent dwellings, and I consulted an architect friend as to the likely cost of so doing. She sketched a plan of a three-bedroomed cottage at the east end, completely shut off from two flats, one above the other, in the rest of the house.

Little alteration was needed to the upper flat, which contained our aunt's and Betty's bedrooms, for Betty had already made part of my discarded bedroom into the much needed extra bathroom. The centre of the long room could form a hall giving access to both flats, to which there was already a front door closed these many years. In fact we would be putting the house back to its original cluster of dwellings.

It so happened that Betty was retiring from teaching that year, and as she had always intended to look after our aunt, she agreed to take over the alterations to the upper floor and, once installed, remained for the rest of her life. Avis, however, needed to sell the east end as soon as it became available, without alterations to it, and a would-be purchaser patiently waited for it during the inevitable hold-up by the Waverley District Council and the reconstruction.

Having impeded the building of my garage for some time, the Council was now quibbling over the creation of three households with only one garage between them, but I was not anxious about the outcome. The Council might think the decision rested with them, but I was certain my mother, whose spirit went with me on all my adventures, was with us still, and in some ethereal form had the matter in hand and sanction would ultimately be given. So it was, after months of delay, when I felt the Council ought to pay the accruing rates.

When my sisters arrived home on my mother's death, I had thankfully handed over all responsibilities and crept into bed, whereon the singles improved, but after the funeral Betty insisted I must go on holiday. Yet if the china had got interrupted during recent months, the book had got totally neglected and Faber's, getting restive, had tied me down to a delivery date.

There followed therefore a most stimulating working holiday at Blakeney, where Betty often stayed in a small hotel which by now only had rooms in the annexe – a line of ground-floor bedrooms and a bathroom, in a field. This was perfect; I parked my 'office' next the end bedroom, got up at dawn and worked on the book, had breakfast in the hotel, returned and worked till lunch. In London I had picked up Kay and Mary Walker, a fellow librarian over from Canada, and brought them to the big Blakeney hotel, and in the afternoon enjoyed their stimulating company either walking or driving in the countryside.

I cannot describe my lightness of heart on that holiday. No responsibilities: Joan Fordham in charge of the china, our cook in charge of the house, and Betty had taken our aunt back to Stroud until my return. My aunt and I had now been living together quite some time in an unusual peace. Circumstances at home were now different and her attitude towards me had changed, but the seemed unaware of the difference.

I got rid of the shingles, but it was a long time before I got rid of the book and its index, and as I looked at my diagrams I wondered how I had produced such firm lines at midnight in the small east end bedroom. I had not found instructive writing easy, and my aunt had agreed to my reading her some of the passages to see if I had made my meaning clear. But it was now the break-up for summer holidays and Betty's retirement in glory from Stroud, and the waggon had to do service in bringing her and all her possessions home.

*

Betty's arrival coincided with the first batch of proofs from Faber's, which I noticed she viewed with apprehension, and I rashly told her I could manage now on my own. All the same, I have a memory of sitting in the upstairs study reading aloud to my aunt but not anticipating Betty's presence trying to find shelves for her books. Such remarks therefore intervened as, 'My dear, you can't get away with that, the sentence doesn't hold together', while my aunt, sitting on the edge of her chair was exclaiming, 'Oh, but I *see* what she means!' In my desire to be explicit I had forgotten the old enemies. By the time I had gone through those proofs with a tooth-comb extracting them – and some endured to the page proofs – I had to pay a tidy sum over the allowance for corrections.

In spite of all these set-backs a handsome volume, *China Mending and Restoration* by Claudia Parsons and Frederick Curl, was published in autumn 1963. It was not by then the first book on the subject, but covered all types of repair to glass and china, from riveting, sticking, modelling, casting, even to museum build-up. The methods of repairing rare porcelain were supported by photos of the various stages, and the book fulfilled our expectations of a modest but steady demand. For a number of years we got a modest but steady income. Ingredients change, as do suppliers, but I am thankful a revised version was never contemplated. Yet I have been interested to discover that among teachers of these arts are some who still rely on this book for information.

*

By the time the china-mending book was published, we were living in a conveniently altered house, and it was wonderful now to have the means to get my part of it just as I wanted it. By making the east end into a separate house, once the party-wall had been completed, Betty, our aunt and I fitted into it snugly, immune from dust and noise while the work was being done on the flats.

My flat now included the west end of the long room, with kingpost and handsome fireplace, and I had a window cut in the south wall and a sun room built outside. The walls of my bedroom I had lined with yellow pine and built on to it cupboards, bookshelf and chest of drawers, a matching surface of matt tone the colour of ripe corn. The kitchen I embellished with built-in cupboards, corner cupboards and a glass-fronted china cupboard, painting these white to match the kitchen walls. It did not make it easier that the walls of old houses are rarely straight. I had an old friend, a cabinet-maker, who took an enthusiastic interest in all this.

Betty had never found enough shelves for her books upstairs, and asked me to make a double row of shelves to fit under the long north-facing window-sill of her study. In view of the irregularity of the walls, it was very necessary to get her help in taking the bare rudiments of this job – two horizontal planks joined at their extremities by two vertical planks – and try them against their future housing.

They were a considerable burden to get upstairs and this, combined with their fledging appearance, sapped Betty's confidence. She could see they would never get under that window-sill. They did. She had stipulated that an embroidered stool must be contained beneath them and they didn't allow enough height. They did. By this time tempers were slightly frayed and it did not help that my old cabinet-maker chose this moment to call, and had to be ushered upstairs, where he had never before penetrated. He sat in an awkward silence while I made full use of this precious chance to shape the job to the wall. He then helped me downstairs with it.

The bookcase filled with her books still stands against the wall under the window-sill, the vertical planks converted to two cupboards supporting the shelves, the embroidered stool fitting neatly between them. I remember the old man as we descended the stairs quoting the adage, which Betty must have heard but was by then in a mood to be amused by it: *Never show an unfinished piece of work to a child, a woman or a fool.*

1959–1969

BACK ON THE ROAD

Once the currency restrictions were lifted, the carefree sixties witnessed a national urge to travel, and busloads of youngsters went east or south, each with his or her bedding roll and cooking apparatus. The established travel firms enlarged their programmes and the later sixties saw many more such firms developing and covering a wider range of travel by planes rather than by sea.

Thus the embellishments made to my flat occupied a number of years as once more my ambitions were in conflict. I was pulling out of china; I was no longer dependent on it and had had enough, but a backlog was still waiting to be done. Also it seemed I had a backlog of clients wanting me to take them abroad in my waggon: plenty of leg-stretch and storage for trophies, and clients mostly of an age to prefer sitting at table for picnic lunches, and with the double doors of the car wide open, one was sitting in a cool, shady verandah. So, however much I wanted to finish my flat, if their interests coincided with mine, I was ready to take them.

During the war my heart had ached for my favourite continental cities, and lucky I had been to know them in their original state. Now, in spite of the poignancy of going back, I had to see what had survived. Of the most shattered it was not until the seventies one saw the patiently rebuilt restoration, stone by stone, but there were also instances of clemency. The Allied bombing of bridges to disrupt transport was confined to the junction of bridge with embankment, so the fine old bridge at Kreuznach – similar on a smaller scale to old London Bridge – only shattered the extremities and left the old houses intact. In fact, as we gazed up at them from the embankment, someone emptied the slops from a top window into the river below, so we felt the spirit of the place had not much altered.

I was then in the Rhine country with Frieda Perrins – Elspeth's stepmother, now a widow – on my first engagement after getting the waggon. It was also my first occasion of flying a car across the Channel as I had so far shunned these frequent twenty-minute flights between Lloyd and Le Touquet as too expensive. I now found the saving of time balanced the cost and rarely went by sea again.

219

We were on our way to the Dalmation coast, where I had never been before, and I approached it by way of the Gross Clockner pass, which I had last seen when Mrs Seddon, Father Austin and I explored it in secret and alone. Now it was alive with vehicles like ants crawling on a wall. These thinned out as we made for the coast, and how beautiful it was, that coast with its colourful rural industries, its vineyards and ancient little towns, some of them with their feet in the sea.

I was delighted to return to the country where I had failed to be eaten by wolves, and Yugoslavia now had tarred roads and good hotels, but the coast south of Split was then visited by people with their own yachts or on the pleasure steamers, so the road was unsurfaced and the hotels not of Frieda's standard. The last stretch to the delightful hotel awaiting us in Dubrovnik was therefore a long one. We got in at 10 p.m.

The enchantment of Dubrovnik and its surrounding country held us there some time. Little did we realize our privilege seeing it uncrowded, the old harbour still existent, and the noble buildings and exotic market of the city enclosed by walls. These had resisted many onslaughts but could not withstand machine-age shelling. What is it like now, that lovely city we were so privileged to see unspoilt.

We put the car on a steamer for our return north, but there was no lifting tackle. This was my worst experience, but also my last, of boarding a high deck, and also coming down from it, by a couple of wooden planks. Frieda boarded by the more conventional means. We intended taking the coast road right round to Trieste, and a further hazard awaited beyond Zadar, where the road climbs to quite a height and suffers at certain times of year a down-draught wind that has been known to blow vehicles off the road. We happened to strike it, and the Volkswagen stood high and was not heavily laden. It rocked ominously but held its own, so we survived to see the colourful little villages that border the road further up the coast. How glad I am to have known this country when the wolves were real ones, not those that are ravaging themselves and their country today.

*

Before reaching out to wider horizons, I should mention the influence of having a car at home. My mother only once drove in it before her seclusion in her bedroom. My aunt, on the other hand, could barely be kept out of it; she would jump into it like a small dog, whatever my mission, and when I drove her in the country she rejoiced in sitting so high she could see over the hedges. There came a day when she needed to be helped up into the seat, which plunged her into a profound gloom. She was into her nineties and knew she was failing; she died at home some six weeks later on the eighth of June, the same date as my mother, only this was five years on in

1964. I find it touching but also typical that her last words were, 'Don't forget to order summer coal.'

Betty was grateful for the waggon on occasions of necessity, but preferred independence in buses and trains; it was Avis and daughter whose destinies the waggon helped to shape. As soon as my flat was sufficiently ready to invite a guest, I at once invited Avis. We had long since sold her portion of the house – the east end – to the waiting purchaser, which had made life easier for Avis up to Balchraggan, and she finally advertized for someone to organize the raspberry harvest. Maurice Cullity, a young Rhodes Scholar studying law at Oxford, had applied and so enjoyed Scotland he now came annually.

While Avis was with me, a small investment our mother had owned gave each daughter a few hundred pounds, whereon Avis at once asked, would this cover a three-week tour in Spain in the Easter holidays? I said it would more than cover, nevertheless that tour rested on a knife-edge. Easter compelled immediate bookings for transport and hotel accommodation, and Avis was no sooner back in Scotland than again in hospital, but certain of recovery in time. Maurice was hoping to join the tour but uncertain of dates, and an outbreak of smallpox was compelling vaccination on the Spanish border.

Recklessly I booked everything, unsure of occupation, yet all these anxieties were dispelled on departure. My speculative bookings were used, and having seen all the right things on the way through France we reached a delightful hotel I knew in St Jean de Luz on the appointed day before Easter. Vaccination was over.

The expanse of Spain stimulated us all; Avis soon looked the picture of health, and there was a growing interest between Maurice and Heather, who though she had just left school was still much of a child. On this tour she decided to train at a school of dancing in London. The dancing proved less valuable than a year away from home, which developed her own natural common sense. Meanwhile Maurice was in Oxford obtaining his law degree, and Betty working equally hard to save an only descendant – on both sides of the family – being swept off to Australia. Eligible sons of Betty's early pupils were put in Heather's way, but to no avail. Two years later Heather and Maurice were married in Scotland in the Benedictine Abbey at Fort Augustus. Maurice came of an Irish Catholic family long established in Australia, but had no aversion to Heather remaining Church of England. Even our aunt had reluctantly confessed to liking him.

I look back on that Spanish tour always with pleasure, and Heather was not swallowed up in Australia after all. After a few years in Melbourne they moved to Philadelphia and then over the border, where Maurice now has a large practice in Toronto, and they live some miles out at Thornhill. By this time the family had increased by two daughters and a son. During these migrations they visited relations in Western Australia, in Wonersh, in Norfolk and, of course, went to Scotland, where the aunts also visited them with the waggon. Yet Heather and Maurice, at the outset of their marriage, had been barely eighteen months together in Melbourne before a doctor's report from Scotland told them if Avis was ever to see her newborn grand-child they must come home soon. A heart-searing separation had taken place, leaving Maurice teaching law in Melbourne, and I met a Madonna-like figure at Heathrow carrying a magnificent baby. Heather and Avis had about two months together before Avis suddenly sank lifeless to the floor. Balchraggan, up at that height, was probably not the best place for a heart patient, but having daughter and grand-daughter with her, that is where she would have chosen to die.

*

When I had been at my busiest, still hampered by the china-mending book, the Soviet Union had allowed foreign cars to reach Moscow by certain routes. I had at once planned an expedition to get there, but it was some time before the chance came, when I invited Marjorie Bell, a fellow member of the Women's Engineering Society and a like-minded adventurer, to join me. She had just vacated a job and had time in hand, but at this point the Soviets clamped down on their offer.

This was a blow, but we replanned the tour, making for Lubeck, a port of great character on the north coast of Germany, then ferry to Gothen-burg, and we motored across Sweden to Stockholm, staying with Barbro and Stig at Alkvettern on our way. Then by ferry again to Helsinki, where one could pick up a Swedish boat on a four-day visit to St Petersburg, so we booked return tickets from Helsinki to see at least this much of Russia. In Helsinki we left the car at a Volkswagen agency to be serviced and housed till our return, and a night journey on the Swedish ship brought us to a quiet country wharf, surrounded by trees. A tramline connected the wharf with the city.

With the ship as our base during the next four days, we could visit St Petersbourg, have tickets for the ballet, and explore the city either in a group with guide, or independently.

We chose independence, which brought us nearer to reality and taught us to manage the tram tickets, with the Russians crowding to help. It meant tagging on to English or French groups, if such there were at historical sites, and it meant walking for miles as the grandeur of this lovely city, built by monarchs of absolute power, is its infinite space. The great circular sweep behind the palaces, where carriages used to drive up to the doors, was empty in July save for a few pedestrians, but in winter it now becomes a massive ice-rink. We found restaurants distressingly sparse and always with

222

a waiting queue, but foreigners were yet so few as to be pushed immediately to the front.

By the third day we were veterans, could reach our objectives by tram and, no longer confined to a diet of sausages, could select food from the menus. The sun was setting well before midnight but its afterglow, mingling with moonlight, spread an ethereal light over the city which we walked back to admire.

At home I hadn't gleaned much Russian from a course I did with the BBC, but got a good grounding in Cyrillic lettering, which is not identical with the Greek. This was invaluable; I could read notices, to find that a lot of words were international, could read the names of the artists in the Hermitage art gallery and the designers of the porcelain shown in the white marble ballroom. All the time I was in that finely proportioned room I seemed to hear music, to be in the proximity of people dancing, and when I met up with Marjorie she had had the same hallucination.

On returning to Finland we drove from Helsinki along primitive roads, through flat countryside fretted with rivers and lakes but rarely a town. Villages had wooden houses and horse traffic, and in that rural area was so little to pollute the air that we noticed the intense green of the grass in the fields, the brilliant colouring of cornflowers, poppies, harebells and buttercups that bordered fields and roadways.

Deprived of Russia, our intention was to climb as high as we could through Finland into the Arctic Circle, and Finns seemed to rely on camping when travelling by road. Camps were well stocked, generally beside one of the plentiful lakes, and I now found I had an ardent camper in Marjorie. Shrewd in marketing, swift in cooking, she would have a fire going and something stewing before I had even rearranged the caravan. We would arrive early, go and have a swim, come back to a meal and be asleep before the place silted up with other campers, whom we would discover in the morning. Migrant Finns were well-trained campers, quiet and considerate. Yet my idea of camping is individual and solitary, but solitary sites were hard to find.

We were making for a fair-sized town, Oulu, some distance up the Gulf of Bothnia. It shared the same name as the area in Malaya where we had studied the aborigines, but the two could not have been more dissimilar. Marjorie was a soroptimist, a member of a club which established introductions between fellow members in different countries, who would welcome and show the visiting member around. Marjorie had such an introduction in Oulu, which showed us how rapidly an expanding country can catch up with, and even surpass, the old.

A Finnish family showed us their town house in a row of houses built since the war, its attic a laundry fitted with all the latest gadgets for rapid washing, drying and pressing of sheets and clothes. Its cellar was a large, well-lit recreation room for badminton and other exercise during the long dark winter, and below this an air raid shelter for a country in such close proximity with Russia. They shopped mostly in Helsinki, to which planes flew frequently like a bus service. I began to see the reason for the paucity of hotels. The Finns offered us the garden of their dacha on the riverside, and their sauna for drying off after bathing. In the morning milk, butter and bread were left for us. The best camp we ever had.

*

When we planned this tour we made some severe blunders. I had anticipated a good deal of camping but believed the waggon would be as comfortable for two people as I had found it for one. Marjorie was so impressed with its fittings she saw no reason to bring her tent, and I was so foolish as to leave behind my sleeping-bag, in which or on which I had slept under so many different skies. Another delusion from which we were suffering was that the Arctic would be cold. It was a summer of undeterred sunshine and, as the Arctic had it by night as well as day, the Arctic was hot. We often slept with the doors of the waggon wide open and, unless parked under trees, we would be woken in the small hours by the sun streaming on to it and have to move into the shade. As camping went on unremittingly, Marjorie said I snored and kept her awake, and I was yearning for what was always a tonic to me, a spell of solitude.

One night, failing to sleep, Marjorie got up and went for a walk, and saw the sun sinking halfway into the skyline, roll along it a short distance and then get up again; she felt had she had her tent she could have comfortably slept outside. I suspected that the prolonged sunlight was the real hindrance to sleep, with so far never a cloud in the sky.

We had now left the Gulf of Bothnia, where the Torneo river flows into it from the north, forming a boundary between Finland and Sweden, and a road runs parallel with the river on both sides. At one or two towns there would be a connecting bridge where the Finns would flock across to buy the much cheaper Swedish food. We did the same, but otherwise kept to the more rural Finnish side, where there were quite a few places for independent camping.

We were now on the edge of the Arctic Circle and our objective was Kiruna, the most northerly town to which there was a road, but though surrounded by Lapps – distinguishable from the tall Finns by being short – Marjorie wanted to see them in their traditional dress. An old man told us in archaic English that we would find them thus at Muonio, 100 miles up-river. Our map showed a bridge at Muonio, and a road giving access to Kiruna, which was in Sweden.

So we continued along the river and were now in view of a new road being built through Finland and Sweden to link with ports on the north coast formerly only reached by sea. This road will have wrought great changes to the area, and was deplored by the Lapps as likely to break up their herds. Yet we noticed the reindeer were already inured to the colossal road-making machinery, saw one in fact browsing beside a mechanical road-digger in action, undisturbed by the shattering noise, which had also drowned the approach of our car. However, the reindeer was still alert to stealth as I quietly opened the door to take a photograph. It looked up, saw me and in one bound was heading off into the distance.

We were now 110 miles into the Arctic Circle. Woods were growing sparse, the fir-trees looking hangdog and dispirited, with a fungus, like green seaweed, hanging from their branches. Marjorie found a pair of almost intact reindeer antlers in the undergrowth, which joined the trophies being taken home. My car compass was beginning to give erratic readings, which I felt sure must be due to the proximity of the North Pole, and a chill wind was now defeating the warmth of the permanent sun.

At Muonio we were at our highest point in the Arctic Circle, and Kiruna, as the crow flies, lay about seventy miles due west. Lapps were still only in dungarees, and the price of petrol and the exchange rate in this small Arctic town were such that we decided to rely on what petrol we had. A rash decision, as we were now in the loneliest pieces of country that I had ever seen: a vaguely green desert, unpopulated, uncultivated, unproductive and apparently unwanted. It was desolation personified and I could imagine the searing winds that would sweep this plain, discouraging all growth. Our map marked petrol obtainable at a point on this track, but we were into more forgiving country, and only twelve miles from Kiruna, before we saw a petrol pump.

Kiruna had all the hallmarks of a railway city, served by the line from Narvic in Norway, through Sweden and Finland to the Gulf, but it had retained features of earlier days, and it gave us what we were seeking. At nearby Jukkasjäve was a wooden church, cut with adze, and here were Lapps in their traditional dress gathered in anticipation of a festival. I had seen them thus when with the Wikströms, for not far from Sundsvall had been a Lapp church on a hill with a clock face painted on its steeple, the hands showing the time of the morning service. At Jukkasjäve all was so traditional that it was somewhat of a shock later to see Lapps in native dress coming out of a food store laden with provisions and putting them into a waiting taxi.

I cannot describe the warmth of the embrace of that grand old wooden mansion at Alkvettern; the weather had broken and after the solitudes of the north, the coast road south seemed crowded. We had by now overspent our estimate of costs, so though hotels were plentiful, Marjorie kept to

225

camping and I was furtively edging towards Karlskoga and Alkvettern. Though Barbro and Stig were away on holiday they had urged us to stop there on our return, if convenient, and apply to the caretaker. The electricity was functioning, our bedrooms were reserved for us and the relish of hot baths and single bedrooms repaid the detour I had made.

My visits to Alkvettern were at a time when it was fulfilling the purpose for which it had been designed, when it housed three generations comfortably, and where we dined and danced and there was an immense annual dinner for all the foresters and people employed on the estate. When Stig retired as chief forester, he handed over to a bachelor, and I fear Alkvettern may now stand empty, if indeed it exists at all as a family house today.

*

There was a Middle Eastern country with a toe in Europe that Kilton and I had been defrauded of seeing on our journey from India by having to take the North African route. This was Turkey, and I had never therefore seen Istanbul. I also wanted to see the treasures of Syria, Lebanon and Jordan, in fact to do an expanded tour of the Mediterranean, a long haul for a single journey and anyhow immediately impossible by the political situation in Palestine.

Marjorie was now battened down in a job, and the problem was to find a partner, for to roam the Middle East with an empty caravan would look like an open invitation. There was no dearth of applications from experienced travellers with plenty of means, but what they all lacked was time, and to pack even a portion of my programme into an interval of leave was not my idea of travel. I believed in a set route, but wanted leisure in which to follow it, and in obtaining this I stirred up a lot of curiosity by going with someone else's husband.

He was a full-time civil servant whom I met at the Ministry in London, and we shared an interest in theatre, until he was sent to India to advise on employment and trades unions. When I saw him next he had retired and seemed to be leading a rather purposeless life going on long walking tours or solitary camping expeditions. I knew he had a wife and family, but not till I was invited to their house did I discover the reason. They had an invalid daughter who occupied most of his wife's time, and John in India, or going daily to London, was tolerable, but permanently at home he was not. It was Mrs Carey who suggested my taking him on my proposed tour.

It was with some misgiving I did this, for I had long since recognized John as one who thought women's whole purpose in life was to work for men. On tours now I hoped to be partner rather than courier but, taking him on, a courier I certainly remained. His inertia at times was maddening, yet caustic comment was no help, only a sweet docility induced goodwill.

226

Those of my friends at home, either suspicious or hopeful that I was enjoying romance, should have witnessed my silent, and sometimes my not so silent, rage. To balance this, I had a companion with all time at his disposal, relishing the splendours of the tour, the information gleaned from some excellent museums and who, in a good mood, could be amusing. One might say I was accompanied by a trusty hound but one apt to get savage unless handled carefully.

Turkey had long been visited by foreigners, but provision for them had mostly come from the supply countries: Britain in the Edwardian era had established a Park Hotel, which remained forever Britain, and America had planted a skyscraper hotel, alien to the surroundings but giving a fine view of the Golden Horn and the Bosphorus. Yet it was still one of the countries of which tourist offices had little information and advised one to go to the embassy. We scoured many embassies in the early weeks of 1966, imposing buildings around Princes Gate and Queens Gate, but rarely did we gain the front doors. A handwritten notice PASSPORTS AND INFORMATION with a pointing arrow, would direct us down a passage sordid with dustbins, and finally a flight of steps to a meagre office. Sometimes even the flight of stairs was denied us by a foreign woman seated at the bottom and activated solely by a telephone. Queries translated were sent up to an office, the information by a reverse process conveyed down to us. Applicants seemed to be looked on as suspect until they had proved their innocence, and only at visa level were we sometimes allowed into the main building through a side door.

The waggon was fully laden by the time I had added John's gear to my own. I had made it abundantly clear from the start that in the event of camping I alone would occupy the waggon. John, a practical camper, scorned the idea of using it; he had a waterproof tent that one blew up with a foot pump, and a mattress like a car seat which, along with other gadgets, saw us pretty well stocked. We flew Lydd to Le Touquet, seen off by Judy and Frederick, living not far from Lydd, and it gave one a feeling of privilege being waved to by friends clearly visible at ground level while one climbed into the sky. Then we drove to Marseilles, took the same Greek ship on which I had sailed with Elspeth to Cyprus, but went on to Beirut, where Lebanon clings so narrowly to the edge of Syria.

*

Though Turkey was the inspiration of this tour, the increase in numbers going abroad made me anxious to go first to Lebanon and then down the route so fertile in history from Damascus to the Holy Land, and on to Petra. We would then come back again into Syria and enter Turkey on its south-east coast in the bay of Iskenderun. And what a galaxy awaited us:

227

ancient cities, crusader castles, handsome mosques, desert palaces, and we seemed to have got there well before the crowds or even the preparations for them. This gave us individual attention but no literature beyond the rather outdated Hachette guide I had with me.

We visited Petra on horseback, on foot and by moonlight; the ancient toll-house near the entrance to the Siq had been turned into a hostel for the management, but they let empty rooms and we occupied these for three nights. I regret that the Siq, the narrow gorge leading down to this sanctuary, has been cutback, where the vertical cliffs came closest together, to allow for passage of lorries. Even so, nothing can destroy the emergence from shadow to the brilliant golden face of the Treasury, a climax arranged between Nabatean sculptor and morning sun.

Nor is the coloured sandstone unique to Petra; we saw it again in the mountains on our way to Aqaba, Jordan's only access to the sea, and at this time of brooding warfare the view across the gulf into Israel was one of barbed-wire entanglements. Yet at the peak of the bay was a peaceful Edwardian-style seaside resort, lace curtains in a sublime little hotel, and coral stuck in the flower-beds to cheer the plants wilting in the heat. There was a post office, and there were cupboard shops that sold goods at such humble prices one wished one had need of them.

Unlike the other countries, Jordan was packed with visitors, and Jerusalem rather oppressive in its divided state, with moreover the beautiful Dome of the Rock under repair, surmounted with an anachronistic crane. Queues of former householders of the forbidden quarter were seeking re-entry at the Mandelbaum Gate, and the anxiety of those waiting, and the agony of those refused, were providing intense entertainment to tourists looking down on them from the flat roof of the YWCA.

I rejoiced in returning to Syria, which combines its historic features with everyday life. The spirit of Queen Zenobia still seems to cling to Palmyra, whose sensible wooden hotel looked out on a colonnade of arches, monumental ruins and a wide scattering of excavated tombs. May Aleppo long preserve its stagic citadel, also its casements hanging over the streets, supported on colossal beams, enabling screened women behind the casements to look along the streets. Here I had to be enshrouded in a wrap to gain entrance to the mosque. The traffic may be noisier at Baron's Hotel than when Lawrence praised it so highly, yet it had remained a most caring and unassuming hotel in view of the famous names in its visitors' book.

With entry into Turkey at the Bay of Iskenderun, we were at once in a Victorian atmosphere where a sedate little hotel looked on to a palm-lined square and a cab rank with coachmen awaiting hire. The climate had also adjusted to the change of scene. In the north-west corner of Syria eagles and buzzards had given way to songbirds and we dined under jacaranda trees. This change was due to snow still lying on the Taurus mountains,

228

which we climbed to visit Konya, but it warmed up again as we returned to the coast near Alanya. Here a lovely empty stretch of moonlit beach inspired a picnic dinner and camping, lulled to sleep by the sound of the waves.

We were now in the south-east corner of Turkey, a refined area containing features both natural and historical, and Turks were beginning to discover there was money in their historical treasures and that they were worth cherishing. With American machinery, they were also repairing their roads, but with miles yet needing to be done. Apart from Cyprus, there was little known about Turks outside their country, so it was cheering to find a happy-go-lucky nation, friendly and anxious to please. Small in stature compared with the Americans, they were physically strong, having to use muscle rather than machine. Would a Western waiter carry a marble-topped table with iron legs the length of a terrace for customers desiring the shade?

At Selçuk – Ephesus – we found members of a Swan tour, brought to the coast by sea and on here by motor coach. Despising the group tours, we kept aloof, but from what I heard of their lecturer, they would learn far more of Ephesus than we would, even if we learnt more about Turkey. They would see nothing of the attractive village of Selçuk, where we were staying in a hotel which seemed to own bedrooms scattered around the village. Mine looked into a narrow street, with an ancient viaduct close to the wall beneath my window, its duct long since fallen away, leaving only the pillars and battered capitals, each supporting a stork's nest. Thus I witnessed a constant domestic scene of parent storks regurgitating liquid into the open beaks of two baby storks and I felt more than ever glad of my independent travel.

*

We climbed out of Turkey via Bursa and Istanbul, where we dallied many days and could have done with many more. Though its markets had been drab and its apparel very ordinary, Turkey contained the bizarre and the beautiful and was divinely cheap. Nor had we seen half of this country that stretches from the Mediterranean to Mount Ararat. When, therefore, a low-priced ferry service started between Venice and Izmir, we decided to go again, and it was like old times coming into harbour at noon and seeing a dozen Turks sitting in the shade, each sleepily smoking his narghile.

We were on familiar ground as far as Bodrum, calling at our favourite restaurant, Blue Corner, on its river-bank, and meaning to follow the south coast eastwards. This road, rich in relics of Grecian and Roman occupation along with later attractions, was nevertheless a terrible road. Only the stretch between Antalya and Alanya was surfaced, the Turkish Riviera. I intend only to mention a few outstanding events of this second visit to Turkey, such as our spending the night in a bird-watching hide in mistake for the hotel in Koycegiz, which I had been warned was extremely primitive. We found a wooden shed with bunks, tap water, candles and a Primus cooking stove. What more could one want? Yet what intrigued me was the view from the window on to a lovely lagoon lying still in the moonlight, wooded hills reaching down to it steeply and no sound save now and again a birdsong. I got up often to look at it, and at dawn there was a tremendous dawn chorus, and I wondered. No one came at morning, so we left our name and what we felt was suitable payment, but as we drove on through the village we saw a seedy-looking hotel, and the truth was confirmed. Yet how glad I am we did it. All that coast may now be quite different; a hotel may stand where the hide stood and that lovely lagoon may be a marina.

Occupied with Xanthos one morning, we decided to lunch at Kas, not far distant, a delightful little village where a man sat reading an English paper, and I asked him, had Francis Chichester got home yet? He replied, 'Francis Chichester? Good Lord, yes! There's been a war since then.' Relatively near the scene of trouble, we had read or heard nothing of the Six Day war. The menfolk at Kas were all sitting under the trees at tables playing backgammon; the women were out in the fields hoeing, with a man timing their progress, their bright clothing enhancing the scene. We were also to see women harnessed with a donkey to the plough, all of which recommended the country to John.

Shades of clouds were racing cross the Anatolian plain, and there were stretches of magnificent country when we turned north from the coast road for the rock tombs and the eroded land round Ürgup. Of these I will only mention Kaymakli, recently discovered, the underground city which we arrived at bent double down a tube-like tunnel, arriving at the first of seven floors reaching downward. Here 60,000 people had once lived. They had air brought to them by a shaft, they had water and they had a church, but they were too early and too numerous for Christians, as this was before the time of Christ. No one then knew their origin and I have never heard if it is known today.

We now go into what I would describe as Turkey in the raw, a commercial area into which we strayed making for Trebizond: communal bedrooms, washrooms, lavatories. Though some of these hotels had WITHOUT written over the door, meaning without bugs, in fact bugs were the only discomfort we did not have to endure. I was, of course, trained to this, but one would have expected some provision for a man travelling with his wife, even if this was only expressed in a washroom for women. One got the impression that no Turkish woman ever left home, that Ataturk's effort at emancipation had failed. Yet in the same area Turkey would have a talented cook. Here they were large buildings, generally with a row of wash-basins inside the door, and it was at first surprising to see men in European clothing come in to wash face and hands and then – shoes removed – put their feet in the basin. This custom was more picturesque seen outside a mosque.

I feared irritation in my fellow traveller at the crudity of these hotels, but they seemed to arouse humour, particularly when the hotel gave no food which led to the discovery of the breakfast-houses in the town, where there was generally an expert in the art of making cheese. Pressed out many times on a marble slab, the cheese reached the refinement of a muslin headscarf, which would be tossed in the air, then rolled up and baked a few minutes in a charcoal stove and then dealt in small slabs to eager male customers and a few women who bought it at the door. Eaten with fresh bread rolls, it was delicious and inspired a smooth start to the day.

*

My last tour with John was remarkable at the outset, but later – in my opinion – eroded by civilization. The idea was to follow the North African coast from Tunis to Morocco, the final stretch of which Kilton and I had missed on our return from India through lack of funds. Besides this, I hoped to penetrate the Algerian Sahara, as neighbours of ours had done pre-war in a specially adapted car. They had described the joy of the people of the oases in seeing new faces and having contact with the outside world: brief visits that did not strain the local amenities.

We let a year go by after returning from Turkey to let the coffers refill and to let Algeria settle down after gaining her independence from France. Even so, its war had left difficulties in obtaining car papers, the Algerian dinar was only obtainable within the country itself, and maps of Algeria were non-existent. I had maps covering the whole area we needed but they were not up to date.

We took the Marseilles–Tunis ferry and went some way down the border with Algeria before crossing into it, for here was a convenient bank for buying dinars, and also a road finally leading into the desert. We now learnt that the nearest bank for buying Algerian money was in Constantine, many miles north near the coast. Luckily French francs were accepted – at a price – and we spent all our French money and much time getting back up there. Yet I shall never regret being sent to this city, this fortress built on almost vertical rocks that were joined at their pinnacles by slender bridges and their steep escarpments again eased by bridges down to the plains.

In Constantine, streets seemed to hang like ropes suspended from one pinnacle to the next, and as I only had a small map of the town in a Hachette guide, I arrived more by accident than design in the Place Nemours,

231

where we located a pleasant little hotel. Next morning the business of securing rights of passage and money were rendered more harrowing by a change of time, robbing us of an hour in which to accomplish all this. Offices were threatening to close while officials were demanding, why was the car registered in my name rather than John's? I foresaw a delay of days ahead, but must add that on this occasion John was fully useful.

In fact we got through on time, to explore the city of palaces, mosques and a cathedral but also a difficult one-way street system. Held up at a traffic light in a street hanging in space, I asked the driver of an adjacent open car how to get out of the town for the road to Biskra. He said, '*Suivez-moi, madame.*' There followed an enthralling city tour over the Pont del Kantara, like a thin necklace it seemed at its peak, to the Kasbah, to a view of the Route Corniche, along the Chemin Edith Cavell, to the Belvedere, the Great Mosque, the main street, and finally the Pont du Diable, a man-made bridge whose slender legs led steeply down to the safe sober road at ground level beside the river. Here we heartily thanked our benefactor – '*Un plaisir, madame*' – and took the road to Biskra.

From now onward the route was a flirtation with railway, river and road, the rail constantly crossing our path and the river running parallel for a time and then wandering off, but as the land grew arid, always visible with its cultivated banks. The cliffs of El Kantara, like a blood-red line seen distantly, grew ever more formidable as we approached. There was only one fault in those cliffs, and road, river and rail were all making for it, coming closely together for the final assault. The cliffs hung over us as we plunged out of the sunlight into a red cave, the river dropping into a ravine, the road clinging to the embankment and the rail mounting a causeway carved for it out of the rock wall. We emerged from those cliffs slap into the desert; river and vegetation had disappeared, the water soaked up in a vista of sand stretching as far as the eye could see, with road and rail continuing in harness for some fifty miles.

Biskra was now a ghost town where Communist views and the struggle for liberty had expressed their revenge. Luxury hotels were either tenements or boarded up, the casino was closed, the headquarters of the Foreign Legion an empty space wired in like a chicken run. Of theatres and entertainments there was not a sign, all statues had been removed as if in an endeavour to stamp out history, but a memorial was retained to the Algerians killed in the war against the French. Picture postcards alone showed what had been, and I sent one to Barbro, describing as it was now, the place where her parents had once stayed. Yet the remaining hotel was comfortable, reasonable and contained good company.

*

Touggourt had huge trees, a luxury hotel and a tarred road all the way, but our next oasis barely deserved the title. Ouarglia was closer to expectation: bleak, dusty, with more barbed wire entanglements than trees, but it had a lorry stop that offered food, a washroom and beds, the latter all booked, we were told. Too innocent to recognize this as a means of extracting bribery, we decided to stay for dinner. We could always camp outside.

When the refectory opened it was a circular room with alcoves in the walls like a serai, and John decided to sleep in an alcove and put his bedding role in one to reserve it. When the management saw this they came forward with offers of bedding, but John slept in his alcove and, with blinds drawn and doors bolted, I slept serenely in the waggon just outside. This bedroom blackmail was prevalent at the time, but to hold out against it was to win.

I do not know when it dawned on me that between the first planning of this tour and the doing of it, modernization had crept in like an epidemic and all but one of the oases we planned to visit were now joined by tarred roads. Even El Golea, the furthest south we could afford to go and marked on my pre-war map as having *eau potable*, was getting fresh water in a series of mobile tanks that we passed on the road. I had never anticipated the oases growing worldly, losing all character; there was no expertise needed in reaching them and the Michelin maps we bought on reaching Algiers showed airfields spread around the desert; thus modern assets were easily available, and a partially made road went right down to Timbuktu.

The only oases of character we saw were the cone-like strongholds of a confederation of Berbers, who had their own language and trades, and built their houses on arcades, one above the other like a pack of stacked playing-cards rising out of the desert – a sight I am sure is well known to the tourists of today. Even so, these tarred roads had their quota of skeleton vehicles lying by the roadside, and there was still the innocent wisp of sand lying across the tarmac, virtually a bar of iron, a sleeping policeman deceiving the unwary, though usually marked by an early-warning notice: *Attention! Sable!*

I certainly have one rewarding memory of this period, when an Arab encampment in course of migration crossed our road some distance ahead. The long line of camels moved gracefully, leisurely, the leading ones bearing palanquins containing, one imagined, wives and their servants. Two long poles stuck into the camel harness stood high above each palanquin like a pair of inverted pendulums swinging slowly and in rhythm to the camel strides. Outriders on camels, and in full Oriental garb, were followed by lesser orders herding further camels, then horses, mules and finally goats. We had pulled up at a respectful distance and watched this unhurried procession fade into the horizon of sky and sand.

Nothing could surpass the fish restaurants down by the water in Algeria itself, the fish coming fresh from sea to stew-pan to plate. Neither wars nor

233

rebellions could deter flowers and trees from flourishing along that riviera coastline, but we broke from it at the Moroccan frontier to take a diagonal course to Fez and Azrou. The snow on the high mountains of Morocco was feeling the effects of the early summer sun; cataracts of water were filling wadis and streams and flooding rivers to near bridge-level. Some roads were closed, others taken at one's own risk. It was the only exciting driving of the whole tour. We were booked on a ship from Casablanca to Southampton and reserved the last eight days to visit Marrakesh and the High Tatra, a date postponed for over forty years.

Sailing home from Casablanca, I pondered the difficult task of breaking up this tandem travel, but if possible without rancour. We had, after all, journeyed some thousands of miles together; I had undoubtedly made use of John, as Mrs Carey had made use of me. He had left me the entire planning of the tours, which I enjoyed doing, and the second visit to Turkey had been almost harmonious, but this last had been just the opposite and very wearing. He knew of my desire to go up the Nile by boat from Cairo to Aswan, and had expressed similar interest, but with Egypt and Israel in a state of stagnant warfare, we learnt from a man seated at our table on this ship that the local pleasure steamers from Cairo had ceased to ply. To sail the Nile, these steamers were my only hope of reaching Aswan, so I now decided on taking a drastic step, in which I knew John would never follow me, and the break-up of the tandem would be his doing, not mine. In any case I was not going immediately so I could let the dust settle before earning his everlasting contempt.

*

The sixties that had brought so many diversions had also brought too many deaths. That first tour to the Middle East took so much longer than expected that we got out of rhythm with poste restante. Betty had no way to let me know my friend Esmond had died, and finally had to represent me at a packed memorial service at St Martin's in the Fields. I had not seen him for some time as, now a Brigadier, he had been five years in command of the West Indies, but we had always kept in touch.

I generally received letters at Christmas, immaculately typed by Clara but obviously dictated by Kilton, and had always replied. Besides a busy practice in New York, he had taken on a smaller one that he attended at weekends at Jenkinstown, an offshoot of Philadelphia. I felt it would kill him, and evidently it did. After two years of silence I wrote to Clara asking for news, and heard from her then that he had died. His group therapy had caught on in America, but anthropologists criticized his methods with the Sakai, and it was Edmund Leach, now Provost of Kings College, Cambridge, who gave assurance that he had done no harm.

234

Verena had won her full honours in engineering, and finally owned her own factory: an ambition since early youth. I wish we could have seen more of each other after the war but we were both too busy with our own ploys. I visited her at the not-too-far-distant nursing home to which she had finally had to retire, but for one who was happiest with the young it was not the right environment, and I could not be wholly disheartened when she escaped in death.

Yet the sixties gave me one special gift, quote out of this world: an invitation to the anniversary of the 200th year of the Drottningholm Court Theatre from Barbro and Stig. I had now visited Sweden by successive progressing means: first by ship, then car and now by plane. This was September 1969.

Stig, on retirement from being head forester in Värmland, had been offered the post of forester to King Gustav of Sweden, then a very old man. The Hegardts were thus housed on the island of Drottningholm, looking out on theatre and palace with the Royal Post Office next door. A gracious Edwardian atmosphere surrounded them, bolstered, however, by all the latest devices for comfortable living. The King was not at his palace, nor was it on view during the festival, nevertheless I was shown round palace and theatre by devoted custodians, and in the theatre saw appealing hand-operated mechanisms for producing stormy artificial waves and other scenic effects. A barn-shaped, all-wooden construction whose only modern innovation was electric lighting, the theatre seated I would say about 800, mostly arriving by motor boat from Stockholm. Here we came many evenings, and I think the dress rehearsal for a Handel opera was one of the most spectacular occasions, with a straw-hatted *corps de ballet*, with orchestra as well as actors in eighteenth-century dress, rivalled by an audience restricted to the islanders in their glittering twentieth-century regalia.

The islanders, nearly all related to or working for the King, enjoyed enormous privilege. I would accompany Barbro, who was eligible for exotic fruit and vegetables cut for her by gardeners in the royal kitchen gardeners, or she could ladle cream by the pint from a vat in the cool-room by the cowsheds. There were royal relatives scattered about in neighbouring estates, some of them not too well off; one would see a Countess in gum-boots and slacks driving her own tractor in the fields who, on sight of Barbro and her guest, would come across and issue a warm invitation to supper, probably for that very night. Spontaneous hospitality had always been a feature of Swedish life and all seemed to possess enormous freezers, washing-machines, washing-up machines, drying machines and the like. By evening the party would have gathered strength, there would be a dream of fair women smartly dressed, mixing sauces, making salads, laying an exquisite table and all talking English on behalf of the guest. Husbands would be battened down in an adjoining room having pre-drinks, and probably selecting a suitable wine for the occasion. Mercifully I had foreknowledge of this kind of thing and had brought with me my entire wardrobe of smart clothing – it hardly stretched – thanked Heaven I had learnt something of cooking and could subscribe mild syllabubs when Barbro herself threw a party.

I wondered what they did when they gave official dinners, as I was sure at times some of them had to do. I learnt the answer from my neighbour at dinner that night. One rang up a certain office in Stockholm and ordered food and wine of one's choice, and this was brought up-river by a private staff who cooked, served and left everything washed up and in order before returning downstream. It was a lot easier than ordinary entertaining, he added, but very expensive and not nearly so much fun.

1970–1990

LAST FLING

We are now well entrenched in the century, past the prosperous, light-hearted sixties and into the seventies, which at first gave no hint of the rise in prices and decline in standards that were to become noticeable, even alarming, as the seventies drifted into the eighties on a downward slope. It was a year and a half since we had returned from Morocco, and I was at home, never more happy, writing a work of fiction and living with it, but fiction allowed for diversions. I had seen John occasionally: lunches in London, a theatre or two, and I had driven him over to watch polo at Cowdray, but latterly I had got immersed in my novel and was sure he had found out, as I had, that there were no local steamers plying in the Nile. Yet there were Swan tours, still sailing to Aswan, with an additional journey to Abu Simbel by hydrofoil across three hundred miles of Lake Nasser.

This covered all I wanted, and I had written to Swan asking the price if I retained my cabin coming back again down the Nile instead of flying home from Aswan. I was unused to having compressed holidays. Not till I heard, and found I could afford it, did I let John know my intention: a carefully written letter but the inference clear, for I knew John would never join a group. I wanted to get this off my chest; the tour was not till late November, *why* did I have to send that letter now?

My letter crossed with one from John telling me light-heartedly he was in a nursing home with jaundice; another from his wife asked if I could go and see him as she was unable to go every day, but referring to an operation of which I knew nothing. The nurse taking me to his room when I went to see him was so tight-lipped I learnt nothing more there. Certainly John looked a very sick man but he gripped my hand with surprising vigour, talked cheerfully and was delighted with autumn roses I had brought from our garden. On the table by his bed was my opened letter. We neither of us mentioned it, and I left, never dreaming I would not see him again. A phone message told me a further emergency operation had been necessary, from which he had not long survived. Mrs Carey was with him when he died.

I never knew all the facts of the case and was left with a feeling of guilt as well as remorse; perhaps there was an underlying reason for his lethargy on those tours, and yet I felt I should have heard about it. Even more I deplored my letter to him when Swan's wrote shortly after, saying they thought it advisable to postpone the tour for that year.

Thus it was not until March 1971 that I occupied one of the single cabins on the MS *Delta*, right over the stern of the ship, where the vibration was such that anything on the dressing-table waddled to the floor. The noise was excessive but did not disturb my sleep, and we generally tied up at night. I would sit out of a morning on the ribbon of deck which encircled my cabin, where breakfast was brought to me, and the view of waving palms and Biblical scenes confirmed me in the opinion that the Nile should be seen from the water rather than the shore.

The *Delta*, the only passenger ship plying from Cairo to Aswan, was of traditional pattern, flat-bottomed, apt to run on to sand-banks and, if the wind was in their favour, likely to be overtaken by the native *faluccas* going at full speed, their tall sails lying over very close to the water. My fellow passengers were sporting types, risking this journey; the war was still unsettled, which meant frequent checking of passports, a great showing of arms, and the glass doors of museum cases plastered with strip paper. These strictures seemed to ease off as we got up-river, and we heartily despised the luxury French tourist ship venturing only between Luxor and Aswan and equipped with orchestra, hairdresser and other such frivolities. I was told later the *Delta* sank, though I suspect no longer on tour, and for a time the superstructure could be seen above-water, a fitting memorial to those more adventurous days.

Meanwhile we were well instructed in Pharaonic history and saw Tutankhamun's tomb in the Valley of the Kings, where Carter had found it, the staggering wealth of gold, the jewellery and colouring all then in pristine condition. By seeing twice over the Valleys of the Kings and the Queens, the temples of Karnak and Luxor, and many other treasures, they were fixed in my memory far better than with a single viewing.

The High Dam, built by the Russians, had converted a desert valley into a lake, and we crossed this 300 miles of water by hydrofoil, seeing not a sign of human, animal or bird life. What looked like rocks at the edge of the lake were the craggy tops of hills not yet submerged, for the dam would not be completely full for another two years.

Abu Simbel stood at the far end of this expanse, and only by seeing it could one appreciate the miracle of raising it from its former position in the lower valley to its present height clear of the water. This temple, faced with its colossal statues, was still sited so that the first ray of dawn fell on the statues and on the altar within, abiding evidence of what can be done when nations collaborate.

Sole passenger on the *Delta* that night, I dined with the management, and next morning found the (then) Cataract Hotel at Aswan, with its strongly

Victorian flavour, the perfect setting in which to write the many letters I owed. At midday the second lot of tourists arrived.

That expedition undermined my resistance to group travel. After this I let Swan, Jules Verne and others take me on long-distance travel by plane, and provided it covered what I wanted to see or revisit, I was thankful for someone else doing all the organizing and hard work. Age and greater prosperity may have influenced this change of mind. (But I was over eighty and suffering from cataract before I made my first conscious move in deference to age. I resigned from various forms of transport I had done for the WRVS ever since I had bought the waggon, and had no idea I was breaking records until, on resignation, I received a handsome certificate as a member still working at eighty-two. However, at this time I was still a young thing in my early seventies.)

*

In 1974, our fiftieth year in The Old House, Betty and I intended to give an old-fashioned garden party – Edwardian style – with printed invitations, marquee, band, refreshments such as cucumber sandwiches, asparagus rolls, iced coffee, and inviting all our friends in and around Wonersh. The size of the marquee recommended was such that I felt it would be impossible to install, but our experienced tent merchant came to measure and view, and by including a small tree *within* the marquee it fitted comfortably into our lawn.

We had lately been introduced to a wonderful caterer, so excellent that appreciation of the refreshments featured in nearly every thank-you letter. Also the early seventies were not so dominated by the refrigerator; food came fresher to the table, no mummified asparagus. We hired a butler, retired but still living locally, who ushered guests to the garden. Finally I think a great factor towards success was that we invited everyone we knew from the Lord of the Manor to the postmistress.

This might suggest an inordinate number but, in fact, though inflated housing estates held an ever-growing population, it was continually changing and now far too vast for all to be personally known. When I started china-mending I would know eighty per cent of the people passing the window, generally on foot. Now they passed mostly in cars and I knew not a quarter of them, so the marquee could comfortably seat everyone at tables for tea. We had been granted a sunny day, but cold.

The party was certainly enjoyed and never forgotten. Many photos were taken and we received a number of handsome gifts. One of our guests was a professional artist of repute living locally, Margaret Palmer, who asked if we would like a painting of the party. We would indeed, but how could it be done?

The answer is an oil-painting now hanging in our hall, containing portraits of ourselves centrally, surrounded by portraits of at least fifty or more well-known guests, shown talking, gesturing, laughing. The artistic eye must have taken in details of clothing and garden-party hats, and she herself had a camera and possibly a scheme already in mind. The painting at the top shows a distant view of the refreshment table, and at the base a fringe of wind instruments breaking the line of guests in the foreground. Many of these guests came in to look at the scene fondly when the picture was hung.

Betty had never been very partial to the waggon, though grateful for its services, and it was partly on her behalf that I sold it. I had had it twelve years and felt bereft at its departure. On the merits of their recent achievements, I bought a Saab and kept this until I gave up driving, for I tended to make friends with the cars I drove and they served me well. Yet though I had made the automobile the backbone of my life and loved driving, I had always seen cars as a potential menace. Shortly after the Balkan tour I had sent an article to the WES magazine which anticipated the state of the roads, holiday resorts and places of interest when nearly everyone owned a car. The article was prefaced by a notice that the WES took no responsibility for the author's views. When I came on it while making some research at headquarters, I found my prognostication very close to the situation at that time.

Not only did I love car-driving but I loved railways; however, as the century advanced I had seen railways being destroyed by road haulage and independent transport. I remembered stations as places with friendly staff and carefully tended flower-beds, and a whistle blown by a guard announcing the departure of the train, with all doors carefully closed. I had listened to the beat of the *Flying Scotsman* scudding northward to the Highlands, but after the Beeching rape, staff and flower-beds began disappearing from country stations, leaving a bleak platform, or none at all as stations closed. To arrive at a large junction meant an anxious hunt for a porter, and I was to see steam haulage supplanted by electric; cleaner and more compact, it nevertheless led to whole trains being left in the charge of one man – the driver.

Betty had shamed me in the early seventies by flying to Toronto to see the Cullity family out at Thornhill, whereas I, the traveller, had so far made no such move though I had it in mind, along with a heartfelt desire to travel across Canada by the Canadian Pacific railway. A friend, Zöe Bankart, who had joined the *Delta* on the return journey down the Nile, was anxious to do this with me on her way out to the USA.

Sailing by cargo boat was now hopelessly out of date, emptied of all interest by their brief delay at ports, but a helpful agency booked us on a small passenger ship that sailed from Poland to Montreal, calling at Southampton. Then from a Canadian Baedeker I had acquired, we made out a train timetable and telephoned it to my niece, who made all reservations. It seemed incredibly simple.

Thus it was we reached Canada and, after a brief visit to Quebec, returned for a day in Montreal before setting out westward that evening, and Canada was not so bomb-strewn that we could not leave our holdalls in a locker during that day.

*

Porters have always seemed to me the essence of civilization and I am thankful that airports have found them essential to cope with the spate of arrivals. It was luxurious to return to the station that evening, to hand keys and luggage slips to a porter distinguishable by a red cap, to join the train later and find him in charge of it, the heavy luggage stowed, our hand luggage in our 'roomettes'. These, barely nine feet by five, had beds which pushed into the wall by day and contained everything one could possibly want for the journey, including an armchair.

It was luxurious in the long twilight to lie in bed looking at the passing scene and the Canadian fauna leaping away from the approaching train. We had chosen roomettes on either side for maximum viewing, and from these, from the dining-salon or observation car, one looked out on great welts of woodland, grassland, mountain and prairie, growing ever grander in scale as we advanced westward. One saw the effect of climate on landscape. Where there was no shelter for the searing wind, plains would be empty of trees save where the owner of some dramatically isolated farmstead had conscientiously fought to tether young trees in the ground during early growth, and a sparse fringe of adult conifers might have rewarded his efforts to shelter his home. Sometimes we followed the course of a river and, in the corn lands, saw the tall, graceful grain stores on the river-bank, from which barges loaded their holds by gravity. I learnt many were now out of use through grain being carried by road.

Large stations allowed a leg-stretch of about half an hour, and a bell gave warning of departure. If a stop was needed at a smaller station, where the platform was barely above ground level, departure was signified by small mounting-blocks put out under the now elevated carriage doors. Sometimes we ran parallel with a national highway, when car and train would ride abreast at about seventy miles an hour. From what I saw of Canadian driving there was no fanatical worship of speed.

After a stay of some days in Vancouver, we returned on the National Railway, which gave equally efficient service on a more devious line. Between Winnipeg and Toronto the land flattens out into a series of lakes and small islands with rarely a dwelling in sight – a fisherman's Paradise. It was a Saturday evening and several fishermen were waiting to be taken

241

back to Toronto, standing on intermittent wooden platforms such as those once used for milk churns awaiting transport. It struck me as a highly considerate service, as arresting and restarting a diesel train cost a lot of money.

Where distance is considerable it is easier to maintain a train passenger service, the comfort of being carried outweighing the fatigue of driving and the cost less than by air. Nevertheless, I made that journey only just in time. I heard rumours that the CPR was anxious to cut down on passengers and take more freight, and I learnt later that there is now only a limited passenger service, and that taken up far in advance by package tours.

That was 1976, the first year of unnatural heat, resulting in a conveniently calm Atlantic. Zöe had flown to America, I had enjoyed ten days of being spoilt with the Cullity family and was now reclining on a deckchair finishing the last of Betty's dining-room chair covers, for embroidery was the last craft I had added to my repertoire.,

The *Stefan Batory* did not thrust entertainment on its passengers but gave them the choice of good music in the afternoons, cinema in the evenings, dancing after dinner and a tour of the ship when the radar screen on the bridge showed the proximity of the icebergs between which the ship was being steered. There were no single cabins but I shared mine happily with a woman who also liked reading in bed.

The *Stefan Batory* plies no more. Too many people do the journey by air.

*

It suited me to go on tours with the travel firms with their shorter absences, for I was not at liberty now to be away for long. Betty depended on me for household shopping and such, and though still clinging to her independence, still taking herself around by bus, an increasing absent-mindedness resulted in her purse being regularly brought to the door by a vigilant bus conductor, who thankfully still existed at that time.

So it was evident we must synchronize our holidays. Betty was still excellent company, and for her eightieth birthday had organized a luncheon locally for a number of her erstwhile pupils, and it was rewarding how many came. Also, soon after this birthday, there occurred an outstanding event.

An Oxford don, Frederick Bateson, had been told by his doctor to lay off all work, and his wife, a long-standing friend of ours, wrote to Betty asking if she had a manuscript anywhere that he might try and get published for her, for he so admired her writing and it would give him something to do. The outcome of this was the publication of *Laura*, by André Deutsch, in 1978. This book not only sold well but the film rights were bought by an American company, bringing in a very large sum. In view of Betty's age –

she was now rising eighty-two – ready money was more important than what Hollywood might do with the film, if it did anything at all. André Deutsch was now pressing Betty for a further novel.

So I took her that year to a favoured hotel in Norfolk where she was well known and had but to walk down a leafy glade to bathe in a calm sea when the tide was in. She had the new manuscript with her and liked holidays on her own, as I did, so I left her and toured Britain in the Saab, with a guilty feeling that I had neglected the splendours of my own country for those abroad.

Leading travel firms were now gaining a footing in remoter countries, and it was advisable to join early before the places got too popular. I refer to them only briefly as they are available to all with the money to pay for them, and in this respect my own finances had considerably changed since the shoe-string days. Indian Military was growing increasingly bountiful – I imagined by now there were not so many surviving benefactors – and I had received another legacy from the Perrins family after the death of Frieda Perrins. Help from that family had always come at a vital moment.

I went to Moscow, which I had failed to visit by car, and the tour continued to Georgia, Armenia and Uzbegistan, where Bokhara had long been forbidden to infidels. Even now, tenure of the region by the Soviets was too precarious to allow the mingling of Uzbegs and tourists, so Bokhara was being drained of a now fairly subdued population, and tourists – more lucrative – were staying at a rapidly emptying shell, in fact a museum town. Samarkand was far more rewarding, to which we flew in an old propeller-driven plane at such a mean height above the desert that I felt I was back in old Baker choosing the best passage through the sand.

I also went back to Iran, but that was a mistake. I much preferred the Persia I had visited with Baker, before they had exploited oil, before there was smog in the air usurping the beautiful colouring.

A valuable outcome of these tours was the meeting with Sigrid Hart, a twice-widowed American with a grown-up independent family, and with all the assets I had once quoted to a young friend who had wanted to join one of my expeditions. I had said one needed to be tough, tolerant and know where the North was, in none of which the young friend qualified, but it had been remembered and often quoted. Here was Sigrid, qualified in all three and more beside, the easiest person in the world with whom to share a bedroom where accommodation was limited.

I met her on a Swan tour of Kashmir, when we lived on houseboats on the Jhelum river. We went to Katmandu, flanked all the way by the Karakoram range of the Himalayas, and in Nepal by even mightier heights, not that there was any guarantee of seeing them. Even while exploring Kashmir the clouds had never lifted from Nanga Parbat, which stood, so to speak, in our own backyard. We wound up in gloriously rural Sikkim: high mountain

243

ranges, rice terraces, markets, monasteries and an old-world post office from which someone sent a postcard to her husband in England which I believe eventually arrived. Sikkim was then a small separate state with its own ruler but it is now part of India. We flew home from Calcutta, which filled me with depression, the Maidan looking like an untidy allotment, the Fort shrouded in barbed-wire. Never go back.

I joined up with Sigrid again later in Iraq to see far more than the Arch of Ctesiphon denied me earlier by the flooded Euphrates. Mallowan was the archaeologist who showed us many of the proofs of Old Testament history, and I hope something remains today of Nebuchadnezza's audience hall so brilliantly excavated. I could not help wondering if it was purely accident that Mallowan had set up his camp not far from the Temple of the God of Writing. We all gazed with awe at the plain wooden shed in which his wife, Agatha Christie, wrote her books in the early morning.

Mixed in with these were a few private tours such as visiting my young friend who never knew where the North was, now doing pottery quite successfully in Madeira; also hiring a car with Sybil Clement Brown in Crete in search of rare birds and orchids. Then suddenly the floodgates opened: a firm with special contacts in the country was offering entry to China.

*

My interest in China was aroused by an exhibition of Chinese art shown in Burlington House in 1935 when I was intoxicated by the scroll paintings. One could gaze for ever at *A Million Miles of the Yangtze River* with its quiet fishing scenes. I wonder where that valuable painting is now.

I had also read the experiences of those who had gone through the rapids of the Yangtze gorges, heard of the former forced-labour crawling along the ledges cut in the rock to haul shipping back against the flow. Lately there had been the drama of the British gunboat, the Amethyst, held up at Wuhan by the Chinese government, whose captain had slipped anchor one evening and in spite of her being damaged by gunfire, had got his ship down to safety in Shanghai. Now there was a tour being offered to Peking which took in the Yangtze gorges. I telephoned Sigrid and we settled on a convenient date, but there seemed every sort of impediment.

There was no Miss Ranby now to whom to turn, and only at the last minute was there approved coverage for my absence. There was then no direct flight to Peking; we had to change planes at both Frankfurt and Karachi, and the ongoing plane from Frankfurt was so late we missed the one at Karachi and there was no other for three days. Our tour manager travelling with us was livid as we were the only Peking passengers, but she laid on a programme during the delay, and in Peking got us an extension so we fulfilled our programme. A rather second-hand-looking plane flew us, in thick mist all the way, but landed us finally in Peking.

We stayed at the Peking Hotel, a great slab of modernized Oriental splendour on the corner of Tiananmen Square. In the Memorial Hall we were lined up to file past the embalmed body of Chairman Mao. There followed a set programme: Great Wall, Summer Palace, Sacred Way, Ming Tombs.... In the pavilions of the Forbidden City we were to see various forms of art and craft that challenged the Fabergé masterpieces of St Petersburg and rivalled the miniature paintings of the Seraglio in Istanbul. Not content with the carving of lifelike figures in ivory, the Chinese had wrought an ivory carpet, a long strip of smaller interlaced links that one would not expect to support a procession or the prostrate body of a supplicant, yet it had survived.

Having scoured Peking we flew to Chunking, where we boarded a river boat which in the course of the journey came to look like a badly packed shopping basket. It was remarkably undemocratic: the entire first-class was consigned to our group – foredeck, cabins, bathroom and saloon. Second-class got food and a few cabins, third-class nothing but a square of deck and had to feed themselves. A lot of strange luggage strewed their decks, barrels of junk and small items of wooden furniture.

The Yangtze was at low water; we would tie up at naked floating wharves with the port of call high on a ledge at the top of an almost vertical river-bank, reached by a flight of steps and a God-given haulage system where exports were balanced against imports, the goods coming down on a rail, drawing those going up on a parallel rail. Passengers climbed the steps, and the object of the unusual luggage was revealed: a market town high overhead was doing a nice line in wicker chairs and exchanged them for wood furniture and barrels. The third-class generally bought groceries and hens with tied feet. Yet all these acquired goods were stored not within the ship so much as lashed to its railings, even wicker chairs.

I could remember the lovely tunics worn by the slim Chinese women when I was formerly in Hong Kong, and I resented now the dull uniform, jumper and slacks, worn by nearly everyone in Peking. Here in the country one found self-expression in clothing, even if it was mostly European.

We had to rise at four in the morning for the first, the most formidable gorge. As I walked the smooth foredeck the evening before, it was obvious that the worst rocks had been blasted out of the passage for shipping, which was marked by a series of electrically lit buoys, and I had an anticipation of disappointment which was fully realized. Though the pre-dawn gave an impression that the ship was approaching a narrow opening between door-posts of immense height, we raced through a relatively wide aperture well clear of angry water, the ship's steering fully in control. Like the Siq leading down to Petra, motorized traffic had demanded revised thinking, and modern machinery had enabled the gorge to be tamed.

Limestone cliffs stood out, naked of vegetation, unlike the nearly vertical mud-banks that had a coating of green like a rug with, near the top, an occasional nervously clinging tree. The lower gorges were wider, with barely a race in the water, and there was little sign of life save where a lone farm could be seen on the ledge, or a battery of communal farms. Then suddenly we were out of the mountains and the Yangtze had opened up into a wide sunny lake where the mood was quite different, and lateen-rigged sampans were fishing lazily at the water's edge. At the far end of this placid lake the Yangtze gathered again into a river heading for Wuhan, our point of disembarkation.

*

It was natural my reading had always been in favour of explorers – Thesiger, Lawrence, Gertrude Bell, Freya Stark, Mildred Cable – and I had been so fortunate to hear Wilfred Thesiger and Freya Stark lecture at the Royal Geographical Society, of which I was a Fellow. Yet it was not till the sixties that I read Sven Hedin's *My Life as an Explorer*, recounting his determination to survey the notoriously dangerous Takla Makan desert, which lies in what is now known as Chinese Turkestan and borders Tibet, India, Afghanistan and Russia. During this eminent explorer's first attempt he lost a member of his team, all his belongings and instruments and very nearly his life. With experience gained, he succeeded, and came on traces of a Buddhist civilization. This information he passed on to Aurel Stein, an archaeologist and explorer working for the Survey Department of then British India, who allowed him leave to go and excavate.

Stein's book, published early in the century, was hard to come by, but the London Library had a copy and Betty, a life member, obtained it for me. *Ruins of a Desert Cathay*, in two large volumes, beautifully printed, with illustrations opening at the pages to which they referred, describes enthralling expeditions, taking drinking-water in blocks of ice, transport by camel, many of which died, and excavating underground dwellings along the border of Turkestan and Tibet. Stein's writing is imbued with enthusiasm that must have given him his superhuman endurance, which one hopes was shared by the rest of the team.

In 1983 there was an expedition that would cover a slice of the Gobi, so ably described by Mildred Cable in her book *The Gobi Desert*; it included a description of her visit to the Cave of a Thousand Buddhas. It was here that Stein had rightly or wrongly 'bought' and preserved for posterity the first printed book, the Diamond Sutra, now in the safety of London. There was to be no encroachment on the Takla Makan desert but the plane

246

would fly over it on what was now a direct route to Peking. Needless to say, I joined this group.

The flight carried us not so much over the Himalayas as through them, a flight which alone made the tour worthwhile. Knowing their habit of shrouding themselves, I was sanguine about seeing them and, as expected, we approached at first light with nothing visible beneath us but what looked like cotton wool. However, as light increased, my view in front of the starboard wing showed the wool to have a tendency to rise here and there in a cone and, I wondered, was the cone covering the top of a mountain? It was. Soon solid rock was appearing out of the cones and a beam from the sun, shining over my right shoulder, suggested we were avoiding Pakistan, now in dispute with India over Kashmir, and were coming in over India towards Jamu, Ladakh, Leh, and not over, but *through*, the Karakorum Pass. For suddenly we were not looking down on mountains, they were above us, on each side of us, harrowing, exhilarating! Our wings seeming almost to scrape the flanking heights as unerringly we came through. K2 had been clearly visible to those on the port side of the plane, but now we were through into Turkestan, and the Kun Lun range of mountains stretched away on our right like a line of teeth dividing Turkestan from Tibet. Takla Makan was sleeping under the cotton wool.

We flew along the Tian Shan mountain range, over the Gobi, and looked down on Mongolia as we approached Peking. Here we were put through the same programme as formerly but we had then had China to ourselves, had seen the unyielding purpose with which the Great Wall advanced across mountain and dale with no concession to the contour of the land. Now one could barely see the Wall for the visitors, and along the Sacred Way the stone statues of animals and famous potentates were draped with sightseers being photographed.

Turkestan, to which we flew back over our incoming route, was another world, where the facial features of the clans of this autonomous state were in strong contrast to those of the Chinese. Han, Hui, Uygup, Kazak.... It was a well-organized visit and I fancy the Kazak women who lunched us in small groups in their bell-shaped yurts were well paid. This was at a Kazak camp tucked into a lovely glade in the mountains, and it wound up with a fine display of horsemanship by both men and women.

There were in fact many places of outstanding character and beauty on this journey, not least Turfan, a market oasis on the borders of the Gobi desert, but travelling in bulk is not ideal. I felt this keenly in this remoter border country where the smallholder had rarely seen anything like us, did not know how we came there, and though he might be reconciled to a single stranger, a coachload was an invasion of cameras focused on his property and ultimately within his yurt. Some of the group resisted, and all intruders felt guilty, but each was spurred by the other. Bulk travel segregates one from the people of the country or else promotes an uneasy contact, unless there is some diplomatic arrangement such as those lunches in the Kazak yurts.

I even felt mean lying comfortably in a sleeper or having a meal in the dining-saloon of a steam train that took us mile upon mile across the Gobi. I thought of Mildred Cable and her fellow missionary often having to walk this hostile landscape to bring medical or other help to desert-dwellers of whatever kind, some of them brigands. I voiced my feelings to one of the group, who smiled at me patiently, and when we left the train at a minor oasis and learnt the coach meeting us had broken down and we had to drive in an old rattletrap bus with broken windows, I was asked, was I happy now? I admitted this was more my line of travel.

*

I had arranged to take Betty to Crail in September. In this fishing village on the east coast of Scotland just north of the Firth there was another favoured hotel in which she was well known. We went by motor rail but drove back, visiting various friends on the way; a holiday on which I was to look back gratefully.

Betty had finished her book but was dissatisfied with its ending and wanted to rewrite it, and the publishers who had refused it were willing to see the revision, but this never got done. My sister became victim to a terrible inertia; there were bouts in hospital when I would be tortured by her expression on being left there but rewarded by her joy on return. Yet inevitably a time was coming when I would be unable to get her out of her chair, and in spite of kind neighbours and paid helps, constant vigil would be needed. I myself was due to have transplant operations on both eyes for cataract, but the long delay to get into hospital was at the moment useful as the eyes were adequate for household work if not for driving my car.

A remarkable neighbour, herself at work all day, gave her evenings to driving me round the neighbourhood to find the seemingly necessary home. The object was achieved, though rather distant: a ground-floor single room in a sensible home with a nice Matron. Betty was to have her own furniture and books around her, and as she was at that moment in hospital the move was to be made while she was away. In a state of gloom I was sorting her things when suddenly I knew I could not do it. It was like murdering her, putting her out of my life, separating her from her home, with no hope at present of getting over to see her at will. I flung myself down on her now empty bed and prayed.

I was no dutiful Christian, I sporadically attended Sunday service only for the honour of the house; but in moments of urgency or ecstasy I prayed to the God I had always believed to exist, an architect of creation. I did not picture this Almighty in the form of a man but rather as a presence outside and within one's soul. I thought of Christ as an emissary who would naturally have to take the form of a man, and if one believed in Christ one could accept miracles, could accept the Gospels. Such was my garbled faith.

The gist of my prayer was for strength to revoke all the time taken, and the kindness given, in finding me this home, where a room was already booked. What I wanted was to be sent a kind, strong nanny who would live here permanently, and I got up with an extraordinary certainty that this was going to be granted. It was. Just such a large, kind Irishwoman was sent to us from the agency from whom I had got temporary helps. By chance Marion Daly happened to be free to stay with us. She nursed Betty for two and a half years, taking over the cooking – she was a wonderful cook, and never idle. A day after her arrival, she was sitting mending Betty's curtains.

Betty died in 1986, a few months short of her ninetieth birthday, and would so much have enjoyed her funeral service. Her godson and second cousin, Sir Anthony Parsons, had just attained his retirement, to which he had been looking forward ever since he left school. Now after a life of high office in many countries, he came readily to give an appreciation of Betty which was both touching and amusing as he recounted memories of her. Added to this he read a letter from an early pupil quoting Betty's remarks in the margins of the pupil's exercise books, which resulted in our leaving church more in laughter than in tears.

I lived on alone, though never alone for long, as I lent Betty's flat to friends who for various reasons needed a temporary roof. The nice help who had succeeded Dora, and cleaned the house for some twenty-one years, was moving to Shoreham on the south coat. I foresaw a parting of the ways, but no, she wasn't going to let me down. She drove a car, and would come up one day a week; so I still have a help with merits I would hate to lose.

It was at this point I resorted to my former habits, and joined a party of five going with a guide to North Yemen.

*

Why did I want to go to North Yemen? A relative who had been there had shown me illustrations of its unique architecture and landscape of volcanic mountains rising from desert level to gigantic heights. They looked menacing but in fact contained water and would grow vegetation of all climates, where there was level or terraced ground. Then it was fairly recently that the former despotic Amirs had been replaced by a President and a government anxious to trade with and receive foreigners into the country. So I felt the natural way of life could not yet have been totally destroyed; meanwhile

249

a road service had been established over this difficult terrain. Foreign contractors had engineered a highway system joining the towns, but leaving the home-grown routes branching off for the smaller hamlets. There now existed an air route from Gatwick to San'a, their capital city, standing at a height of 700 feet.

San'a, the meeting-point of Yemeni and Western civilizations, had a good deal of mediocre architecture in its new town, but at least restrained in height. The Sheba Hotel, a creditable feature, rose to six floors only, but heavy transport had brought noise and congestion to streets in which empty tins, plastic and dust swirled about. The pearl of the city was its old town with its markets, old houses and museum, where scribes at the door were penning letters, at a price, for those who could not write.

Only in hotels or buildings frequented by foreigners was there modern sanitation, but though we had been warned to take anti-malarial pills, there were no mosquito nets, mosquitoes or even flies, so someone was attending to hygiene.

This country posed a question often raised in my mind when travelling: at what point had we reached, or were we going to reach, the peak of civilization? On the perimeter of this group of mountains were villages whose citadels were poised like storks' nests on topmost crags, almost impregnable, the villagers living on cultivated terraced land not far below. Fully independent and not really under government control, these villagers knew nothing of plastic or modern invention, were living as they had at the time of Christ, their day measured by the rising and the setting of the sun.

I am thankful to say our Toyota could not reach them; their survival depended on segregation, which they sought to maintain. The natural strength and unaided faculties of those surviving to maturity presented a useful yardstick for comparison with generations dependent on modern doctoring and the surgeon's knife.

The same thought occurred to me when we lunched on the top floor of a tall narrow building of imposing height and typical Yemeni architecture. Built of blocks of brick apparently without mortar, the windows and frames increased in elegance as they rose from the domestic floors to those of the Amir and his family who had formerly owned the house. Its spiral staircase, however, sparsely lit and built of great slabs of stone of unequal height, I could never have scaled but for the help of our guide, nor was I alone in finding it tortuous. Yet a Yemeni woman with skirt down to her toes and carrying a small boy in her arms climbed it with unconcern, which made me ponder the deteriorating influence of lifts and mechanical transport.

In this country I was thought to be very old, having to walk with a stick. My fellow travellers had also been duly impressed on learning I was eighty-six, an age which added spice to later antics when we were down at sea level on the coast of the Red Sea. The temperature was climbing high in the nineties and we were making for a mosque through streets too narrow for our Toyota, and all in the blazing sun. Suddenly I knew I could go no further but was unwilling to cramp the rest of the group. Our resourceful guide, however, knew a man with a motor cycle; would I ride on the flapper bracket back to the Toyota under the trees? Gratefully I did so, though it was some years since I had performed this exercise, and I had to embrace the young man round his waist for want of other hold over very uneven ground. The rest of the group were taking photographs, which I later received. Then having slept in the car all the way down to the port of Moccha, I was delighted when we drove almost on to the beach and joyously went to splash water on to my face and hands, not realizing how steeply the sand shelved down. I fell straight into the water to over my waist, to be swiftly yanked out again by two stalwart members of the group. The whole action was so prompt that we all roared with laughter, and my clothes dried on me within half an hour.

This tour was the nearest I ever got to the Empty Quarter, the desert Wilfred Thesiger had lived in and described so vividly in his book Arabian Sands. As we drove towards Maarib in a land cruiser, the mountainous dunes moulded by the winds of the Empty Quarter were clearly visible; but only briefly, as we were on our way to see the remains of the ancient dam that had earned its regim the name of Arabia Felix, also the new dam that had restored the title again. The remains of the old dam were as impressive as the achievement of the new. Bearing in mind the lifeless waters of Lake Nasser in lower Egypt, I was astonished in this area of sand, sand, sand to look down from the top of the new dam on to a lake of still blue water in a wide green valley.

The flight home from San'a was a gift I shall never forget, on a Sunday when as far as Athens we had the plane to ourselves. It was a brilliant cloudless morning; we seemed to advance with stately leisure, so wide and so distant was the enormous panorama lying below with no landmark from which to measure our speed. We flew above the Arabian coastline, looking down on Jeddah, on Sinai, on the Gulf of Aqaba and the insignificant little Suez Canal, and I felt this to be a farewell survey of a large chunk of my travelling life. Now we passed over the Pyramids, looking like table napkins folded for a dinner party, and as we lost height in descent for Piraeus I could almost see the ground where Sybil and I had found our best orchids in Crete. Then a slice of the old continent I had so frequently driven, France so orderly, the Channel, and Gatwick obscured in rain.

*

My return from the Yemen was the first time in my life I had come home to an empty house with no one there to greet me or listen to my enthu-

251

siasm, and though I normally enjoyed solitude, which gave one freedom of action, I did miss Betty. She pervaded my thoughts to the exclusion of memories of the Yemen, and there floated into my mind a conversation between us before that terrible inertia had claimed her body and mind. It had been her considered opinion that I should write an autobiography. I was utterly astonished.

I had certainly entertained my great-nieces telling them my adventures, but writing them for a sterner public was a different matter, and it amazed me that Betty thought it worthwhile. I may have been a natural craftsman, and I loved writing and adventure, but beyond that I looked on myself as a clownish character and a charlatan in most of the jobs I took up, though managing to be successful in the end. Betty saw me as one who had broken the ice of convention that held women down to certain jobs but denied them others, and at a time when to the majority of people the world was unknown.

Everything now had been left to me, and I felt overwhelmed by my wealth but did not resent getting it so late in life as my early adventures had been more exciting without it. I had sold the Saab when my sight became impaired and let my neighbours have my garage and yard for their two cars, thus relieving the congestion of parking in the street. With eyes restored, I meant to buy a light car, but had found the buses so convenient, starting almost at the door and saving the drudgery of parking, that I never bought another car.

It occurred to me now that my life was going to be void of many former activities. What if I did set aside my novel and write the story of my life? I had little to which to refer except my long memory for the unimportant and the ridiculous, and I had diaries kept since 1924. To these, however, I had sometimes poured out my soul beyond the dated page, thus to refer to them for specific information was rather like excavating old tombs. Nevertheless I was soon engrossed describing events firmly fixed in my mind, but being far too expansive, for the life story of someone not famous nor working in any great cause must not be too long. To get ninety years of activity down to digestible length has taken four years of writing, rewriting and condensing. In fact, autobiography is specialized work.

During this time I took one brief holiday, going down the Danube in a lavish motor cruiser to beyond the Iron Gates, the locks that bring Danube water to the lower water-level of the Black Sea. I had longed to do this but it had been too far off our course when motoring to Bucharest forty-seven years before. At that time special pilots had been necessary to see ships through the Kazan Pass, the narrows where the Danube had fought its way through the mountains and Hadrian had built a bridge whose plaque may still be seen. Now there was no need of special pilots; the pass had been

252

widened, a mighty dam controlled water-level and a powerhouse supplied electricity over a wide area.

As we approached the first of the Iron Gates, every high-standing projection on our cruiser at a single control lay flat, and I could see the need for strict control of water-level as, with what seemed like barely an inch to spare overhead, as well as at the sides, our cruiser entered the lock. A blustery following wind was threatening to blow the stern sideways but this was controlled by the knobs, telephones and computers plus human intelligence within the glass compartment that had supplanted the old-fashioned bridge.

At river level we were released to penetrate what had been a solid barrier but which had broken in half, the lower half sinking out of sight, the upper half giving the minimum of headroom as our colossal craft glided majestically downstream. A brilliant exercise between controllers of ship and lock. Yet downstream beyond all these innovations, I noticed the dear Danube had rather lost heart: no longer that exuberant spirit that left trees standing in water at one point and high on the banks at another, no longer the little sawmills or the romantic raftsmen shepherding tree trunks down to the sea. It had become a rather ordinary river and I was glad this was relatively near its journey's end.

*

I have loved my century, but it got tarnished by the two world wars. At the start we were mainly honest, God-fearing and content with the natural resources for our needs. Only the steam trains streaking across the country gave hint of the tremendous revolution in rapid communication that was to be firmly established within its first quarter.

Our efforts had formerly been constructive, but the First World War turned to the destructive which mounted with a terrible crescendo in the Second World War. By this time we had mastered the atom and dropped the atomic bomb; soon we had nuclear power, satellite communication and had landed on the moon. There seemed to be no boundary to what we could achieve, giving the feeling that it was we who ruled the earth. How wrong we were.

Can we pull out of our present dilemmas? Have we the wisdom to reverse our thinking and employ human intelligence above that of the machine? Can we preserve the God-given from major exploitation, or shall we continue to destroy? I fear I shall not live to know.

I had meant to wind up this saga with our garden party, but there was too much flowing beyond. So I shall wind up with the lunch party given me by the village on my ninetieth birthday – a treasured memory. It was superbly organized, far larger than I had anticipated, and I was exhilarated seeing everyone looking so nice and so obviously enjoying themselves. The food table was sublime.

I have no urge to go on further journeys. I am happy to wait for the undiscovered country, whenever that may be.